Allied Strafing
in World War II

Allied Strafing
in World War II

A Cockpit View
of Air to Ground Battle

WILLIAM B. COLGAN

McFarland & Company, Inc., Publishers
Jefferson, North Carolina, and London

LIBRARY OF CONGRESS CATALOGUING-IN-PUBLICATION DATA

Colgan, Bill.
   Allied strafing in World War II : a cockpit view of air to
ground battle / William B. Colgan.
      p.   cm.
   Includes bibliographical references and index.

   ISBN 978-0-7864-4887-6
   softcover : 50# alkaline paper ∞

   1. World War, 1939–1945—Aerial operations. 2. Fighter
plane combat—History—20th century. 3. Close air support—
History—20th century. 4. Air interdiction—History—20th
century. 5. Raids (Military science)—History—20th century.
I. Title.
D785.C57   2010
940.54' 4—dc22   2010026624

British Library cataloguing data are available

Front cover photographs courtesy United States Air Force

Manufactured in the United States of America

McFarland & Company, Inc., Publishers
  Box 611, Jefferson, North Carolina 28640
   www.mcfarlandpub.com

Acknowledgments

Due to the broad scope of events and actions in this book, many specific recognitions and credits are made within the text. I am deeply grateful to each individual and agency involved. I give loving thanks to my wife, Anita, and family members Bill Jr., Sandy, and their children for moral backing and overall aid; my thanks go especially to grandson Dallas Lowe for vital time and wizardry in overcoming computer malfunction.

I express particular appreciation to Dr. Daniel R. Mortensen, Office of Air Force History; Dr. Robin Higham, Kansas State University; and Brereton Greenhous, Canadian National Defense Headquarters, for personal attention and support. All personnel of the Eglin Air Force Base (FL) Library were most helpful.

My deepest thanks go to combat pilots Gilbert Burns, Glenn Moore, and Jack Porter and armament officer Bob Greninger for firsthand accounts; also to Alfred E. Schey for providing his view from the ground on the German side in the war; and to David Livingston for review and input from his more modern era as an F-15 pilot.

For a vital collection of gun camera film, which played a key role in this book being undertaken and is used extensively in it for explanation and evidence, my gratitude goes to all personnel of the 86th Fighter Group, World War II. More on the story of this film is in the text.

Most welcomed and heartfelt to me was encouragement to do a book on strafing from so many people, which include most of those mentioned above and other readers of my prior book, *World War II Fighter-Bomber Pilot.* Some of them wished to know more about strafing, but mainly they were fellow combat pilots and unit ground personnel I served with in the U.S. Army (Air Corps) and U.S. Air Force (1941–1972) who knew that life ever so well.

Table of Contents

Preface

This book is written by a strafer about pilots and aircrews being strafers in their air war in the deadly low-altitude skies, where they fought with aircraft guns and cannon in battle with the enemy and his weapons on the ground.

Many specific actions and missions, heavy on firsthand accounts and backed by extensive gun camera film evidence, combine to show strafing's major and varied role in war as well as the core story of warrior duty, valor and sacrifice.

The writing of this book was much the same as it would be for a book on a particular football Super Bowl where readers might know very little or nothing about football and other Super Bowls. Yet, that is the case for this book on World War II strafing, as some of its readers might have little knowledge of strafing. To remedy that, the tie-in history contained in salutes to prior and later wars includes limited basics of strafing in those wars as a primer on strafing history. These are my summaries, as a strafer, of what I gleaned from references on World War I and from my own and other pilots' experiences in later wars, which should help readers better see and appreciate "our story" in history.

The writing of this book could also be compared to writing one on fishing for readers who know little about fishing. For understanding fishing—a subject of broad scope—authors invariably divide it into separate components: salt water and fresh water, then further by types of fish, locations, and "how to"—offshore, inshore, lake, stream, trolling, casting, fly, etc. With strafing, a broad subject too, I did the same, using major categories of "air," "support" and "ground/surface" rather than a chronological account of strafing events in the war.

The primary goal of this book is that readers will learn things about strafing and strafers that we strafers did not know ourselves before we did them, things not found in previous books, media, movies and even video games.

My prior book, *World War II Fighter-Bomber Pilot*, received universal acceptance as lucid, accurate, long overdue, vital history. It has been used as a textbook at the U.S. Air Force Academy. Above all, it was totally endorsed by

1

Top: Strafing an enemy aircraft. In World War II, only a small percentage of gun camera film, including this example, was officially retained for public information and archives (U.S. Air Force). *Bottom:* Strafing enemy railroad locomotives on film collected on their own by units and pilots (gun camera, 86th Ftr Gp, World War II).

pilots and ground crews, those whom the book was about, as definitive: it "tells our story."

Certainly strafing was a key part of that book. For many readers it was the most gripping and astounding action, a fact which encouraged my undertaking this book. This is a greatly expanded and more in depth look into strafing in the war—more actions and experiences of more pilots and aircrews, more units, major victories, and other theaters—all devoted to strafing, along with a tie-in to the history and heritage of strafing in other wars.

A significant additional coverage includes extensive use of a special 60-plus minute reel of World War II gun camera film that was not available before. During the war, most gun camera film of the U.S. Army Air Forces was (by regulation) "unclassified, non-permanent record." Some of the best quality and most spectacular footage was sent to public information and archives; but most film never left combat squadrons and was often given to pilots or destroyed. A few units saved some on their own.

In the 86th Fighter Group in Germany at the war's end, Colonel George Lee, Majors John Dolny and Bill Colgan, and Captain Clyde Hailes had film from each squadron put into a collection. Pure combat footage, it contained many hundreds of strafing passes (some air fights, too) from a wide variety of missions flown. A few copies were brought back to the States, but their fate and whereabouts were unknown to most 86th veterans until determined effort by Hailes located one in an attic in Pennsylvania some 50 years later.

Attempts to have the film reproduced found no firms that would work with the old 16-mm black and white movie film. It was put on tape and the original placed in U.S. Air Force archives at Maxwell AFB, Alabama. In turn further copies have been made by 86th veterans and donated to schools, libraries, etc. Numerous still photos of action in this book are taken from these VHS and DVD copies and from DVD of a second reel found in 2001 in the high school library at Norwood, MA. In all cases, viewers still see history—what pilots saw after missions in the war—rather than the generated images of today.

Similar to footage from surveillance cameras at car washes, parking lots, and convenience stores—as well as in-flight video of precision bomb and missile strikes in the Gulf and Iraq—the photo quality may be lacking, but what is shown can be quite clear as record and evidence. That is the role of the gun camera film in this book. Thanks to Colonel Lee and personnel of the 86th Group for preserving that film; otherwise, without it for proof in a subject so unknown and misunderstood as strafing, I would not have undertaken this book. All sequences of gun camera film from a particular strafing pass are arranged bottom to top. This allows the reader to see the action in the same direction and order as it appeared to the pilot.

In *Allied Strafing in World War II,* just as I did in my prior book, I stress that flying and fighting operations could vary widely in World War II between theaters, time frames of the war, and situations, as did tactics of air forces,

These pilots were featured in a World War II European Theater news release published in numerous home front newspapers in April 1945. The original caption reads in part: "USAAF Fighter-Bomber Base, France—Uncle Sam holds a hand of six aces that are hard to beat—a sextet of P-47 pilots whose combat missions total exactly 1,000. Left to right: Captain Jesse R. Core, Little Rock, Ark., 126 missions; Major William B. Colgan, Waycross, Ga., 195 missions: Lt. Col. George T. Lee, Norwood, Mass., 245 missions; Captain Bushnell N. Welch, Wellesley, Mass., 189 missions; Captain Walter C. Taylor, Newark, N.J., 119 missions. Not in the photograph: Major John R. Dolny, Minneapolis, Minn., 126 missions. Add them up. Total 1,000." These men held top command and operational positions in the 86th Fighter Group and continued to fly combat missions, almost all strafing, until the war's end in Europe, with final top theater totals of Lee's 258 and Colgan's 208. Captain Taylor was killed in action on his 126th mission. Most of the gun camera film in this book is from missions flown by these and other pilots of the 86th.

groups, and even squadrons. The content of both books is made up of specific actions and missions just as they happened, with the tactics used and the results, for better or worse. The broad scope of the book tells of war against enemy air forces, enemy support forces, and enemy ground and surface forces and recounts strafing victories, valor, and overdue glory—with much about "voluntary," "being our 'own' generals," and "aces in the hole, saving the day." The goal of this book is to tell a definitive story of strafing and strafers in war.

By doing that, may this book make the story of these brave pilots and aircrews better known and appreciated.

Introduction

During my military career and on into retirement, through contact with the public and with military scholars and buffs, I have found strafing to be probably the least known and the most misunderstood type of flying and fighting in all air warfare. Other combat pilots of strafing experience agree. This circumstance certainly is not caused by a lack of strafing done in war, which has a record of great use and contribution from World War I to the present date. But it simply has never received publicity and acclaim. As Dr. Daniel R. Mortensen, Office of Air Force History, said to me years ago (back when that office still existed), "As we all know, strafing [its history] has not been done."

This book is written to give a readable, understandable, and definitive story of strafing and its warriors in World War II, with salute to other wars. The "flying and shooting" and "calling the shots" are told about in specifics and explained, along with note of high command impact on our low-level fighting.

I will cite the official definition of strafing from the *United States Department of Defense Dictionary of Military and Associated Terms* (JCS Pub 1-02): "the delivery of automatic weapon fire by aircraft on ground targets." While concise, this covers much. It specifies actual firing of weapons, not a doctrine or concept. And it is "automatic weapons"—machine guns/cannon—which eliminates rockets, missiles, bombs, clusters, and other munitions (except gun pods) as strafing armament. It neither designates who does it nor states who cannot. It can be done by any branch of service and any type of unit, pilot and aircrew, or aircraft on any kind of target anywhere and in any role, task, or mission. In actuality strafing has been used that broadly. If this definition were widely known to people, that in itself could prevent some common misconceptions. For example, one writer friend questioned my plan for this book: "With a subject of strategy, how can it be exciting for readers?" A retired airline/military air transport pilot commented: "Yeah, 'strafing,' a term for close air support." On the other hand, a woman neighbor said, "Don't know it, but sounds nasty," She is the only one close to being right.

The name "strafing" is traced in the *United States Air Force Dictionary* as

If it was an aircraft and had machine guns/cannon aboard—in all units, all services—it surely has had a part in strafing's great and varied history in air warfare and shares in strafing's story of unsung glory. These aircraft of one unit, 39th Squadron, covering World War II, Korea, Vietnam, and subsequent wars are an example (painting by Ronald T.K. Wong, print by 39th Test Sq, Air Armament Center, USAF).

German—"strafe, to punish," with original World War I application to air-ground attack, then evolving to such attack only with guns. The dictionary notes that the term was unpopular with some Allied countries after the war but that once the association had been made with the peculiar action of an airplane suddenly striking from above with guns ablaze, it served a need that no older or alternate word seemed to fill. Apparently that has remained the case, but with a strange record in usage. Most U.S. combat operations, units, aircraft, and pilots and aircrews historically have been designated by function—fighter, bomber, reconnaissance, etc.—which reflects the primary thing they do. But that is not so for the conduct of strafing and its unique name. No U.S. units, aircraft, or pilots and aircrews have ever held "strafing" or "strafers" as official designations. Thus strafing suffers a lack of name recognition in both histories and news releases.

One use of its name has not helped at all. An officer's club bartender asked, "Strafing—do you mean in the air or in the bar?" In strafing a firing attack on a target is called a "pass" or a "run." Perhaps it was inevitable that pilots and aircrews also would put a tag of "strafing" on a pass or run of a social nature made in the bar. However, the fact that a pass and a run is the same thing can alert a reader that accounts of strafing experiences will contain language out of the ordinary.

With that, I will leave official definitions to files and archives. The main story here is of duty, valor and sacrifice. Out in the low-altitude skies, strafing carries a quite well known definition, a real world reputation earned in battle over its history: "air war's bloodiest gunfighting." It is also an "art."

· 1 ·

The Pioneers
World War I

This salute is aimed at the beginning of strafing and the heritage of duty and honor passed on to us by strafers of World War I. What they started, and accomplished, defined much of strafing's enduring nature and reputation. "Their story" is a key to understanding "our story" of World War II.

In August 1910, at Sheepshead Bay Racetrack, New York, Lt. Jacob Fickel, U.S. Army, fired an issue rifle from a pusher airplane at a target in the infield. Four rounds were fired; two were hits, and the crowd roared approval. The press praised the feat and forecast great things for guns in airplanes. Military spokesmen said single shots may be fired successfully but any rapid fire would upset the flying machine and cause it to crash.

In 1912, Lt. Col. Isaac Lewis, U.S. Army, inventor of the Lewis machine gun, proposed an unofficial experiment to Capt. Charles Chandler, commanding officer at College Park, Maryland, to fire a fully automatic Lewis machine gun from an aircraft at a ground target. Chandler approved and volunteered to fire the gun. In a Wright pusher aircraft, short bursts were fired at a piece of cheesecloth laid on the ground. They were accurate on and near the target but Chandler could not see the impacts. He fired a burst into a nearby fishpond where the bullet pattern would show. Lewis, on the ground, feared this unplanned shooting was accidental and uncontrolled. He sent observers dashing for cover in adjacent hangars—or, according to some versions, they didn't wait to be told.

With explanation by Chandler after landing, a second test was made the next day. It was highly successful and accurate. The press again took note. The machine gun had not upset the aircraft. Speculation on guns and planes as tools of war was widespread. But War Department officials declared that aircraft were suitable for scouting only, along with this explanation (from *The Machine Gun* by Lt. Col. George M. Chin, USMC, Dept. of the Navy, 1951): "Any dream of aerial combat was simply the product of too fertile imagination, a failing often found in younger men with insufficient service to recognize cer-

9

The beginning: in the low-altitude skies over the Western Front of World War I.

tain things as utterly absurd. Besides, the experiment had been run without official sanction, which, as far as the military authorities were concerned, left it in the category of having never happened."

Similar firings were made in 1912 and 1913 from aircraft in England and France and from zeppelins in Germany; but in August 1914 when British Royal Flying Corps pilots went to France at the start of World War I, neither their planes nor those of the Germans were equipped with guns. Pilots and aircrews of both sides just began to shoot at each other with pistols, rifles, and carbines.

On 22 August, Lt. Strange and Lt. Gaskell, RFC, put a machine gun aboard their plane, took off and sighted a German pursuit (fighter) plane. Unable to close on it, they fired a drum of ammo at it from some 1,000 yards. No hits were observed but two milestones were recorded. A machine gun went aloft in war and was fired in combat. The mission report stated a belief that machine guns could replace the pistols and rifles being used. The result was the opposite. An RFC high command order was issued prohibiting machine guns in aircraft, noting that the extra weight of the gun degraded aircraft performance.

That was the status of machine guns in aircraft when strafing was born. And the above order may have had a part in the start of strafing with rifles and carbines rather than with machine guns. A mission of 14 September reported that British pilots, unable to get shots at higher flying German pursuits, turned in frustration to firing their individual weapons at German troops on the ground. Thus the British could be originators of strafing, or the French or Germans about the same time. The public can get the date of the first bomb dropped in war from almost all encyclopedias, but some of those references have no entry at all on strafing. Then, too, veteran pilots of strafing gunfights have always wondered if the enemy on the ground shot first. Regardless of that uncertainty, once one fired, the other did too. Gunfire both ways has been a constant ever since.

Two facts do stand out. First, strafing did not have a celebrated birth. Second, strafing did not originate in high commands, schools, academies, or industry. It was purely the brainchild of pilots and aircrews in combat. Subsequently those pilots and aircrews were the driving force in the early phases of the war for aggressive use of it against the enemy.

Any and all prohibitions on machine guns in aircraft were short lived. Machine guns quickly were put aboard planes of both sides in the war. Air-to-air and air-to-ground machine-gun combat grew rapidly from birth. Early use was firing in about any direction practical and not hitting your plane or propeller. Air-to-air dogfights created the need for forward firing. Guns were mounted on wings above propellers. They were fired through props, chancing hits. Armor shields were then put on props; then synchronizer systems were developed to fire through the prop arc without hitting the blades.

Fixed forward-firing synchronized guns mounted in front of the pilot became normal armament on pursuit and observation planes; flexible guns were on pivot or ring mounts at rear cockpits or other positions of multi-crew planes. With fixed forward guns, the pilot flew the aircraft in the direction he wanted to aim the guns. For flexible guns, gunners manually swung the guns for aim. The majority of the guns were .30- and .303-caliber, although larger caliber machine guns and even cannon were used in the war. Rate of fire of most guns was between 600 and 800 rounds per minute. Ammunition loads varied but reports show pursuit pilots having 30 to 40 seconds of firing time. From the beginning that "time of fire" became of paramount importance to pilots and aircrews and has remained so.

Air-to-air gunfighting quickly gained its enduring gloried status. It was aptly dubbed "dogfighting," with records of "air victories" and famed pilot "aces," all well served and deserved. Air-to-ground gunfighting quickly and strongly earned its bloody nature, but it and its nondescriptive name of "strafing" gained an opposite public image from that of air-to-air gunfighting—one of "overlooked glory," even though it would become by far the more extensively employed of the two.

These two stayed closely entwined in flying and fighting operations. The pursuit units did both with the same pilots, planes, and guns. Not even one

The two fixed forward-firing synchronized machine guns show on this replica Fokker tri-wing pursuit (author, from the Bill Parish collection).

cockpit switch or lever had to be changed to go from dogfighting to strafing, or vice versa—just fly the airplane to aim the guns as needed. Those units did most of the strafing in World War I, but observation and other units were strafers too; and in later years specialized ground attack units and aircraft were also used. Experiences of pilots and aircrews set the enduring character and nature of strafing. These ranged from pilot and aircrew voluntary impromptu attacks on targets of opportunity to high-command ordered massive strafing efforts later in the war—all done in an amazing variety of strafing actions.

A pilot flying with German "ace of aces" Manfred von Richthofen reported that on one mission Richthofen dove on a flight of British Sopwith Camels, shot one out of the sky, then kept going to pull out just above the ground and strafed, directing his machine-gun fire along a column of British troops. The British returned fire with machine guns and rifles and put numerous holes in the wings of the "Red Baron's" famed Fokker pursuit. Ernst Udet, Germany's second leading ace, achieved at least one victory against a British tank as well. He made some five strafing passes, firing directly on the tank; as the crew attempted to fight back, the tank rolled down a steep embankment. Udet made a sixth pass, putting bullets into the "softer" underbelly of the upturned monster as he ran out of ammo. Canadian ace "Billy" Bishop was out ground machine-gunning when he earned the Victoria Cross for air victories. As he strafed hangars and personnel on a German airfield, four enemy planes attempted to take off. Bishop shot down three and damaged the fourth.

On the morning the battle of Ypres opened in 1917, British No. 56 Squadron went out in strength to strafe airfields of Richthofen's "Flying Circus" in very bad weather. Lt. R.A. Mayberry, flying an S.E.5A pursuit, with a synchronized Vickers and a top wing Lewis machine gun and carrying four small Cooper bombs, was one of the first off. Leaving his base under the low clouds, thick smoke over the lines cut visibility to zero. He detoured to a known point, and then followed a road toward his target area. Flying at 30 feet, which he could do only because battle destruction had knocked down all the tall trees along the road, he navigated into better visibility near his first target airfield. He was spotted by two German fighters but he was determined to make his ground attacks before any dogfighting began. He evaded the enemy planes by maneuver, a few bursts of his Lewis machine gun, and another substantial detour.

At the first of his targets (all near Courtrai, Belgium), which was Heule, field of Jasta 10 (a pursuit squadron), he dropped three of his small bombs on a line of aircraft sheds. The fourth bomb hung up and he took it over the rail station at Courtrai and got it released on that target. He then turned back to Heule to use his machine guns. While bombing there he had received enemy machine-gun fire from two positions on the field. His first strafing pass knocked out one of these but he could not locate the other. Nevertheless, he turned to making low runs across the field, firing into entrances of the sheds housing the German planes. In tight turns and repeat passes of less than 30 feet, changing ammo drums on the Lewis gun along the way, he actually flew into the ground in the center of the field. Apparently it was a glancing impact of the fixed landing gear that skipped him back into the air without damage to the prop or engine.

Still flying, he went to Cuere, field of Jasta 4, and strafed it with both guns. On one pass he spotted two German officers on horseback nearby. He darted over and gunned them down. Flying to his next planned target of Bissenghem, field of Jasta 6, he also strafed a column of German troops marching along a road. A German two-seater plane appeared overhead flying just under the clouds. He went up and shot it down. Circling over the wreckage as German troops gathered around, he strafed them. This was back near Courtrai and the rail station he had bombed earlier. As a troop train arrived there, he made diving runs, strafing it until he ran out of ammunition. His return to base was in the same hazards of low clouds and thick smoke as his outbound flight. Of note, he was just one of many pilots flying those missions and strafing the enemy in such conditions that day—and doing the same many times in other major battles of the war. It's obvious that strafing's history of great versatility had strong roots in missions such as that of Mayberry.

The extent of strafing grew tremendously as the war progressed. "Strafe the enemy wherever found" became common in pilot briefings. The British distinguished between "trench strafing" (battlefield) and "ground strafing" (behind the battlefield). For ground warriors of both sides, being under machine-gun attack from the air became a regular and unwelcome part of warfare. "Air trenches" for protection from strafing were added in trench networks. Behind the lines, targets ranged from airfields to troop columns, trains, and vehicles, and even out to sea. Both sides reported serious destruction and casualties—with descriptions such as grievous loss of men and equipment, frantic efforts to take cover, horses going wild, traffic jams, dashes to escape to open fields, and more.

The bloody nature of strafing was not just for those on the ground. Pilots, from early 1915 on, cited return fire from the enemy as being deadly to low-flying strafers. This included antiaircraft fire, called "Archie," but especially the fire of enemy machine-guns and rifles, which was encountered in great intensity from troop concentrations and positions at many times and places. There were other threats. For example, in the battle of Cambrai, nine British Camel pursuits set out in bad weather to strafe enemy airfields. They were jumped by German pursuit pilots, who shot down two Camels. Then, while strafing, two more Camels were lost from flying into trees.

Various pursuit pilots said they would rather take on several dogfights with the best German fighters than face a single trench strafing mission. One pilot said be was shot down three times in logging his first seven sorties. Losses in units on low flying operations in major ground actions after mid–1917 are recorded as averaging 30 percent per day. British No. 80 Squadron, in such work for the last 10 months of the war, lost 168 pilots killed in that period. With a normal strength of 22 pilots in the squadron, they needed replacement of the entire complement every 39 days.

The lack of glory showed among pilots, too. An Allied strafing attack on a German airfield destroyed 11 new Fokker D VIIs and put an enemy squadron out of operation for days. The few Allied pilots who did this knew that they would be acclaimed heroes if they had destroyed that number of enemy planes at one time in the air. But as it was, they had no more fame than when they arose that morning. They were scheduled to go strafing again first thing the next day, expecting no fame then either, unless by the very likely means of their names appearing on the day's casualty lists.

Pilot feelings on assignment to a specialized ground attack unit versus a regular pursuit squadron were evident too. When Manfred von Richthofen's younger brother Lothar completed pilot training, Manfred used his national hero influence to insure that Lothar did not go to a ground strafing unit but was assigned to Manfred's own pursuit group. However, that did not keep Lothar out of strafing, just from a full-time job of it.

With the start of the Great German Offensive in March 1918, strafing reached yet greater intensity in the critical days that followed. By 26 March practically all British pursuit squadrons had orders that very low flying was mandatory and all risks must be taken. Some squadrons were using one plane on patrol and all the rest on strafing. One report notes that British airmen fired 540,000 rounds of machine-gun ammo on the 26th and 27th in this action on the British Front.

In April, Marshal Foch, Supreme Allied Commander, directed British and French air services to make support of ground forces the primary task of fighter airplanes, with air fighting looked for and engaged in only as necessary to allow the accomplishment of the ground support. Emphasis was on attack of enemy concentrations at the front, on roads and in bivouac. For that "ground support" by "fighter aircraft," a list of all objects dropped or released from aircraft on the enemy in the war would include about anything from bottles of gasoline and grenades to special incidents such as firing rockets from and at aircraft. However, small 20–25 pound bombs (as mentioned on Lt. Mayberry's mission) were about the only "standard" items normally dropped from pursuit/fighter planes. When and if carried, that was a load of about four per plane. On the other hand, the aircraft guns were always there—every time, every place, every plane. Guns were overwhelmingly the main means of ground attack in World War I by fighter and observation aircraft.

Nieuport fighter shown strafing near the Somme in a diving pass firing down into the enemy (painting by Henry Fane, USAF Art Collection; print by U.S. Government Printing Office).

Of course, the overall German offensive on the Western Front was stemmed by the total effort of Allied forces, with French and American troops fully involved and battles of Belleau Wood and Chateau-Thierry prominent in doing so. The United States went into World War I ill equipped for air warfare. When war was declared on Germany (6 April 1917), our armed forces had no first-line combat aircraft and only a motley collection of less-than-modern machine guns for either air or ground combat. The gun situation has developed amazingly since American Hiram S. Maxim invented the first fully automatic machine gun—the Maxim—which was widely used in several versions of aircraft guns in the war. They included the synchronized British Vickers (a Maxim design), the German Maxim and Spandau (Maxims made in that town) and the flexible Parabellum (a modified Maxim). The Allies' primary flexible aircraft machine gun, the Lewis, was also invented by an American. Both the Maxim and Lewis had been turned down as aircraft armament by the U.S. military but accepted by European nations. However, the United States did bring the American Marlin aircraft gun into the war, and the American Browning later became the superior ground machine gun of the war.

When U.S. Air Service pursuit and observation units entered combat in late March and early April 1918, it was with French and British aircraft and a mix of .30- and .303-caliber guns and foreign synchronizers. This was in the "Toul Sector" of air operations. By June American pilots Eddie Rickenbacker and Douglas Campbell had become aces of five air victories each. Regarding strafing, Brig. Gen. William Mitchell, chief of Air Service, Group of Armies, AEF, described in his memoirs a view of the French airdrome at Toul after German planes had machine gunned and set fire to several planes on the ground and shot up the whole place, killing a number of men.

By July American air units went into the mainstream of the war in front of Paris, notably at Chateau-Thierry, in desperate fighting to hold back the German offensive on the Marne. I have never forgotten some figures I once read that veteran French flying officers gave to American pursuit and observation pilots going into that action. One was that the average life of a flyer in the type of work to be done was two and one-half hours. That work was not air combat with the best German pilots. It was low-level strafing and corps observation. Another figure was the average life of a pursuit pilot overall as 17 hours, a grim figure in itself. But obviously the more time spent in air-to-air combat and the less in strafing the better the odds of survival—if not very good either way.

Major Harold Hartley, commanding officer, 1st Pursuit Group, called Chateau-Thierry the first big test. In meeting that test, he said he would never forget July 15, 1918, as long as he lived—as it seemed the entire German Army desperately flung itself into the Allied lines. He recalled the frantic orders for his high-flying pursuits to go down to ground level and fix positions of the German advance. In praise of all his constantly flying pilots, he specifically cited (Lt.) MacArthur and that pilot's one-man effort to stop the Germans by strafing troops crossing the pontoon bridges at Dormans and other locations on the Marne. MacArthur flew seven and one-half hours on repeated missions that day, expending all his machine gun ammo on each, before rushing back for more fuel and ammo to go again. Hartley said he would dearly like to know just what damage MacArthur did in that single day.

By mid–August the Allies were on the offensive, and their air power had grown more dominant in order of battle, control of the air, and support of ground forces. At St. Mihiel, Brig. Gen. Mitchell employed close to 1,500 aircraft in an attack on German ground forces. The official history, *The U.S. Air Service in World War I*, contains this entry on strafing at St. Mihiel on the first day, 12 September 1918: "All day long our pursuit airplanes harassed their troops with machine gun fire, throwing the enemy into confusion."

Flying in a mission of 14 SPADs of the 93rd Squadron, Lt. Walter Case reported finding some 3,000 German troops and many motor lorries in and around a small town. He dived, machine-gunning into troops in the town center, which resulted in a frantic dash for cover and a jam of troops trying to enter one door of a building. He concentrated fire on that door, sure of killing and wounding many as he could see them fall from his close range of less than 150 feet. However, return fire from other troops in the area made this no "turkey shoot" of easy pickings. And on a following pass as he dived, firing on a column of troops outside the town, he could see they were at the ready and about a second later wondered if his time was up as smoke erupted from many rifle barrels. Still, he pressed on firing both guns until he had to pull up to keep from hitting the ground.

Lt. John Young, pilot, and Lt. Henry Bagel, observer, 90th Aero Squadron, in a Salmson observation plane, flew an infantry patrol mission for the 42nd Division. In bad weather under low ceiling, after more than an hour over enemy lines calling targets for artillery fire, they decided to take on some of those targets themselves. They strafed a convoy of horse-drawn vehicles and troops; the pilot used his front guns in the pass, then the observer added fire from his flexible gun as the plane passed over. The column was sent into total disarray and fled into nearby fields. The two next attacked a German gun battery, unloading their ammo with further spectacular results. In an interlude to reload the observer's gun, an enemy bullet struck their water-cooled engine. A shower of hot water told them the engine was short lived. It barely got them to an emergency landing among lead elements of advancing American infantry.

At St. Mihiel the U.S. 1st Bombardment Group had orders to bomb and machine-gun hostile troops opposing U.S. infantry. Thus bombers and their crews became part of strafing history in this war. American aces were involved too. Lt. Edward Rickenbacker and Lt. Reed Chambers, flying under low overcast, spotted a large movement of German forces from the lines, including a

America's top ace, Rickenbacker, and SPAD 13 pursuit. The fixed round "iron" gun sight for two guns shows just below the top wing (U.S. Air Force).

distinct column of artillery pieces. They immediately strafed it, using a series of short dives and pull-ups in placing machine-gun fire along the length of the column. Horses and men were gunned down and the column broke into panic. The aces stopped strafing only when out of ammo.

Brig. Gen. Mitchell's memoirs tell that Allied attack of rear area rail and road traffic resulted in routes piled with wreckage and carnage that hindered German movement and allowed capture of many enemy troops. He noted some gruesome results of German strafing on our forces too. A German two-seater strafed a French troop train of wounded and sick soldiers; some 200 were killed by a single plane. A German pursuit strafed two American engineer companies lined up for mess; 87 were killed and 200 wounded before they could take cover.

"Balloon busting," the machine-gunning of observation balloons in the air or when cabled down into their "nests" on the ground was considered among the deadliest of missions. While pilots were credited with an "air victory" for destroying a balloon, the shooting was in a strafing setting—low level, in the intense antiaircraft and small-arms fire always in position to protect balloons. American ace Frank Luke was noted for making repeated machine-gun passes to destroy balloons. When no more were in the air or nest to shoot, he regularly turned his guns on the nearby antiaircraft crews and other ground support troops.

In Meuse-Argonne action of late September and on, American pursuit and observation units reported ground machine-gunning as regular work. In more specific terms the citation for award of the Silver Star to an American pilot for strafing a German artillery unit read in part, for "killing 60 horses and a like number of men."

The U.S. 1st Pursuit Group flew numerous low-altitude patrols to counter German squadrons of specialized ground attack aircraft, called "troop strafers" by American troops. Flying under 500 feet, our pursuits broke up numerous such attacks. But these heavily gunned and armored enemy planes also caused Gen. Pershing, commander of the American Expeditionary Forces, to state a need to Washington for a larger caliber, higher muzzle velocity aircraft machine gun to best shoot them down.

A specialized U.S. air unit was the 185th Aero Squadron, flying Camel pursuits. It was trained to engage German Gotha bombers operating at night. Yet, when bad weather frequently halted these German raids, the 185th turned to low-level night attack of the enemy on the ground. On one mission a German train was strafed as it steamed along unsuspecting of such attack at night. Also, staff officers of Brig. Gen. Mitchell, driving at night with lights on, took hits in their vehicle by machine-gun fire from a German aircraft above.

Firsthand experiences in the following chapters on World War II delve into the "doing, how and what like" of strafing. However, some of the underlying principles and nature of that "doing" came directly from World War I strafing. For example, in the film and video *Thunderbolt* (sponsored by the U.S. Army Air Forces [USAAF]) on World War II air action, P-47 pilots are shown shooting up trucks, trains and other targets of opportunity with their aircraft machine guns in Italy in 1944. As the narration states, "Every man his own general!" Found in a film production, these words may hint at "theatrical," but they are fully valid historically. Much text in this book is about that cornerstone of strafing, and I'll start here to give credit and honor to those who originated it.

Examples of British, German, and American strafing show varied missions flown. Lt. Case was on a 14-plane mission. Rickenbacker and Chambers operated as a pair. MacArthur and Udet flew one-man efforts. But regardless of how many planes left home base together, once into strafing action it was done as single planes or small elements—and those pilots and element leaders became the decision makers in their searches for and attack of targets, now their own generals.

But that is not the full story. We need to identify just what was being employed in this air-to-ground machine gunning as these decisions were made. Was it planes and aircrews, and guns and ammunition? Yes, but more specifically and accurately from the pilot's and aircrew's view, it was the "time of fire" of the guns. That time of fire was inherent in gunfighting. It was there in some amount of time, continuously available for use on the enemy. On the other hand, that time of fire could not be used all at once. It took that long to generate it—as opposed to bombs, rockets, etc., that could be released all at once or almost so if desired. Thus aircraft gunfighting (dogfighting and strafing) had a built-in decision factor for pilots and aircrews in applying its time of fire. For strafing, whether trench strafing, ground strafing, airfield strafing, or hunt and find strafing, once out over the enemy there was always that amount of time up for decision on how to use it.

With his time of fire, Lt. Mayberry moved about strafing a variety of targets. So did Case. Udet stayed in one place with repeated passes to destroy a key target there. MacArthur went back mission after mission, pass after pass, to shoot troops crossing a river. Rickenbacker and Chambers stayed with their large convoy target, as did the Allied strafers who destroyed 11 new Fokkers on an airfield. Young and Bogel and Richthofen were not even on strafing missions; they just decided to strafe.

The majority of the pilots and aircrews in these examples used all their firing time, applying it in multiple passes. In every case, they had a specific target that they had found. Their shooting was aimed right into that in-view target. They wasted little or none of their time of fire toward anything except bullet holes in enemy equipment and hides. That maximum number of such holes per airplane employed seems a very valid and effective concentration of force and firepower on the enemy—even though the warriors doing it were spread out in small numbers at the time.

Then, too, the capabilities and characteristics of aircraft and guns demanded on-the-spot decisions for the situation in each pass. The best pursuit planes of World War I had top speeds of around 130 miles per hour. Thus strafing passes ranged from diving speeds above that to much slower in early war pursuits. Hoverer, one fact about speed and flight attitude, (which is not obvious to many people) is that fixed forward-firing aircraft guns could be fired regardless of how fast or slow they were flown, or whether flown straight down, some lesser dive, or flat, or with wings level, in a bank, or even inverted. The guns fired wherever they pointed when the trigger was pulled.

Thus strafing did not require tables of speed, altitude, dive angle, and the like from which to plan attacks then closely execute in order to achieve accuracy. The pilot was free to aim the guns in any way desired or needed. To concentrate bullet impacts on a target, the aircraft nose was held on it while firing, usually requiring some degree of "dive" to do so. To spread bullets along or throughout an area on the ground, the aircraft nose was made, or allowed, to move while firing.

Lt. Mayberry flew near level on the deck in order to aim his guns into the open ends of sheds housing enemy planes. To aim those same guns on the troop train among buildings in town, he had to dive down from above to have an unobstructed line of fire. Lt. Case stressed he "dived" to hold his gunfire on troops at the door. Rickenbacker and Chambers "porpoised" down an enemy column. Had they flown along level above it, their guns would never have pointed down on it. A steep dive was necessary to shoot downward on troops in trenches. Yet, shallower dives were more common on troops in the open and numerous other targets. There was an endless variety of target situations.

References report that World War I pilots felt that certain altitudes were very dangerous in strafing passes, particularly 300 to 500 feet. Starting higher, 1,000 to 1,500 feet was considered best; then when pulling out down low, 100 feet or on the deck, to stay down in leaving the target area. It can be assumed that was a desirable pass. But the examples vary greatly from it. They show passes flown as needed and chosen to achieve effective results on particular targets and also for repeat runs, and strafing under weather of low ceilings of 500 feet and below—with many passes made entirely in the highest danger zones—all decided by pilots in the air to accomplish the mission. Certainly there were numerous other factors, including equipment as well as flying and aiming techniques, involved in decisions, and these are primary subjects of

Salmson 2 A.2, an observation plane with two rear-cockpit flexible guns and a forward synchronized gun (U.S. Air Force).

later chapters. But recognition of this underlying great flexibility in use of fixed, forward-firing aircraft guns from this war is felt to be essential background to those chapters.

Flexible guns of rear-seat and other aircrew gunners had their story too. Primarily for rear arc protection against enemy aircraft, examples show much of their strafing was done in that rear arc as the aircraft passed over and beyond a target. But they also had a capability unique to them. A pilot could bank the plane and circle above a target while the gunner fired downward on the inside of the turn to concentrate fire on that target; and he could hold it there on target as long as the plane circled above.

The German specialized ground attack planes had forward-firing and flexible guns and, in certain cases, downward-firing guns mounted in the fuselage. However, if these "downward" guns were fixed position or limited in fore and aft traverse, bullets would always impact along the ground in raking or "walking" fire; a gun had no real capability to aim on a specific target. This type fire was useful in places, and pursuit pilots at times "walked" bullets too. But downward-mounted guns were one element of World War I strafing that did not go on to standard use in future wars (although some slightly depressed guns have been used).

Summaries on American strafing in *The U.S. Air Services in World War I* include the following: "[T]he enemy's troops were attacked by our pursuit airplanes with machine guns and bombs.... [T]his aid from the sky in assisting during an attack by our troops or in repelling an attack or counterattack by the enemy greatly raises the morale of our own forces and much hampers the enemy. It will be well to specialize in this branch of aviation." Thus there was postwar high-level recognition of the contribution and value of strafing, where prewar judgment of it had been "absurd." However, that recognition was in broad military terms, without publicity on strafers and their accomplishments.

Maj. Hartley had said he would dearly love to know just what damage MacArthur did in a single day. Since Hartley did not know, it is unlikely the world will ever know either. A citation noted one pilot killed sixty horses and a like number of men on a mission, but no figures are found for how many he killed in the entire war, nor of accumulated scores of damage done by other individual strafers during World War I. Of the names in examples covered, only those of the top aces, with their confirmed scores of air victories, are known to the public. The "unknown" names mentioned here are not even a token of the total strafers in the war. Yet, examples leave no doubt that their duty, valor and sacrifice ranks with the greatest in all history. This is certainly the ultimate story and legacy passed on by these pioneers, and it is a legacy of honor ingrained in and inseparable from the strafing of later wars.

It is fact that strafing was a pilot and aircrew creation from which they set the way in utility and tackled varied targets, situations and weather, much done voluntarily. This established strafing as a "pilot and aircrew and cockpit" business. Expertise in and conduct of strafing operations, and the knowledge thereof, was from the start, and remains, located at combat unit level, not at high headquarters, schools, and archives. Strafers are largely their own generals in this respect, too.

In writing this chapter, I found no books dedicated to World War I "strafing" to use for reference. The examples here are based on material in books on "aces and fighter planes," including *Von Richthofen and the "Flying Circus"* by H.J. Nowarra and Kimbrough S. Brown; *Rise of the Fighter Aircraft, 1914–1918,* by Richard P. Hallion; and other works listed in the bibliography. These volumes on aces and fighters include much on strafing; yet, they do not mention "strafing" or "strafers" in titles, nor in most cases in tables of content. The same is true for general histories and other accounts of that war and subsequent wars. Fortunately, most of the following chapters rely very little on published references. They are primarily material from the "horse's mouth"— experiences gained out in the gun smoke.

· 2 ·

Pearl Harbor
World War II

During a recent book signing at an Air Force base exchange, as I showed gun camera film of strafing on a monitor, a group of high school youngsters stopped and watched for several minutes. One asked, "I thought strafing spread bullets across the ground like you see in movies, but this film isn't like that. What gives?" Before replying, I couldn't resist saying that my high school history teacher once told us, "Don't believe all in a newspaper and much less in a picture show." That led to a bit of side discussion that eliminated the Internet as a factor in the 1930s and established that movies were "in" back then, in fact, were one thing we could afford during the Great Depression. An amazing outcome to these youngsters and me was that I, when in class in 1938, had believed exactly the same thing about strafing as these students today, some 66 years later. We all had thought that it meant the "spraying" of bullets across the ground. In answer to the question, I explained the shooting in the combat film. The students agreed that was the real thing, and they departed knowing that strafing was not just "spraying." And one girl had a separate comment on the film: "They [the enemy] must have hated you guys, like awful."

For me in high school it was several years after graduation before I knew other than "spraying." In print and movies of the 1920s and 1930s about the past Great War, most all air warfare covered was on the famous aces and "dogfighting." Who would not admire the challenge of head-to-head air gunfights, the skill and cunning, and of course the courage needed? On the other hand, when and if strafing was shown, it had no tie to fame or heroes. It gave no image of superb skill, cunning, and courage. It came out in mind as just flying low, shooting bullets along the ground, which shouldn't be hard to do.

Strafing was seldom in the news before the American people in the nearly 21 years between the two World Wars. That did not change much with the start of World War II in Europe in September 1939. Early on, this was dubbed a "phony" version of the last war—foes mostly eyeing each other on a new Western Front. But in just months this one lost all resemblance to its predecessor. "Lightning war" was headlined, featuring "armored" and "mechanized" thrusts on the ground supported by "dive-bombers" in the sky. The German terms of blitzkrieg, panzer, and Stuka became household words. By late 1941, German and Axis forces had overrun and occupied Europe from the French coast on the west to the outskirts of Moscow on the east, and from the northern tip of Norway to the Mediterranean and on into Africa on the south, leaving the British Isles as sole Allied bastion on the west.

In those German ground victories, air power had made some news. Newsreels showed level high-altitude bombers in action, as well as impressive fighters such as the Bf/Me 109 covering the battlefields. However, fighters and their gunfighting (air and ground) were not top news in this war as in the past one. The new headline makers were dive-bombers and even troop-carrier planes of German paratroop operations. There was one major exception: the Battle of Britain, where British fighters immediately regained gloried status. British Hurricanes and Spitfires became the best-known fighters of the war until then, as their pilots (with help of "radar") successfully fought off the German air campaign (designed to set the stage for invasion) and won the Battle of Britain, thus insuring that "island of freedom" still remained. That same great air battle also put strategic bombing, to include attacks on cities, in the news forefront for the rest of the war.

One major land campaign had again put strafing back into its "high use" status of World War I, if not in the news. That was a lone bright spot in ground fighting in those grim days. In December 1940, Italian forces threatening Egypt were attacked by British and Commonwealth forces and were sent reeling back across North Africa. Fighter and other aircraft were key players in British success with low-level attacks and strafing of Italian armor, vehicles, guns, and troops. Then constant strafing inflicted a "mass kill" on the retreating enemy. Also Italian fighter planes were repeatedly strafed on the ground while refueling and rearming. Both Italian air and ground forces were decimated, mainly by strafing, in this victory. (But it was not a final victory in Africa yet. "Rommel" and "Afrika Korps" became household names as the Germans pushed the British back into Egypt.)

From 1940 and early 1941, U.S. National Guard and reserves of all services had been called into service and the military draft put into full effect. Newsreels of units in training on large maneuvers invariably had scenes of troops in columns suddenly scattering to ditches, fields, or woods as low-flying planes made simulated attacks down the column. This brought some public attention to strafing as part of air warfare, but it also reinforced views such as mine that it was scatter or raking fire down a column.

Many of us heard rumors at the time that this training did not always end with just the simulated attack. Accounts and memoirs of veterans over postwar years have confirmed that soldiers were told to hold in the positions they had scattered to in ditches and fields after the aircraft flew over. Vehicles came by and passed out life-size cardboard "soldiers" to place where each real soldier was positioned. Then the real soldiers departed the area as aircraft came back and this time raked the column's position with live machine gun fire. The real soldiers returned, each man to his cardboard "self." If "you" had no bullet holes, you could pick up "you" and go back to ranks in column. But if "you" were among those hit, you stayed put for medic decision on your fate. Most memoirs reflect lasting impact on both the casualties and those back in ranks from this "being strafed."

United States forces became involved with real strafing in World War II at the initial moment our nation was launched into the war on December 7, 1941, with the Japanese attack on Pearl Harbor and other installations on Oahu, Hawaii. (There had been earlier unofficial involvement by the U.S. Navy in the Battle of the Atlantic.) Of course, in Hawaii, Americans were on the receiving end of strafing fire by Japanese carrier pilots and crews, carried out thousands of miles from any ground war. That strafing was in support of the main goal of torpedo and bomb attacks on major U.S. warships in Pearl Harbor, with much of it against aircraft on our air bases on Oahu, but also spread to many other targets.

This was not history's first strafing of Americans by Japanese. In 1937 the USS *Panay*, on the Yangze River in China, and accompanying vessels were bombed and strafed by Japanese aircraft. Abandoning the sinking *Panay*, the crew made for shore in the captain's launch and a sampan. One strafing run of "sewing" fire on the launch (described by Capt. Charles Barton, USN [Ret] in *Retired Officer* magazine as stitching a path of bullets across the boat) added only one sailor wounded to substantial casualties in the overall attacks.

Certainly, Pearl Harbor is remembered foremost for infamy. The scenes of battleship row in Pearl Harbor under attack and the terrible toll of lives lost make it so, but there were also attacks on other installations that day. When accounts of individuals serving in Hawaii that morning are reviewed, the horror of sights such as the USS *Arizona* exploding, entire flight lines in flames, and comrades being killed are prominent in memories. At the same time, rarely in these accounts is there failure to mention machine-gun bullets raining down around them as well—whether one was onboard ship, in the harbor area, on an airfield, in base housing or elsewhere on an installation.

One reference alone, *December 7, 1941*, by Gordon W. Prange, which contains hundreds of statements of American military personnel and families, plus those of Japanese pilots, reflects such frequent citing of strafing fire during both waves of the attack. Personally I don't recall ever talking with a Pearl Harbor survivor who did not make some mention of machine-gun fire from the air.

At a 50th anniversary memorial service in my hometown of Waycross, Georgia, on December 7, 1991 (in which I participated), Army veteran Robert J. Ussery told of his experiences during the Pearl Harbor attack. At Schofield

26   CURTISS P-40

P-40s were first-line inventory USAAF fighters in Hawaii on December 7, 1941 (U.S. Air Force).

Barracks (adjacent to Wheeler Field, 10 miles inland north of Pearl Harbor), while he was taking a shower, he suddenly thought someone had thrown a handful of rocks into the shower room. As he looked around, all thought of rocks vanished as shattered plumbing fixtures and bullet holes in the walls, one just two inches from his head, registered as the source of the sounds he had heard. He raced outside "as was" to see what was going on.

Ussery is confident the time was 0745 when the bullets hit. That is three minutes before the time usually reported for the first attack on Kaneohe Naval Air Station (NAS) across the island from Pearl and almost 10 minutes before the first recorded strike on Ford Island Air Station in the harbor. It is about 15 minutes before the first torpedo plane attacks on battleship row. Ussery's theory is that Schofield Barracks was the first major military installation the Japanese planes coming from the north across the island reached—and some eager Japanese pilots strafed the first target they saw. Ussery indicated that a tablet mounted at that spot on Schofield Barracks announces it as the location of the first enemy shots fired on U.S. military forces in World War II. Those first shots were strafing.

Howard Beverly, a Waycross native, was also at Schofield Barracks that morning, serving with the 11th Field Artillery. Dressing in anticipation of a breakfast of pancakes, a treat available by special order on Sunday mornings, he caught a glimpse of an airplane flying through the yard beyond his barracks. Dashing outside he met a soldier who had been hit with a strafing round that literally parted his hair with a scalp wound, perhaps the first American soldier wounded in World War II. Beverly reports the area was strafed several times thereafter that morning. Once he was saved when the trunk of a palm tree took bullets while he lay flat on the other side. As the Japanese Zero/Zeke fighter passed over he had the further experience of an ammo link plopping to the ground right between his legs (*Waycross* [GA] *Journal Herald*, December 4, 1991).

The following smattering of brief accounts on strafing actions of general recorded history may reflect some extent of the strafing.

In the first wave of Japanese attacks, fighters first strafed Kaneohe, then dive-bombers came in, followed by more fighters strafing. Eyewitness accounts cover machine-gunning of planes and ramp and hangar areas as well as autos, individuals, and the mess hall, which was shot full of holes,

At Ewa Field, Zeros made up to eight repeat strafing passes. Marine Corporal D.J. Shaw reported he first knew what was going on when his barracks got tattooed with bullets. Moving vehicles were targets, including constant shooting during a heroic trip by personnel on a fire truck across an open field and ramp to reach burning planes.

Wheeler Field, the main Army Air Forces P-40 base, was hit by 25 dive-bombers, each plane then returning on four or five strafing passes. Witnesses from the ground described the air as being full of enemy planes circling but making strafing passes and shooting in no apparent pattern, some so low they flew into and cut telephone wires. As Zeros arrived to strafe, the field was already a sea of fire.

Japanese pilots of at least one carrier had been briefed not to attack downwind and then to shoot into the closest row of parked planes. Attacking in this manner would send a screen of black smoke over all the other planes and block view of them on following passes. The photo with this text, whether by plan or accident, shows that the upwind rows of planes in the photo remain clear of the heavy smoke.

The (U.S.) Army Air Force's (AAF) Hickam Field, adjacent to Pearl Harbor, was attacked by dive-bombers, who also strafed parked planes and hangars. Again eyewitnesses reported a much wider range of shooting, to include cars in parking lots, quarters, and a specific blast of bullets into the doorway of the officers' club. Zeros over Hickam mixed in some air-to-air-shooting on unarmed AAF B-17s arriving from California low on fuel. One B-17 hit by enemy fire on approach crash landed and burst into flame. Escaping airmen were strafed. Others on the field were gunned down.

This photograph, identified in *The Army Air Forces in World War I*, Vol. 1, as taken by the Japanese, shows several rows of closely spaced P-40s on the upwind end of the ramp at Wheeler Field still visible to enemy strafers during their attacks. Heavy smoke from burning planes and hangars blank out visibility of the downwind portion of the ramp (U.S. Air Force).

In the harbor, as Japanese planes released torpedoes just above the water at U.S. battleships and then passed over those targets, rear gunners strafed ships and about anything on Ford Island. One plane pulled up over the stern of the USS *Nevada* just as the color guard was raising the flag. The rear gunner cut loose at band and color guard, spraying the deck with bullets and putting holes in the flag but failing to hit anybody. Less fortunate were three sailors from the overturned USS *Oklahoma*. Clinging to the pontoons of an upside-down catapult plane in the water, two were killed by strafing fire on that plane.

As 18 Zeros arrived over Kaneohe and nearby Bellows Field, three pilots of the U.S. 44th Pursuit Squadron attempted to get P-40s into the air in opposition but one was killed getting into his plane, another was shot down on takeoff, and the third was shot down just after getting airborne. Witnesses report six zeros made strafing passes on a taxiing P-40 but could not hit it, but once airborne the enemy fighters shot it down. Overall, the strafing of Kaneohe and Bellows was described as inflicting much damage, but with wild flying and seemingly inept skidding and yawing in passes and turns, spraying bullets all over the bases.

Second wave strafing at Hickam inflicted some of the highest casualties among Army Air Forces personnel as airmen worked desperately to ready and load any serviceable A-20s and B-17s for missions to seek out the Japanese carriers. Grim eye witness reports came from there and nearby Fort Kamehameha where a number of soldiers were killed by strafing. More suffered the same fate when a low-flying enemy plane crashed into a tree and wreckage flew into a group of men on a road.

In the overall history of strafing there is little about the Japanese strafing in Hawaii that is representative of most other strafing in World War II. A few points on that are worthwhile to keep in mind for comparison with later U.S. strafing in the war. U.S. aircraft were parked close together on ramps for protection against sabotage. This made ideal targets for air attack of any kind, certainly strafing. The surprise of the first-wave attacks and the general lack of loaded weapons in place and in the hands of U.S. personnel made even easier "pickings" for low-flying attackers.

The Japanese early-model Zero/Zeke fighters (A6M2, A6M3) at Hawaii were normally equipped with forward-firing armament of two 20mm cannon with 60 rounds per gun and two 7.7mm machine guns with 500 rounds each— about six seconds of 20mm fire and 30 seconds 7.7mm fire. With evidence that pilots made five to eight passes, the conclusion is that they had to make very selective use of 20mm firing time (if not saved for air combat) and do much strafing with only the 7.7mm guns. The Val dive-bombers over Hawaii (D3A1) had two forward-firing 7.7mm machine guns and one rear cockpit 7.7mm flexible gun. Japanese Kate bombers (B5W1, B5W2) and torpedo planes in the attack had one or two aft-cockpit flexible 7.7mm guns. Thus, despite the Zero's solid gain in firepower over World War I fighters, overall much of Japanese strafing in Pearl Harbor attacks was rifle-caliber fire, or the same as most World War I strafing.

Repeated eyewitness mention of "wild flying and spraying of bullets" reflects cases of pilots holding the "trigger" down while flying across bases, through yards, and in hard maneuvers, which certainly will send bullets far and wide. Such shooting may account for the post-mission admission of one Japanese dive-bomber pilot that it took him three passes at Ewa before he could hit any of the parked planes with his gunfire.

While neither the armament nor the tactics of the Japanese strafers at Pearl Harbor match firepower and results of U.S. strafing later in the war, unfortunately it was effective enough in this situation to contribute heavily to devastating loss of aircraft and many casualties on bases and in the harbor. And far-flung bullets took lives well removed from flight lines and ship decks.

The story of U.S. personnel fighting back is the most significant one in this history. Hawaii was a case of extreme "advantage" to the attackers. From that it might appear the challenge to Japanese pilots and crews was "no sweat, a turkey shoot." It may have been such to some extent at the start, yet it did not end that way.

Stories of individual heroics are legend. They include well-known ones such as that of mess steward Doris "Dorie" Miller of the USS *West Virginia*. Amid the flames of his burning ship, he took over an unmanned machine gun, a weapon he had never fired, and got it firing. Eyewitnesses report he shot down at least two and probably four low-flying planes. On orders to abandon ship, he kept firing. It took a direct order to make him leave. For his actions he was awarded the Navy Cross.

Among lesser known actions, Marine PFC Mark Fisher came off guard duty on the floating dry dock that morning. Trucked to his barracks overlooking the harbor, he joined his unit in breaking out 90mm antiaircraft guns packed in crates for deployment to Wake Island. Quickly set up in an adjacent field those big guns were put into action, along with bolt-action rifles by all Marines not on the 90s. According to Fisher, what they could have used was something in between, but without it they fired away relentlessly with what they had (*Waycross* [GA] *Journal Herald*, November 25, 1991).

Many more weapons—antiaircraft artillery (AAA), "in betweens," and individual—were put into action by all services. Much of this involved finding keys for locks or forcing a way into gun rooms and ammo bunkers. Perhaps the most graphic example of determination to shoot down enemy planes was the pulling of aircraft guns from storage, maintenance, wreckage, etc., and firing them as never intended—outside airplanes, propped on anything available, and even by hand with human muscle as gun mounts.

Japanese losses have been cited as low, 29 out of 355 attackers, or 8 percent. The first wave of 185 lost nine planes (5 torpedo, 3 fighter, 1 dive-bomb). The second wave of 170 planes lost 20 (6 fighter, 14 dive-bomb). These Zero and Val losses were a marked increase over the first wave; and the difference in Val losses, 1 versus 14, is fair evidence that the second wave was a much different fight—more like the deadly nature of World War I strafing.

The Japanese used strafing extensively in opening attacks on U.S. forces in other parts of the Pacific. Wake Island was hit about noon, 8 December, by low-flying aircraft. Bombs and guns combined to destroy seven of the 12 F-4F-3 Wildcat fighters of Marine Squadron VMF-211 based there. Casualties included three pilots who made heroic attempts to reach planes and get airborne, but none survived even to the point of taxiing. The Japanese attacks on Wake spread well beyond strafing aircraft to include fuel tanks, the Pan American Airways hotel, and one of Pan Am's big flying boats. Despite being punctured with two dozen bullet holes, that strafed plane (Philippine Clipper) was flown out a few hours later carrying a massive load of civilian workers and wounded Marines.

In the U.S. struggle against Japanese invasion forces, a few Wildcats kept flying until the last was destroyed three days before Christmas. Marine pilots

23

SEVERSKY P–35

Pilots of P-35s were among the earliest American strafers of the war in valiant missions in the Philippines. These prewar fighters had only two synchronized machine guns, which show in the nose (U.S. Air Force).

had scored bomb hits on two cruisers, one transport, and the destroyer *Kisaragi*, which exploded and sank with all hands. Among strafing attacks on enemy ships, the Japanese force commander, Admiral Kajioka, was almost hit himself when his flagship, the cruiser *Yubari*, was machine-gunned by a Wildcat's .50-caliber guns.

In the Philippines the initial Japanese high-level bombing attack on Clark Field on 8 December did extensive damage to base facilities. Yet most of the U.S. B-17s there actually escaped destruction or major damage and remained flyable. But when enemy Zero pilots, who had received recent intensive air-ground gunnery training in Formosa, followed up with aggressive and effective low-level canon/machine-gun attacks, most all B-17s were burned or otherwise destroyed. Japanese Zeros played a similar role against P-35 and P-40 fighters of the 24th Pursuit Group in the Philippines. For example, on 10 December, after U.S. P-35 pilots pressed attacks on enemy landing forces at Wigan, they returned to base at Del Carmen. In came Zeros—strafing. Some eighteen P-35s were left as wreckage, useless for any further action. The 24th Group carried on gallantly in action with ever fewer aircraft, transferring personnel to the infantry as air capability was lost.

Beyond doubt strafing played the key part in destruction of U.S. aircraft in the early days and months of the war in the Pacific. It seems obvious this was preplanned in most opening attacks, especially for the Zero/Zeke fighters, and particularly so in the Philippines. Equally obvious is that the Japanese were the only nation to plan and rely to that extent on strafing at the start or initially to apply strafing experience of World War I to this war or, as some World War II veteran strafer friends of mine have said over the years, "had sense enough to do it." (Obviously that could lead one to wonder how things would have gone if the Germans had opened the Battle of Britain with massive low-level strafing against British air defenses, aircraft, transportation, shipping, etc. instead of high-level bombing. But "ifs" aren't history and other than one or two tempting cases we will try to stick to things that did happen and leave out speculation on "could have happened.")

There is no wondering involved in the valor and sacrifice of American servicemen and servicewomen in the Pacific in late 1941 and early 1942. No other war fighting ranks higher, by all services in actions on land and on sea and in the air. In a story of strafing and strafers, it is a milestone in two ways. One, this was the most strafing done by an enemy on U.S. forces and the most capability lost to strafing in one short time frame. Two, the earliest U.S. strafing missions of World War II were flown. These were done against great odds with whatever units had left for planes and ordnance, down to single fighters with guns doing battle alone with enemy navy cruisers. This was the opening fire of immensely more U.S. strafing to follow in that war.

A very special remembrance of the Japanese Pearl Harbor attack is found on Hickam AFB. The PACAF headquarters building located across the street from hangars and flight line still carries the scars of that day. Many bullet holes and shrapnel gouges in the masonry and concrete building have never been patched or covered over. They remain as inflicted on 7 December 1941.

· 3 ·

Behind the Gun Sight
Gunnery

In late spring 1942 I was a newly promoted corporal, U.S. Army (AC), assigned to the U.S. Army Air Forces (USAAF) Armament School, Lowry Field, Colorado. As did many others of my generation who finished high school during the Great Depression years, I reluctantly turned down scholarship offers and postponed college in order to add to the support of our family, a widowed mother with four children. By 1941, I was playing professional baseball in the minor leagues with a winter job as railroad fireman on steam locomotives. I enlisted immediately after Pearl Harbor. While attending armament school I applied for and was accepted in the Aviation Cadet Program, and then was held at the school awaiting entry into that program. I had two duty assignments: flight line instructor on synchronized machine guns and field captain of the school baseball team. Fellow instructors were sure that my jump from buck private to two stripes was due to the second job, a jockstrap promotion.

In armament school much training had been on outdated aircraft and configurations because everything current was desperately needed for operational use. Planes such as the P-37 (which I worked on), the P-35, with only two guns, and the A-24, with only one forward gun, were hardly what students of 1942 would handle in this war. Yet, there were equipments taught they most definitely would work with, live and die with. A good part of that was found in the school's gun display hall, much of it dedicated to the inventive genius of John Moses Browning. His military arms shown included a Colt .45 automatic pistol, a Browning automatic rifle, a Browning machine gun (caliber .30), a Browning automatic cannon (37mm) and, at center stage, a Browning machine gun (caliber .50).

That last gun was the result of Gen. Pershing's urgent requirement for a new aircraft gun to use in dealing with the armor of enemy attack planes in World War I. The need specified a machine gun of at least half-inch caliber and muzzle velocity of 2,700 feet per second. Browning's design was rushed into being but not deployed before the Armistice. With a shaky existence during the between-war years, it survived and was developed into the Browning machine gun, caliber .50, basic. That gun allowed manufacture of one receiver (capable of left or right feed, manual or electric firing) to be used in seven different types of guns during World War II. It was produced by nine major arms/industrial firms during the war and used by every service in every theater—land, sea, and air.

For USAAF and Navy/Marine air units—and this story of strafing—the version of prime use in World War II was the Browning aircraft machine gun, caliber .50, M2. Almost all combat aircraft had it as armament. About the only aircraft guns of importance that were not Browning designs were 20mm cannon, mainly Hispano, used in certain U.S. aircraft and British planes flown at times by Americans. Mr. Browning's contributions to his country, and his place in the history of warfare, including strafing, went on far beyond this war, too.

As opposed to World War I, where typical aircraft gun armament of friend and foe were much the same, World War II saw a major change between the United States and many foreign nations. The wars of the late 1930s sent the world into crash programs of increased firepower in aircraft. With options of bigger guns or more guns, each approach was involved, but both together became more the standard. Most foreign nations went to multiple cannon, 20mm to 30mm and even larger, plus limited machine guns in most cases, often synchronized in the aircraft nose. Cannon were primarily in wings or barrel-through-prop-hub on single-engine planes, and clustered in the nose of multiengine types. Germany, Japan, and Great Britain stuck with this approach during the war, with four or more cannon on late-war fighters—for example, the German Me 262 jets with six.

The United States did feature cannon in some late–1930 designs such as 20mm for the P-38 (in the nose between twin engines) and 37mm for the P-39 (through the prop hub), both plus machine guns. The later-war P-61, primarily a night fighter, had four 20mm cannon plus machine guns. Also, B-29s were cannon equipped. However, the bulk of U.S. fighters had machine gun armament, caliber .50, with all guns located in wings, firing outside the single engine propeller arc. Most P-40s had six guns, P-51s the same, and all P-47s had eight. Most Navy/Marine fighters had similar armament, six .50s in the wings, and a few exceptions with cannon.

The United States' decision to use machine guns in aircraft as opposed to cannon of other nations has been the subject of debate in some quarters, but it is not a debatable subject here. It is purely fact, history, and the gun types and locations used play a major role in pilot and crew gunnery and gunfighting procedures and challenges.

Armorers were much affected by those gun factors, too. Among published memoirs of an armorer (which are rare) is one by Willard Bierly, 357th Fighter Group, ETO (European theater of operations). First working on P-39s

Thirty caliber guns were the norm in fighter aircraft, and bombs, for the most part, were in 100, 250, and 500 pound weights. War accelerates technological development, however, and it was not long before .50 caliber and even 20 mm replaced the 30s, and bombs grew in to the 1000 and 2000 pound categories. Special purpose ordnance proliferated, for example; armor piercing casings, shaped charge explosives, and sophisticated fusing.

During the initial stages of World War II, armament and ordnance were little changed from the munitions common to World War I. Air delivered bombs had increased in size as aircraft had increased in carrying capacity, but the technology was little changed.

Air Force Armament Museum display of Browning Cal-.50 M2 and Cal-.30 aircraft machine guns. The Cal-.50 (lower) is in flexible gun configuration.

equipped with prop-hub 20mm nose .50s, and wing .30s, he seemed quite pleased when his unit switched to P-51s with wing .50s only. Now there was just one type gun to service and its design and access from the wing top simplified that. Other complexities also were gone. Synchronizers no longer applied and pilot gun charging and clearing provisions had been dropped as no longer needed with the highly reliable Browning—a gun Bierly referred to as "61 pounds of engineering marvel" (*American Aviation Historical Society Journal*).

That marvel, the Browning caliber .50 M2 (some were designated Colt MG 52/53) was most widely known as simply the "Fifty." Technically its rate of fire was 750 to 850 rounds per minute, but which was popularly known as 800 (the later M3 model, 1,200). The "school" answer for muzzle velocity was 2,840 feet per second, with standard ball ammunition, although higher with later combat ammo (more on ammo to follow).

By July 1942 I was in Aviation Cadet Program for pilot training. It has been said the four phases of that experience—Preflight, Primary, Basic, and Advance—can be summed up as Get undivided attention, Learn to fly, Then learn the Army way, and Grasp the purpose: flying and fighting. With the first three phases common, the last divided into "twin-engine" and "single-engine,"

The author in a P-40L of the 79th Fighter Group, Italy, MTO, 1943; the Cal-.50 guns in wings and optical gun sight are in front of the pilot.

the twin orientated to bomber and other multiengine aircraft operations, the single to fighter combat.

Gunnery training took two forms as well. One was flexible and turret guns, mainly bombers, where the gunner did the aiming and firing. This training was done in centralized gunnery schools, plus crew training in units. The other was fixed-forward guns, fighters and certain others, where the pilot flies the plane to aim the guns and fires them too. This was done in with other pilot flying and fighting training. Once a pilot entered fixed-gun gunnery, it was of two basic types—air-to-air and air-to-ground. In training, then and thereafter, he fired at targets both in the air and on the ground—firing "Aerial Gunnery" and "Ground Gunnery," the official gun firing training terms and events for air combat and strafing respectively. However, that is all they were and they were done under set patterns and procedures on ranges and not intended as simulated combat gunfighting, air or ground.

My cadet class (43-C, Eagle Pass, Texas) fired our first gunnery in advance while still cadets, done in AT-6s with Browning caliber .30 guns. This was normal for early war classes. In later war classes gunnery was not fired until in fighter transition. Despite problems of many flyers in early gunnery to hit targets, modesty has not been prominent in recounting experiences. One old fighter pilot wrote a book in which he did not claim he was the best shot in his class. This being considered unusual, others asked, "Why?" He replied, "No way, people might think that is all I was, just best in that class, rather than best in the entire USAAF."

In March 1943, wearing 2nd Lt. bars and pilot wings, I moved on to fly fighters. Any summation of fighter or other training in World War II is subject to exception. No single program was followed by all. Some pilots went into an Operational Training Unit (OTU) and overseas with that unit. Others went to a Replacement Training Unit (RTU), or later in the war to a Combat Crew Training School/Station (CCTS), then as fillers to overseas units. Some trained in the same type or model aircraft they flew in combat, many did not. Early years had few combat returnee instructors, late years had many. Early RTU pilots got 40 to 60 hours in fighters, late ones often more. Early years used Grade 100 fuel (100 plus octane combat fuel) with no restrictions on engine operation; late years used Grade 90 (less than 100 octane training only) with severe limits on maximum engine power and aircraft performance. Overseas needs at any point influenced policy as did a shocking overall accident rate. In the first 32 months the USAAF lost over 11,000 planes in noncombat crashes in the United States (*USAF Flying Safety*, January 1992).

Then, of course, training other than as a fighter was involved. That included attack aircraft such as the prewar A-24, A-31/35, and the A-36, which trained for ground attack. However, most of these "dive-bombers" were not being used in combat. The A-24 had seen some action early in the war against Japan; it was gallant but costly. One mission of seven A-24s at Burma on 29 July 1942 had six fail to return, about their last use by the USAAF. Yet, Navy and Marine counterparts such as the SBD were effective mainstays in the Pacific throughout the war. Against Germany these prewar dive-bombers had never even been deployed to Europe. The A-36 was a different story. It was a P-51 with dive brakes, bomb racks, etc. They were used in combat, if in limited numbers up through mid–1944, two groups against Germany, one against Japan, and they will show up here in later chapters.

One other category of aircraft was definitely involved. These were planned "strafers," light and medium bombers—A-20, A-26, B-25—which had been heavily armed with double digit numbers of fixed forward-firing guns, mostly Browning caliber .50s, plus some 20mm, and even 75mm in some B-25s. Early use of A-20s on low-level attack against German airfields, more courageous than successful, was short lived. Thereafter, level bombing from medium altitudes by all these planes was their main role, and a major effort, in the war against Germany. Against Japan the "hard nose" gun-bristling configurations were regularly used in low-altitude gun attack on sea and land targets. They were a major factor in destruction of enemy shipping and aircraft and are a distinct part of the history of strafing.

Other categories also will show up in strafing action of later chapters,

33   NORTH AMERICAN B-25

B-25 hard nose "strafer," with multiple forward-firing guns in the nose and fuselage blisters, plus turret guns (U.S. Air Force).

many of which had primary missions other that air-ground gunfighting, to include Navy patrol aircraft and USAAF heavy bombers carrying firepower such as 12–13 cal-.50s in most B-17s and B-24s, plus the 20mm cannon of B-29s. I will not attempt to cover specifics of flying training and gunnery for all of that, but only look at a few examples from my experience, which most others encountered in some form, too, and that had an impact on later air-ground gunfighting.

When I arrived for fighter training in April 1943 with the 337th Fighter Group (Sarasota AAF, Florida), which was serving as an RTU flying P-40s, I don't recall that we new pilots were advised of the USAAF's early war finding and decision: "The more versatile fighter-bomber—a straight fighter equipped with bomb racks—proved much more useful [than specialized attack planes/dive-bombers] (*The Army Air Forces in World War II*, Vol. 6). There was no need. We were well aware of the P-39/P-400 "fighter-bomber" work at Guadalcanal and other Pacific actions. We knew that the USAAF had nothing in place in North Africa and Alaska except fighters to do the dive-bombing and strafing. Also, any concerns that we might be separated and some trained as "fighter" and others as "fighter-bomber" were quickly erased. We would be trained "fighter" to the core. Thus the USAAF decision to use fighter planes to do ground attack did not reorient the priorities or objectives in fighter training.

Of course the fighter mission was first and foremost for air combat, but it included additional mission of ground attack and strafing. And that is how we trained: much disciplined aircraft operation, formation flying, etc., then aggressive air combat, simulated hostile skies and all-out dogfighting (without hot guns)—amid constant reminders to "be alert" and "fly the airplane right." At this stage of the war, command policy and grade 100 fuel allowed us to use full engine power and maximum performance flying. Then we went into use of aircraft guns and some bombing.

It may seem logical that air and ground gunnery would have been approached as two separate operations. They used different range facilities and procedures: Aerial—shooting at a banner target towed in the air by an aircraft, normally with a turning "curve of pursuit" attack requiring aim out in front (lead) of the target, done over open water or desert or swamp away from populated areas; Ground—shooting at a panel target mounted on the ground, usually with shallow straight-in dive attack and direct aim on the still target, done both on large reservations such as Eglin, Florida, and small local ranges such as Sarasota on a key or island near populated areas. However, they had far more in common than they were different, and they were undertaken together—a fact that strafers would greatly appreciate later in combat. From the very first briefing on gunnery, it was clear that the object, the same as on a rifle range, was to hit the target with every bullet fired. The number of hits per total of rounds fired gave your score. We were not going to just spray bullets somewhere.

Obviously technical features of planes, guns, and sights controlled much of the "what" and "how" of pilot tasks in gunnery. Yet, these are seldom mentioned in literature on air war combat, aircraft, etc., and thus they are rarely thought about when one reads or views movies or video. But keeping them in mind can shed different light on the action, as in the case of gun sights. The most publicized information on World War II gun sights naturally came from the fame of air victories and aces. For example, Brig. Gen. Chuck Yeager has said, "In the latter part of World War II and Korea, lead computing gun sights like the K-14 in the P-51 made it easy to lead a guy and do it right. We no longer had to depend on instinct. We had to train a little to learn the new equipment" (*USAF Flying Safety*, November 1992).

That milestone in sight development has led many people to believe all shooting was so enhanced during the war. Even if the K-14 aided air-ground gunnery were to equal extent of air-air, which it didn't, very few USAAF fighters ever had that sight. The great majority had sights of unrenowned designations such as N-3, N-9, and MK VIII—which computed nothing. Even so, these sights were real advances over World War I "iron sights." These were optical or "reflector" sights. A stationary sight image, usually an outer ring with a dot (termed the "pipper") in the center, was projected on a sight glass directly in front of the pilot, who could sight through it and the windscreen without lining up one eye precisely behind the image. He could look over the entire view up ahead and still keep aim on a target. Certain fixed information was provided the pilot. For example, the MK VIII sight of most P-47s was a 100-mile-per-hour sight. In deflection shooting, one radius of the ring was proper lead for a target crossing velocity of 100 mph. An enemy fighter crossing 90-degrees at 300 mph required three radii lead. In mils, at 1,000 yards range out in front, the ring covered an area 100 yards in diameter; at 1,000-foot range, 100-foot diameter. The pipper was two mils; at 1,000 feet it covered two feet.

The overwhelming majority of air-ground gunnery in World War II was fired with that fixed, or caged, "ring and pipper" image, with the "pipper" itself the sole aim reference. Corrections for varied conditions of range, wind, moving target on surface, etc., were purely by pilot judgment for the situation, not any computation in the sight.

Another major factor was "harmonization," or "bore sighting," the alignment of guns and gun sight into a gunfire system. Where guns and sight were located together in front of the pilot (most World War I fighters, nearly most World War II P-38s and some gun nose bombers), this was a minor alignment with relatively slight impact on pilot gunnery. But for the most common configuration of World War II USAAF fighters—internal wing guns only—guns and sight were well separated both laterally and vertically. Major alignment was involved, and so was impact on pilot gunnery.

Had the only objective been to "spray" bullets on enemy troops or to "scatter shoot" at enemy planes, the guns and sights could all have been left pointed straight ahead. But that was not the concept behind six- and eight cal-.50 machine guns in U.S. fighters. Combined rapid-fire of all guns of each plane hitting a single point together compounded into enormously greater impact energy, force and destructive power than might be possible with merely machine gun fire (more about this later). To achieve the desired result all guns were aligned to converge and intersect the sight "pipper" line-of-sight at a point out in front of the plane.

The chart shown here is for the P-47D. The center point of the four guns in each wing was just over 18 feet apart, firing outside a 12- or 13-foot diameter propeller. All guns were about four feet below the gun sight. Each gun had to be aligned inward to take care of some nine feet in azimuth, plus corrected for four feet in elevation. The procedure to do this was no quick adjustment on a parked aircraft. Each plane had to be jacked up and carefully leveled; then sight and guns were aligned by "bore sighting" (looking through barrels with a special device) to converge on a common point. Three systems and types of

P-47 GUN HARMONIZATION (BORE SIGHT)

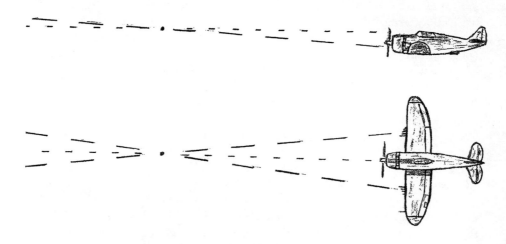

— — Gunsight "pipper" alignment. —— —— Gun barrel bore alignment. • Harmonization point/distance.
Specifics and their great importance to pilots are covered in the text.

facilities were normally used for the procedure. First, by far the best was "firing in"—bore sight at full measured distance of desired convergence point on a firing range/butt, then firing all guns in proof test. Second, and next best, was the full distance procedure, any suitable location (ramp, between taxiways, etc.) without firing in. Third and least desirable was bore sight on an intermediate pattern where full distance was impractical (in or between hangars, etc.) using a Technical Order 1,000-inch procedure. Some local ingenious methods were devised too. In most units each plane was run through bore sight when received in the unit, periodically thereafter, and any time it was suspected of being "off."

A standard figure of bore sight distance for all fighters in World War II would make concise history, but not precise. I fired gunnery in P-40s bore sighted at 750 feet, flew combat in both P-40s and P-47s bore sighted at 750 feet, and P-47s at 900 feet. A range of 500 to 1,000 feet would cover most cases—early in the war more likely 500 to 750, later in the war probably 900 to 1,000. However, changing distances was no routine step such as a change of bomb fuses; each plane had to be completely re-bore sighted at the new distance.

Obviously the effective range of cal-.50 ammo far exceeded these bore sight distances, thus it was not a factor in selection. Many factors could be discussed: aircraft types, theater operations and type mission being flown, air-air or air-ground gunfighting, and unit commander decisions. But certain broader demands overplayed specializing to any extent. These were fighters. They had to do both air-to-air and air-to-ground shooting; shorter distances favored air-air, a bit farther out helped air-ground. Also, as close in as practical produced better pilot aim and greater velocity of impacts. Bore sight distances were geared to the across-the-board best way to blow the most enemy aircraft and other targets all to hell rather than just pepper them. In the same light, World War II fighters could be bore sighted with the guns depressed a bit to aid ground gunnery or elevated some to add lead in aerial gunnery. But doing either one degraded capability and safety to do the other, which was loss of ability to do the full mission and thus unacceptable.

Harmonization/bore sighting had one other preselected input: airspeed. For a P-47 it was normally 270 miles per hour. That speed, the basis of leveling the aircraft for bore sighting, gave the pilot a base point at which everything in the system was in optimum alignment. In the air, 270 mph was about the middle point of pilot operating speeds, stall to maximum, overall a hub around which varying speeds in air combat maneuvers would be expected to occur.

In one respect, harmonization speed had no effect on shooting. Guns and sight were firmly fixed in aligned positions. Wherever the pipper was aimed the guns held their relationship and convergence pattern, whether flying 150 or 430 mph (or even more in dives). However, that speed was important to gunnery. At or near that speed, there were no angle of attack effects for the pilot to cope with, and precise "trim" (with no yaw or pitch errors) was much easier to hold than at speed extremes. For example, a P-40 on takeoff required much right rudder, in a high-speed dive much left rudder, but at cruise very little rudder and less pilot effort.

Some other effects from harmonization speed will be noted in combat, but first a pilot had to qualify in gunnery to get there. And actually both aerial and ground gunnery were orientated to help him do that. Shown is a typical World War II ground gunnery pattern. A primary goal was for a pilot to arrive at the proper firing point (bore sight distance) at the proper firing speed (bore sight speed) in a shallow dive, around 15 degrees. Then, from practice, he had to learn and repeat firing on all passes at that firing point. Normally two guns, companion in each wing, with ball ammo plus tracers, were fired in training. Ammo loads were frequently 50 rounds per gun, a figure that facilitated both loading and scoring, and allowed the pilot to get some 4 to 6 passes of "trigger touch" short firing bursts per mission. However loads, use of tracers, etc., could vary considerably by units.

With guns bore sighted at 750 feet, firing both guns at that distance would have hit a standard target (10 by 10 feet). But if a pilot fired early at 1,500 feet out, the rounds from both guns would cross over halfway to the target and then spread out enough to totally miss on each side. Firing inside the 750 feet would not allow both guns to converge on target, but a pilot missing that way was in grave danger of flying into the target or the ground. A foul line for break off of fire and immediate pull up was used, but pilots were lost flying into the ground in training.

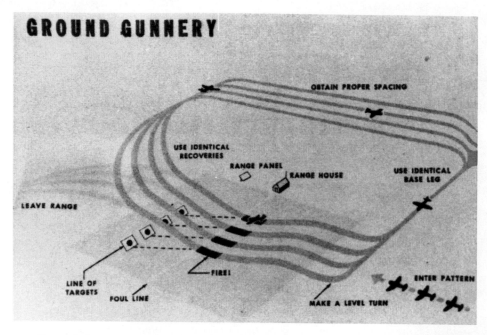

Ground Gunnery Range and Flight Pattern (AAF Manual 50-5, P-47, World War II).

The cold hard fact is that harmonization of wing-gun fighters made ground gunnery very close-range shooting in an aircraft still diving toward the target and the ground. This created an inherent hazard, one overcome only by full attention and no slips in judgment. Pilots in training, with only the task to qualify at the moment, could already foresee how this hazard would be greatly compounded in real air-ground gunfighting.

The P-47 has been used for example of gun harmonization because it was the USAAF fighter most used as a fighter-bomber and strafer in the war. Also, almost all gun camera film stills shown later were by P-47s, thus this material will apply directly to action in those illustrations.

A few instructions on ground gunnery are extracted from *AAF Manual No. 50-5, Pilot Training Manual for the Thunderbolt P-47*:

> Pattern 1200 to 1500 feet ... first passes dry runs ... trim in dive, leave it set. Keep ball centered. No skidding. Dive at bore sight speed ... gun switch on, fire near as possible to foul line ... mere touch of trigger ... short burst 5 or 6 rounds. Start pull-up when bullets strike. Then forget firing, attention to flying the airplane. Recover above 75 feet [which wasn't always done] [as] lower unsafe because of "mushing" tendencies of P-47. Gun switch off [also, specific warnings were given on "target fixation" and flying into the ground].

In addition to poor scores, various flying problems ranging from sloppy patterns to safety violations would fail a pilot to qualify in gunnery. Shooting

The author in a P-47D, a strong fighter "strafer," this one from the 86th Fighter Group, over Germany's Rhine River shortly after VE-Day, 1945.

techniques also could result in failure. In ground gunnery, "walking" bullets at a target would do it. "Pinpoint" impact of rounds was demanded; the pilot hit or missed that way, no "spraying" or "hosing" allowed.

On completion of RTU, I did not go overseas with my counterparts. The 337th was short of permanent pilots until more combat returnees were available. I was assigned there with duties of towing targets, flying maintenance test hops, and leading gunnery missions, aerial and ground. Guidance to me on the latter was "have them shoot like you do." With three trainee pilots (or some holdovers from my class yet to qualify) on each mission, I first of all tried to set an example: to fly and lead each mission right, and shoot my target full of holes on each one, while also working with them to "get holes too." Along with a rehash of manual and other prior instructions, a few personal hints were offered, including these on ground gunnery:

Pattern important—if we fly it right, dive and speed falls in place—special note, watch altitude in final turn, losing any there ruins pass, too flat. Trim by feel—I trim a fraction off neutral—keep light back stick pressure in aerial passes, light forward pressure in ground passes. Learn "sight picture" for correct range—splitting looks front and side can help "good range," but hurt "good aim." Trust the sight, look there, not at tracers—subconsciously you might follow the tracers, thus when "touching" the trigger stay steady in "eyeing" the sight pipper on into the target. Keep flying—some pilots "lock-up" on the controls when the guns cut loose—don't. As in skeet follow through—stay on target on through trigger release and all rounds are underway. Never think of or try to correct aim after trigger touch—with proper range, short burst, it's too late. Fraction of second steady follow through leads into a safe pull-up, attempt to re-aim there can send you into the ground. Precise airplane control in aim is necessary, pure roll will not hurt but any waiver in pitch and/or yaw will. A world of details involved, but we are going to work to "fly the airplane right"—stay ahead of and avoid glitches, and develop a total and repeatable flying maneuver in mind and feel that does the job pass after pass—rather than fly a mass of details each time. Everybody do that, get hits, 10–20 percent, qualify—then we'll all compete for expert status—50 percent and up.

We talked of Mother Nature challenges, too. One was wind in ground gunnery. Correcting for it might appear simple, no different from other flying. However, it was not just airplane track or path to be concerned with; it was also the bore sight point out front that had to arrive on target when firing, not the airplane. That was controlled more by position of the aircraft nose than aircraft track over the ground. For crosswind corrections, "banking" was better than "crabbing" but took alertness for safe pullout. Unless planned for in passes, head winds flattened the dive and could result in needing the nose up to miss the ground while needing the nose down to put the pipper on target. It was impossible to both score and survive from there. Unless planned for, tail winds could cause increasing nose down in a pass to keep the pipper from drifting beyond the target, jeopardizing score or safety. Of course, in training, winds were monitored and passed to pilots by range control and visual means.

The pilots I flew with for the two months I was held at Sarasota all qualified in gunnery. By late July I was back in the overseas movement process, carrying deep appreciation for full acceptance and treatment as a permanent party member of the 98th Squadron, 337th Group, while there, and for the additional flying and gunnery accomplished. That additional work had included more mock dogfighting too, which was valid simulation of the real thing in execution (if not in the finality of result in combat) and camera scoring was used in some units. Ground gunnery and a bit more low-altitude flying than in training were about the only extra flying work toward strafing. Rarely were pilots turned loose anywhere to fully simulate strafing as we heard it was being done in combat. Most background on that came from "talk" with combat veterans, not mock flying. Among such instructors while I was at Sarasota were one from Alaska, one from the Eagle Squadron, and several from the Pacific.

Few fighter pilots headed overseas without openly hoping for an assignment to a unit mainly engaged in air combat (such as P-47s, England, 1943, escorting bombers, fighter sweeps, etc.) rather than to a unit mainly doing air-ground work (such as P-40s, North Africa, 1943). Perhaps things had not changed greatly since von Richthofen kept his brother out of ground attack in the last war, and for the same reasons, which had already become well known in this one—gloried tradition of air combat versus the no fame and better odds of being killed while strafing. Either way, one thing was certain. The guns in wing-gun fighters would be harmonized about the same overseas as in training. All the skill and technique necessary to hit banners and panels here would be just as inherent over there whether shooting airplanes in the air or on the ground, locomotives, gun positions, or tanks. But for ground shooting there would be no more aid of preset patterns, lead-in and foul lines, wind socks and smoke pots, and familiar nearby landmarks of stateside ranges to help. And ranges do not shoot back; targets from now on would.

On a short leave home, I could not help but remember that from movie versions I once thought strafing was only spraying bullets, something that took no skill, nothing to it, just fly along with the trigger pulled. Well, that might still be valid if that's all a pilot was doing, but if he had to put his bullets into a target as in ground gunnery that youthful thinking had been way off its target.

Just as with the high school students at a book signing, I have had numerous opportunities over the years to show gun camera film of World War II P47 strafing to various groups of people. Often they remark on two things. One is surprise that the shooting was directed at targets rather than the "walking" fire they see in movies. The other is amazement that we had equipment that converged the "pinpoint" patterns of gunfire so accurately on targets. However, after receiving a briefing on "bore sighting," most all viewers of combat film say they then see it in an entirely different light. Once people realize that the guns converged in that exact same pattern every time fired, they are astonished that pilots could fly their planes so accurately as to put the shot on targets. This includes, of course, the same feeling of admiration for the ground crews who made all this flying and fighting possible, including the armorers who did the bore sighting, gun and sight maintenance, and ammo loading.

· 4 ·

Behind the Gun Sight
Strafing

Overseas orders in World War II did not give destinations, only project and movement numbers or codes. Saying good-bye to my wife, Anita (we were newlyweds but long-time hometown sweethearts), I boarded a train in Tallahassee, Florida, along with other pilots headed overseas. We could assume that if the train went east we were headed to the war in Europe; if it went west we were Pacific bound. However, a rumor spread that a local woman had just said a train on this track would not go west. And it didn't.

Experiences of replacement pilots on arrival overseas could vary greatly by theater and time frame of the war, from receiving a unit assignment at large processing depots to reporting to a headquarters. Mine was the latter, 9AF, North Africa (Tripoli), in August 1943, where a colonel considered assigning me to a P-38 unit but decided the need was greater in a P-40 unit where the original pilots were due rotation home. That was the 79th Fighter Group, located in Sicily, flying P-40Ls, an American unit operating in support of the British Eighth Army.

Whether a pilot went directly to his unit or received more training in theater first could vary too. In my case, I flew a few noncombat missions in P-40s with the 324th Fighter Group at Cape Bon, Tunisia. Lessons from combat experience was the main gist of flights and discussions with 324th pilots, with their note that each group and even squadrons in the MTO did many things quite differently, from combat formations to attack tactics. We simulated some strafing, with warning you could kill yourself mocking it on our side of the Bomb Line as well as doing it for real. Destroyed or abandoned German vehicles and armor spread about over an isolated area served as targets. Following 324th leaders, we made passes of varying approach, turn-in, dive angle, and the like, which was new stuff to us. Then we were turned loose to make passes on our own—even newer stuff.

In gunnery training only the "right way" had been tolerated. We had never seen where the bullets went if the "right way" was violated—such as fire further

This chapter cites mainly actions in the Mediterranean and European theaters of operations, where the author served in World War II, but all theaters worldwide are included later in an effort to tie our action in with that of other strafing and strafers during the war—to give the full story (Karen Sluman).

out, in deliberate skids, in turns, etc.—all of which the 324th pilots said could be useful in combat. Now we saw bullet patterns on the ground from such shooting. Most intriguing to me was skidding bullets into targets and abruptly stopping a tight turn to concentrate fire on a target. We made level on-the-deck passes, too, and saw how wide the bullet impacts spread, most hitting desert instead of vehicles and many ricocheting into the air. Flying faster than bore sight speed did angle the nose down a bit but unless the target was elevated above the pass altitude there was no way to concentrate fire in one place on a flat low pass.

This was our first time to have all guns loaded with combat ammo. Trigger pull fired all of them. There were no provisions for the pilot to select just two or four guns in the P-40, P-47 and P-51. The pilot instantly felt recoil of all guns through the airframe, most often described as "shudder." (In my later experiences with firing the guns of all these planes, I would rate "shudder" as most distinctly felt in the P-51, a fraction less in the P-40, and a bit dampened, but still definitely there, in the heavier P-47.) Other fighters had their own sensations of gunfire. One pilot described triggering all guns and cannon in the P-39 as a "tremendous roar and cockpit full of smoke." While "shudder of the guns" was common pilot lingo, seldom was "sound of the guns" mentioned for the wing-gun fighters—except in one case. That was when a round "cooked off" (a chambered round fired on its own in a hot barrel without a trigger pull). This unexpected blast was heard so loud that a pilot's first thought was that there had been an explosion in his plane or a hit by enemy fire in combat.

"Walking" fire across the ground and through targets encouraged pilots to hold the trigger down in long bursts. This often "burned out" gun barrels. Once that was done, effective fire was lost for that mission. Barrels had to be replaced on the ground. Long bursts also generated more "cook offs," which could occur in air over the target, on return to base, and during and well after landing. Awareness usually prevented casualties from "cook offs" in flight, but not always so for ground personnel back at home base. Besides those negatives, just my first glimpse of "long burst" spraying fire led to an immediate, and everlasting, conviction against it as wasting ammo (too many rounds that hit only the earth's surface, not enemy equipment and people).

One sure lesson learned from these few missions was visual proof of combined impact power of the cal-.50 machine guns. I put one short burst (1–2 second) at bore sight range into a German half-track. There was a bright flash as bullets hit the thing. It actually bounced and moved, pieces and parts flew off, and a gaping hole nearly cut it in two. With such pinpoint shooting, six-gun P-40s and P-51s put 80 bullets per second into a target; the eight-gun P-47 put 106 per second. However, many pilots did not experience these things until on a combat mission. They arrived at their overseas unit with only stateside ground gunnery training; and in rare cases, one in Italy in late 1944, a

The author in World War II, captain, U.S. Army (Air Corps), with his wife, Anita (Allen), May 1944, as he returns to combat in Europe after a short leave home.

few showed up who had never fired ground gunnery at all. They simply were skipped on the schedule for it while at gunnery camp.

A new pilot's arrival in a multi-mission combat unit put him in a very time-compressed learning situation, He had to absorb all details of command/unit operational procedures and tactics and lessons of past combat and learn the enemy and his weapons, the current situation, and maps and features of the enemy territory he would fly over. And he had to constantly know the location of and fully comply with the "Bomb Line"—the bomb safety line plotted on all maps to prevent cases of "friendly fire" on our troops. Finally, he would find out whether to except more air or ground gunfighting. My assignment to the 87th Squadron of the 79th Group in early September 1943 reflected mostly air-ground gunfighting at the time. This fighter group was doing "fighter-bomber" work and "fighter-bombers" did the most strafing. However, they did air-air gunfighting too, which could be by a change in situation, a mission's objective, and anytime enemy fighters showed up.

No aircraft or pilots were officially designated "fighter-bomber" in World War II. A few units held that designation until most were changed to "fighter" by May 1944. However, "fighter-bomber" still became the universal and common term for fighter units, aircraft, and pilots in multi-mission support of ground forces during the war. ("Fighter-bombers" were forerunners of today's multi-role fighters: F-16, F-15E, F/A-18, F-22, and F-35 Strike Fighter.)

The 79th entered combat as a group in March 1943, crossing North Africa with the British from Egypt. In varied operations, including bomber escort, ship cover, fighter sweep, and anti-shipping, they had scored air victories of 54 destroyed, 5 probable, 22 damaged—a 9 to 1 victory ratio—mainly over German Me 109s, FW 190s, and Italian MC 202s. This record was certainly of note to new pilots, but some other history hit with more impact on what we would be doing.

By this stage of the war, early German air operations characterized by dive-bombers, paratroop drops, troop and supply carriers, and the like were no longer—unable to survive among Allied fighters and fighter-bombers and AAA (antiaircraft artillery) and ground fire. For example the Stuka dive-bomber of early-war fear had been run out of the theater. The only German air opposition expected now was high-performance combat aircraft. Support of ground forces in the low-altitude skies by both sides was being done by fighter-bombers in the theaters where American forces operated, the ETO and MTO (Mediterranean theater of operations).

Certain Allied fighters were mainly handling air defense and long-range bomber escort and sweep, others were mainly doing ground attack. Units with P-40 Kittyhawks and Warhawks (older, short range, non-high-altitude fighters) were now mostly the latter. Thus, I'd be "fighter-bomber." What was not clear at the moment was to what extent that would be, and how many thousands of other USAAF fighter pilots would also become primarily air-to-ground gunfighters. North Africa proved fighter-bombers did well both protecting themselves and hunting the foe in air combat, winning gunfights with enemy fighters. That left the Germans with heavy dependence on another means of fighting back against fighter-bombers: massive FLAK from heavy AAA (88mm and larger) down to small arms, but above all the automatic weapons—37mm, 20mm, 15mm and machine guns, with multiple-gun 37mm and 20mm systems foremost in threat, the quad-gun 20mm at the forefront.

Ground attack was in the 79th history too, leaving no question of its nature. Before the critical battle of El Hannna (Mareth Line), British Air Vice-Marshal Broadhurst personally briefed 79th pilots on a pivotal task. The ground battle plan called for air strikes to eliminate German artillery in one area. Unless that was done, the spearhead attack division, New Zealand, would be exposed crossing open terrain and subject to "slaughter." Those lives, the battle, perhaps North Africa depended on the 79th knocking out the key enemy guns. Unit history on that reads as follows:

> (26 March 43) The 79th Hawks roared up and down the road, showering the "88" gun positions with 50-caliber bullets in spite of deadly hail of small arms fire up at them. Some pilots made the suicidal run again and again.... The 88's were silenced during that critical 2½ hours, the New Zealanders broke through and forced the Germans to retire in disorder from the Mareth Line and beyond the Gabes Gap, the battle was a brilliant success. The objective justified serious losses but the hearts of the Hawks were heavy [4 pilots lost, 1 wounded].

Normal P-40 fighter-bomber ordnance was a 250- or 500-pound bomb (1,000 at times overload), six 20-pound frags, and the guns. But for this particular task only the guns gave mission leaders and pilots proof of achieving the mandatory shut down of each German 88. The cal-.50 accuracy assured hits on guns and crews, gave close-range cockpit assessment of results, and provided "time of fire" for repeat and follow-up attacks as needed to keep the 88s silent. The other ordnance, while effective and useful overall, failed to compare with aircraft guns in those respects—a clear case of ace in the hole saved the day. Other unit history entries were close to reprints, such as subsequent support of British attacks at Wadi Akarit: (6 April 43) "[O]nce again the Hawks were called on to strafe a path through the foe for the Highland Division ... in face of the same terrific ground fire encountered at El Harnma.... [O]nce more the brave Hawks paid the price of strafing [4 pilots lost]. (8 April 43) The 79th was to support by strafing the enemy's transport and artillery in the rear ... pressed attacks home with same fury as at El Hamma choking the roads in the enemy rear with flaming trucks and armored cars and annihilating many gun crews [1 pilot lost]." The unit history contained the following items among others in summary of North African operations, some encouraging to a new pilot, others not necessarily so. Results follow: "Escorted 2125 medium bombers over enemy territory without loss to enemy fighters ... 2¼ enemy destroyers sunk ... (and much more). [Unit losses:] 27 aircraft lost ... 19 pilots

German automatic-weapon flak guns, quad-barrel 20mm; these in southern Italy were knocked out by U.S. fighter-bombers (U.S. Air Force).

killed or missing in action—12 by ground fire while strafing—1 by AAA, 6 by enemy fighters ... percentage of losses to sorties: strafing missions 7.27 percent; all others 0.15 percent." The summary of operations in Sicily listed 1,523 sorties on anti-shipping and sea rescue/escort, many in the notorious intense flak of Messina Straits, and 260 sorties on strafing/armed recce (reconnaissance). Pilot losses were 4 by ground fire while strafing and 1 by AAA in anti-shipping. (All unit history here is from *The Falcon*, 79th Group.)

While these figures were not briefed to each new pilot, if they had been, the message from them would have been quite similar to that given by French pilots to American pilots in World War I on life expectancy while strafing versus dogfighting. However, veteran pilots in the unit did pass on much verbal history on strafing and that was something to the following effect: a hell all its own; it is something separate, over and above other combat; and the surest way to get killed. If any saving grace could be found in that, it was that all strafing had not been the same. One half of the 79th strafing losses had come in two "shows," El Hamma and Wadi Akarit. All other strafing had much lower losses, but still higher than other type missions flown, thus it remained overall by far the most deadly. The next really "rough show" surely loomed up ahead.

New pilots had the particular aircraft and armament systems of their unit to learn, too. That was the P-40L in the 79th, normally with four guns; but these had been retrofitted to six guns. U.S. forces entered World War II with the following cal-.50 aircraft gun (Grade AC) ammunition: ball, armor piercing, incendiary, and tracer. Incendiary, or mixes with other rounds, was normal air-to-air load. German FW 190 head-on attacks of USAAF bombers over Europe triggered the need for a round that would both penetrate the radial engine of the FW 190 and carry incendiary action on into the airframe. In four months (June–October 1943) the armor-piercing incendiary round, API, was developed and supplied overseas.

Highly effective against the FW 190 and other aircraft, API was equally so against ground targets—locomotives, trucks, guns, armored vehicles, people, and more. This single type round became the standard in operations worldwide. After late 1943, "API and Tracer" was the common pilot jargon for their ammo. My strafing from then to the war's end was solely with that, as is all strafing in gun camera film in this book. A further refinement in API incendiary action and yet higher muzzle velocity was made for use against the German Me 262.

Tracer rounds provided valuable (essential, in my opinion) information in combat. Their visible trajectory, while not identical to the API rounds, did follow bore sight alignment. They confirmed good bore sight to the pilot when tracers maintained that pattern, or showed him if one or more guns were "off" when they didn't. And they confirmed good gun barrels when all tracers repeated the same trajectory, or showed worn or burned-out barrels when tracers "floated" or "knuckle-balled" in no semblance of the same trajectory. Early war ammo linking often had tracers 1 to 5 with other rounds. Later many units cut that down to 1 to 10 or even less tracers with API rounds, just enough to serve the above purposes. This was because tracers did not hit with either the accuracy or the "kill" of API. Some units linked several tracer rounds together near the end of an ammo load to show it running out.

Then there was time of fire of the guns. Ammo capacity of plane type and rate of fire of the guns would appear to neatly provide that. Unfortunately for neatness, ammo capacities were not the same for all models within types of planes, and loads actually carried frequently varied from capacities. A few samplings of "time of fire" include: P40s, 281 rounds per gun, about 20 seconds of fire; P-51s, two capacity figures, 400 for the inboard guns each wing, 270 for the other guns each wing, about 20 seconds of 6-gun fire and 30 seconds of 2-gun fire. The P-47 had two capacity figures all guns, and a third involving external loads—425 "capacity," 300 "design," and 267 "restriction" (with maximum external load, any ammo amount over 267 per gun imposed flight maneuver restrictions). Common P-47 loads actually used were 350 and 300, and numerous units loaded only 250 per gun as standard in order to totally avoid flight restrictions. Firing times were about 32, 22 or 20 seconds, with the lower figures most prevalent. An example of Navy and Marine fighters is the F4U, capacity 390 per gun and close to 30 seconds fire if fully loaded.

Ammo loads at times were set in multiples of 50 because the ammo came in cans or boxes containing 50 rounds of linked ammo. Only hooking those 50-round belts together without break up and then relinking of individual belts reduced loading and aircraft turn-around times.

Cannon plus machine gun USAAF fighters (P-38, P-39, and P-61) probably averaged in the same ballpark for machine-gun time of fire. Cannon in early-war planes used ammo magazines—60 for 20mm, 30 for 37mm, about 6 seconds fire for 20mm and 10 seconds for 37mm. Later systems used belt/link ammo with some increased loads and firing times and varied by space available and weight limits.

The inherent pilot decision factors in employing time of fire remained from World War I. It still took that long to use time of fire and time of fire still could not be expended continuously because of gun overheat, particularly those mounted internally in wings. Actually, some new ones were now added, at least in degree. With airspeeds in attacks 2 to 3 times faster, many passes did not last anywhere near "time of fire" available. The enormous increase in gun firepower over World War I (cited as "nearly 600 percent" in *USAF Flying*

Armament and maintenance personnel: the ultimate ingredient in weapon system capability. Here, gun maintenance is being done (79th Ftr Gp, World War II).

Safety, November 1991) did not need more than a "touch" of fire to destroy many targets. That type of fire in World War II put greater responsibility on pilots to "generalship" strafing.

The remainder of this chapter will look at a few of my first experiences in air-ground gunfighting. These in themselves are no more than a minute speck in the story of strafing in World War II. However, revealing my initial findings on strafing (with a few explanations) should provide better background for understanding the full range of pilot and crew challenges in widespread examples later in the text and avoid readdressing various common combat aspects later.

Shortly after the 79th moved into Italy on the east side with the British Eighth Army, 13 September 1943, I flew my first mission. The night before, it was scheduled as normal ground support of that army. Next morning it was an urgent diversion, a max range mission across Italy to strike German forces opposite the Salerno Beachhead, which was under strong attack and threatened with disaster. On arrival, looking down through smoke and haze, the leader confirmed the gun position target on the enemy side of the Bomb Line by coordinates and terrain features. We dive-bombed, then semi-looped for a steep strafing pass, pumping bullets down into the target area without being able to see guns or crews; then we sweated fuel on return, a flight over enemy territory between Salerno and our base. Next morning I flew another mission to Salerno. Again it was dive-bomb then a steep strafing run. In a bit better visibility, this time a gun position was spotted and the strafing was pressed on in, converting from strafing the area to strafing directly on the position, and that followed by another fuel-sweat trip home.

The strafing on both missions was at steep angles. Even foxholes and quickly dug-in equipment offered some protection from flat passes. On the first mission, with no specific target sighted, our strafing fire was directed to cover the immediate area around the coordinates, a 200 feet or so radius. Our ground forces had said that was an enemy position, thus there was something to be shot—guns, ammo, troops, etc. "Scatter" and "shotgun" were pilot terms for the type shooting done. The terms described deliberately dispersed gunfire, but in a controlled pattern. Pass parameters didn't really matter, except it had to be a dive, just fly the plane to distribute and contain bullets in the desired area, then pullout when necessary to miss the ground. Typically a pilot might get off three 2-second bursts in a quick pass of this type, about 450 rounds per plane, but this could vary widely for situations. In such shooting it was common to set off fires or explosions from sources never seen due to smoke, camouflage, trees, and other obstacles and to kill troops. The second mission started as "shot-gunning," an area, then turned to "pinpoint" on specific target, which was not uncommon in battlefield strafing. On these missions of critical need for air support we would have made repeated passes firing all ammo if fuel had allowed. Once done, we were landing with fuel gages showing nothing left.

Gun camera film. This is the first in our extensive use of stills from the old footage. These buildings behind the battle line in Italy's Apennines were used by the Germans as a rest billet. A diving pass is flown by this pilot to shoot down into troops in the courtyard of the left building (gun camera, 86th Ftr Gp, World War II).

A frequently asked question on strafing is "How fast?" These passes in a P-40 probable started about 4,000 feet in about a 60-degree dive, speed building from around 200 to 300 mph. However, if pilots had been monitoring airspeed indicators, they most likely would not have seen the gun position when they did on the second mission. I never once looked into the cockpit to check on speed. Pilots knew their planes well enough to know about what the speed would be in varied maneuvers and power settings. Full concentration went to viewing through the gun sight and flying to put the pipper where it was wanted to send bullets there. This applied to every pass I, and most all other pilots, ever made thereafter.

Attack geometry and techniques varied widely in strafing passes, and other fighter-bomber tactics by situation and type of aircraft. No specific description applied to all, only to that particular case or as representative here and there. For example, P-40s could "split-S" (half roll to inverted, pull into vertical dive, and then pull out level in the opposite direction) from 6,000 feet with no sweat. Such dive attacks were made in combat. But a "split-S" in a P-47 could lose over 15,000 feet or more; and depending on entry speed, altitude, and power setting was a prohibited maneuver. P-47s "mushed" more and more often than P-40s and P-51s on pullouts. P-40s and P-47s were known to withstand G forces well above published structural limits, and pilots were known to frequently do so; but that could be suicidal in some fighters. Thus, there was no such thing as "standard" tactics for all. Stating tactics in generalities can make very bad history.

On these missions to Salerno, enemy fire was judged by veteran pilots as meager flak (88mm) and moderate auto-weapon. Some "jinking" was done amid 88 bursts on the way in, but not so in attack. The mission was to hit the target, not to dodge flak. A fighter plane's strength, engine power, and resulting agility allowed varied approaches, fast or hard maneuvering, which posed multiple challenges to enemy gunners in detecting and acquiring and tracking and leading. This was pumped into planning and tactics. Beyond that, the same as bombers on bomb runs, once in attack nearing firing point, a strafing pilot could not let enemy fire infringe on his resolve to fly the airplane right and hit the target. Since each pilot was his leader for his gunfire results, his duty was unmistakably clear.

This was a first experience with, and look at, German flak: the orange fireballs and black greasy smoke of the 88s and the orange tracer streams of auto-weapon fire and the blankets of blue-white flashes of 20–37mm round bursts. Most machine gun and small arms fire was never seen in the air. Its presence was confirmed only by finding holes in planes after landing or by planes going down with no 88 or auto-weapon fire visible. Evident on the spot was that low-altitude operations, including all strafing, were subject to every air defense weapon in the enemy arsenal—aircraft and AAA from 88mm and even larger, down to machine pistols and handguns—and that anyone who said AAA guns of 88mm size were not threats to low-flying planes was an idiot.

The Salerno Beachhead survived. Immediately we were back operating on the east side of Italy as German forces withdrew from the heel and toe of Italy. This was not in rout, but a general movement north, much by night but demanding day travel too. Combat units, not bunched up, spread out on each route and dispersed among routes. This provided few if any targets for effective use of bombers or fighters with bombs, but many for fighters with guns and "time of fire."

Our missions were almost all armed-recce—go hunt targets of opportunity: vehicles, armor, half-tracks, staff cars, motorcycles, anything else and certainly troops. A period of clear skies aided us, the hunters. But lack of recent rain aided the enemy, who could leave roads for dispersal and drive around road cuts and downed bridges across fields and through small steam beds. Finding numerous "movers" assured that enemy operators or troops were aboard. Top priority for mission leaders was to destroy enemy equipment and kill troops of first-line combat units while in the open before they could regroup and fight again.

Missions were typically eight planes—one flight of four strafing, one covering, and then swapping. Search of roads was offset to one side, often weaving side to side (when flying directly above a road, the view of it was blocked by the nose of most fighter planes). Altitudes were leader decision. Of course the first need was for pilots to see and identify targets. Obviously the altitudes to do that could vary widely for situations. On a clear day a pilot could see moving tanks kicking up dust in the Western Desert of Egypt from 10,000 feet or higher; but he might have to go down to a few hundred feet to spot camouflaged fighter planes amid thick trees and in the frequent haze of Germany's Black Forest. Any general statement on armed-recce altitudes in World War II would have to stretch from the deck to a mile or two up. Many leaders changed altitudes frequently while on armed-recce.

Terrain was also involved. Recce off to the side of a road in a valley could have you flying just above a parallel ridge line, silhouetted, showing altitude for enemy gunners, which you did not want to do. In flying low across a ridge on an early mission, I had 88 bursts erupt much too close for comfort all around my plane while also blasting rocks and trees to bits on top of the ridge. It was desirable to recce above the stated maximum effective range (5,000 feet) of the enemy 20mm flak, and individual weapons fire. Yet most targets couldn't be seen well that high, and 20mm fire was experienced bursting up to 10,000 feet or more. Regardless of all these factors, in order to acquire targets and get results, almost all recce was done well under 5,000 feet.

The 87th Squadron (and all others) had strong commanding officer policy on strafing, which was over and above the constant attention to all combat procedures and tactics. It was recognized that mission and flight leaders had to "generalship" many things in the air, especially strafing's great flexibility and its bloody nature. CO policy on that was not published in manuals or checklists; it was never-ending discussion and guidance on a multitude of situations leaders could encounter on missions. Many of these will come forth in later text as actions take place. But a major point was clear from the outset. Policy on ordered, preplanned, pre-briefed missions on specific targets was of course firm for all leaders: accomplish the mission, period, while holding losses as low as practical. However, missions without specific targets (those of opportunity, armed-recce, add-on strafing after bombing, extra or repeat passes, etc.), which were largely voluntary attacks while in the air, put wider "generalship" tasks on leaders. The policy here stressed judgment and tactics to inflict maximum hurt on the enemy, without taking undue risk of hurting yourself. And new pilots soon learned each mission and flight leader's "generalship" characteristics in doing this.

Most of this post–Salerno recce was in the ballpark of 1,500 to 2,000 feet. Passes were not made by set dive angle, speed or direction (for strafing they did not have to be). When a target was seen, you went from where you were and put your guns on it, particularly for "movers." Getting there quickly, before the enemy could take cover, before operators and passengers could get out and escape, was the primary tactic rather than taking time to fly a particular type of pass. In pulling off one pass, often other targets were spotted under trees, amid buildings, etc. Passes back on these were hard-flying "maneuvers" that usually had no semblance of the original pass.

The normal situation for these missions was a start from recce altitude, high cruise power, guaranteed good speed in passes, well above bore sight, which was desirable except that extreme or max limit speeds degraded precise flying and aim. Pilots quickly adjusted to firing accurately at speeds well above those used in gunnery, and they never wanted speed to be below bore sight. In addition to greater exposure to enemy fire, this increased nose up angle of attack and that was bad. In that attitude you needed nose down to aim on target and nose up to miss the ground—odds of both a target kill and survival of the pilot about nil.

The normal situation of recce off to the side produced mostly "side" or near 90 degree passes into targets. This was desirable for results and often caught people trying to get out of doors for cover; attacks across roads exposed strafers to fewer enemy guns than down them. Many of these passes came out about 15–20 degree dives and 280–300 mph for the P-40. The P-47 and P-51 would generate another 50 mph or more in similar passes. Other times and situations saw much higher speeds.

Only vehicles that burned (termed "flamers") or exploded or were seen to wreck over cliffs, into ravines, etc., could be claimed as destroyed. Definite hits, parts and pieces flying, smoke, or other indicators had to be observed in order to be claimed as damaged. These missions were all pinpoint strafing, close in, and the objective of every round fired was to hit the target. Short bursts of one to two seconds, did the job fully on most vehicles. This also allowed up to 15 or so passes per plane per mission or left ammo in reserve if needed on harder targets or enemy fighter threat. These missions averaged about 10 passes per plane and claimed 20 or more vehicles destroyed and many more damaged. Fuel rather than ammo limited passes as the enemy moved further from our base until we moved and caught up again.

These P-40s had no gun cameras. The photos shown here are to depict types of strafing, not document this action. All combat photography that is credited to the 86th Ftr Gp is from P-47s of that unit, flown October 1944 to February 1945, MTO, and February 1945 to May 1945, ETO. Pilot descriptions were more vivid than wording in official mission reports. They often varied in emphasis, too. Naturally, big gun haulers, half-tracks, big trucks, and similar vehicles being blown out of the war was of interest to all. But especially challenging was shooting at speeding dispatch riders on motorcycles or officers in staff cars; literally blasting them off the roads into gullies, trees and fields made better pilot tent and bar talk. So did fights with flak guns. One of my early passes was on a truck in a stream of auto-weapon tracers coming from dead ahead. The enemy quad 20mm was spotted just beyond the truck. The second element of my flight bypassed the now burning truck and zeroed in on

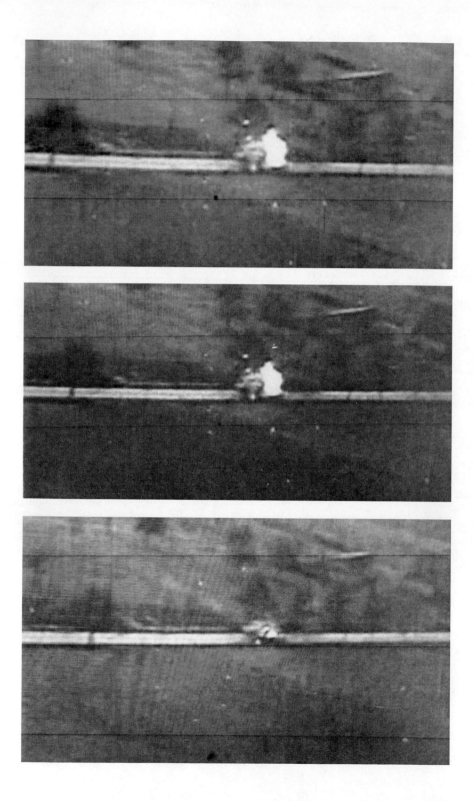

the gun. The truck and gunners were seen to be hit by firepower of two planes; the truck and the gunners were totally wiped out, gone from the war. Maneuvers to knock out such guns when seen during passes resulted in some of the most violent, max-performance of all fighter flying in order to get the guns in position to kill the enemy gun and crew before they got the fighter flying— flat out head-to-head gunfighting.

It was clear that even in spread out movement like this, flak would be encountered, especially from the highly mobile automatic weapons, anywhere, anytime, whether plotted and briefed or not. On these missions there had not been the intense defenses of massed enemy units, airfields, rail hubs, cities, and other critical points, and we had avoided losses so far; but as some pilots said, "If Germans are there so is the flak—you will be shot at." Actually, this was a good intelligence briefing for all armed-recce missions.

By October our operations became far more varied. We escorted bombers a few times. We strafed the German airfield at Pescara. The Germans switched from withdrawal to holding ground and making counterattacks. More missions were flown in direct support of major ground actions such as Termoli and San-gro River. Tanks and other armor (which had been encountered in the movement north) now became more frequent targets and in battle situations. We began working with Forward Air Controllers (FACs). We also flew deeper into enemy territory, bringing marshalling yards, locomotives, rolling stock, supply dumps, and other targets into our strafing operations. Adverse weather and mountainous terrain entered the picture. We encountered enemy fighters and shot down several. The air-ground gunfighting in each of these and others had its own complexities and challenges, as will be shown in detail later, almost all of it much rougher than the armed-recce mentioned to this point.

A prime example of strafing utility came on the first mission I flew leading the squadron. Departure of veteran leaders demanded new pilots take over as leaders. I led flights with 10 missions, the squadron with 20. On that first lead, the mission orders and briefing were for normal ground support to bomb a bridge, then armed-recce strafing to disrupt enemy buildup for attack. When we were already in our cockpits to start engines, the CO and ops officer rushed up in a jeep, climbed on the wing of my plane and handed me a map, saying, "This is now your target." That new mission was to cross the Adriatic Sea, the target being three ships—freighters—reported off the coast of Yugoslavia south of Split. Briefing to the other pilots was by ground crews and nonscheduled pilots running plane to plane to give the new target and the instruction to "maintain radio silence." The reason for that was that eight P-40s without

Opposite: Enemy vehicle. This sequence (bottom to top) is a classic short burst, concentrated and accurate hits, that "kills" the enemy vehicle—in pilot talk, "the way to do it." A few bursts of enemy 20mm ground fire (white smoke puffs) show (gun camera, 86th Ftr Gp, World War II).

Enemy ground fire. *Upper:* Nothing but a poor-quality photograph to many people; but it is a pilot's view of a core and deadly element in strafing—the white smoke "puffs" of 20/37mm enemy automatic weapon flak bursts (light to moderate intensity here). *Lower:* This 20/37mm round exploded just in front of the wing, almost in the camera lens (gun camera 86th Ftr Gp, World War II).

escort or other support would be attacking ships under the nose of enemy fighter threat.

In the air nearing the coast the ships were spotted—the targets judged to be one oceangoing and two coastal. Skip bombing into hulls would have been the first choice, but our 500-pound GP bombs were fused for $\frac{1}{10}$ second delay for a bridge, which would blow us out of the air on a low release. Dive-bombing had to be used and pullout had to be high enough to avoid bomb blasts. We may have got the big one with bombs, close impacts to hull, but no direct hits. No ships exploded or went up in flames. Thus no positive results were evident.

But we had the guns left. Four planes strafed while four covered, and then they automatically switched, some four passes being made by each plane before ammo ran out (firing total of about 5 seconds each pass). Initial strafing knocked out the observed auto-weapons onboard. From there on pilots picked their own ship and aim points on them. I didn't remember anything from training that said where to aim on a freighter to best hurt the thing. I chose the bridge head-on, firing steep enough to send rounds on down into the bowels too. Other pilots aimed for the assumed location of the engine room, others into hatches to set fires and explosions and into hulls at the waterline. Some got in shots on two ships in a pass through hard maneuver. Just missing masts and rigging in runs was common. And throughout not one word was said on radio.

On return to base one thought in my mind (other than being out of ammo, still subject to enemy fighters and with low fuel that demanded precise navigation to base) was that we could report no hits by bombs, only near misses. We could say nearly 100 percent hits by strafing, but with still unknown results except the ships were stopped and smoking. At debriefing those were our claims, and it was very disappointing to me that no ships were in the report as "sunk" or "destroyed." But about an hour later our squadron was advised that reconnaissance reported the larger vessel abandoned, burning and sinking; the other two had beached on islands and were burning. I was glad we had the guns as ace in the hole. They saved the day this time, too.

In my experience to this point, enemy gunfire alone had further erased any prewar thoughts of strafing as simple, safe and unimportant. Yet, the other inherent challenge in strafing (while anticipated for combat) had come through far stronger in compounding pilot demands than expected. That was the earth's surface and all it encompassed—nature's clouds, restricted visibility, wind, and obstructions of varying terrain and trees—plus man's doings of buildings, poles, wires, cables, barrage balloons and more. At times some of these could be "friend." They might block enemy view and detection or aid surprise approach and shield from enemy fire. But far more often they were "foe." They cut pilot visibility, delayed target identification, caused wild variations during passes and made shooting more difficult. Any of these (and more so in combinations)

Close calls: nearly flying into the ground. *Upper:* This pass pressed to the max on a truck took a violent high "G" pullout to survive. *Lower:* This pilot flew through these treetops by pushing in to put max firepower on a tank on the road (gun camera, 86th Ftr Gp, World War II).

sent pilot challenges, both decision and flying, to greater heights and skyrocketed the hazard level.

First of all hazards was just flying into something. In training with all the safety aids there, pilots had flown into the ground. A plane at 270 mph traveled from optimum firing point (bore sight distance) to target in two seconds. The pilot had less than those two seconds to act and execute pull-up before reaching the target in order to miss it or the ground.

For combat speeds of 300 mph and more, pilot act and execute time was still far less in order to miss the ground. Add hills, cliffs, trees, buildings, poles, etc.—whether between pilot and target, around it, behind it, or in combination—and now act and execute time is affected by more than speed and distance. Height of any and all obstructions near the target cut the distance available to clear them on pull-up. Act and execute times were reduced to fractions of a second. Unknown winds could squeeze even more. Poor visibility hurt, too.

Pilots had to recognize all this on the spot, and judge just how far they could press on in and still safely pull out. Above all they had to recognize when firing at bore sight distance was too close for a successful pull-out. In other words, they had to determine when what they had done in ground gunnery could not be done here. In those cases it was up to pilot judgment to fire farther out and hit the target with the most effective fire possible for the situation. Such judgment was part of each and every pass made. (A year later, when I had the P-47s of my squadron bore sighted at 900 feet instead of 750 feet for strafing in the Alps, that gave about ⅓ of a second more in time for act and execute of pull-up at 350 mph, a fraction that was a valuable aid in difficult passes.)

It was the combination of enemy ground fire and targets on the earth's surface so near below that compounded to make the low-altitude skies so deadly for strafers. In that, the earth's surface became the "solid" enemy. You might well be hit and shot down by enemy fire at any time, any pass, or you might not, even in intense enemy fire. But if you misjudged on the earth, you would—not might—hit something that could be truly solid. Regardless of how tough the enemy fire, you had better not let it or anything else distract from full attention to flying the airplane right or you would be dead whether the enemy ever hit you or not.

Then there was an extra challenge, one that had no way of being recognized in advance, nor had any reliable defense against when it happened. That was a target exploding in your face—usually munitions such as ammo, shells, and bombs or fuels and chemicals—whether in or on vehicles, rail cars, watercraft, gun pits, armor, or dumps. Tactics could lessen risk of full disaster in some cases, but not where close-in pinpoint shooting was necessary. As young people today might say, this was "like insidious"—the better the shooting done to hurt the enemy, the more likely the target to explode and blow your plane and you out of the air.

Upper: A target "blows," a gratifying result of good shooting, and has the added benefit of not being a big enough explosion to engulf pilot and plane. *Lower:* This "blow" blurs the photograph but the camera records debris flying up well above the blast (and past the plane), another common hazard (gun camera, 86th Ftr Gp, World War II).

Flying right: the conviction that the doing of strafing was flying and fighting decisions and performance. Air-ground "gunfighting" was much more like dogfighting
than other types of ground attack. Here, flying right to "zero in" on locomotives
amid rail cars and nearby buildings (gun camera, 86th Ftr Gp, World War II).

My prewar view of strafing had not been simply erased. It had been
reversed. Instead of strafing being as different from dogfighting as once
thought, what it really was so different from was other ground attack. Pilot
challenges, decision, and flying overall were far more the nature of dogfighting
(developments in the air in action) than the nature of ground attack (set procedure type of attacks). In looking back on training, I am most thankful for
emphasis on "flying a fighter right" in mock dogfighting and both air and
ground gunnery. These fighter skills came out as best serving the needs of
gunfighting with the enemy, whether in the air or on the ground. I went on
through the war, and have ever since, viewing and treating the two forms of
gunfighting—air combat and strafing—as the brothers they were.

I served with the 79th Group for a just over a year, 10 months in the position of flight leader, and then transferred to the 86th Fighter Group as commanding officer of the 525th Squadron. I held that position for a full year, on
through VE-Day and into the occupation of Germany. However, subsequent
chapters do not just track me and those units. Coverage broadens to strafing
actions worldwide from the war's start to its finish. Strafing is what is tracked.

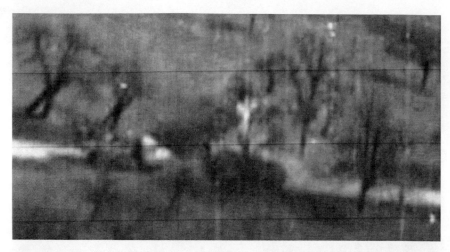

That is not done chronologically, but is in three major areas of air operations: against enemy air power, against enemy support forces, and against enemy ground and surfaces forces, with the objective of giving a definitive and clear remembrance of victories, valor and sacrifice in the war.

One front note to that story might be in order on the extent of strafing done as the war progressed. An example of ammo fired by a P-40 squadron in late 1943 was 130,000 rounds per month. A P-47 squadron in early 1945 fired over 500,000 rounds per month (79th and 86th group records).

When the postwar documentary *Thunderbolt* showed American P-47s strafing targets of opportunity in Italy as the narration stated, "Every man his own general," I could say we learned that phrase early on as inherent fact in most strafing.

Opposite: **Varied targets: vehicles, aircraft, locomotives and much more—an early foretaste of much more (gun camera, 86th Ftr Gp, World War II).**

· 5 ·

Gunfights
Enemy Air Forces

Before the war I had misjudged strafing in another way. I thought of it as being used only against ground troops and people. Pearl Harbor corrected that thinking. A lot of fighting around the world since has added overwhelming evidence that not only were enemy aircraft on the ground, airfield facilities and personnel regularly strafed but they were with high priority.

The early months of the war still had us on the receiving end of strafing in the Pacific. The last days of Allied operations in Java are an example. On 1 March 1942, the struggle by piecemeal employed units against too many of the enemy included one of the last missions flown from Java as it was evacuated. Nine P-40s, six Hurricanes, and four Brewster Buffaloes attacked at low level to strafe Japanese landing craft. The P-40s, of the USAAF 17th Pursuit Squadron, lost three shot down, and the other six were riddled with enemy fire. After the P-40s returned to base, as crews worked to repair planes, Japanese fighters roared in strafing and destroyed every remaining P-40 in the unit. Another incident occurred on 3 March, when U.S. bombers and Dutch flying boats attempted to evacuate personnel from Broome. Japanese fighters shot down one B-24 on takeoff and destroyed 12 flying boats in the harbor, plus two B-17s, two B-24s, and two Hudsons on the ground. At least 45 Dutch workers and 30 American airmen were killed.

War news to the American people changed for the better with the great sea battles of Coral Sea and Midway. Who was doing the most strafing began to change too. At Midway the Japanese carrier *Hiryu* was hit by U.S. Navy dive-bombers and mortally wounded; but before its end the next day six USAAF B-17s sighted it. They attacked from some 3,000 feet, and then strafed the deck of the carrier. This is one case among many in the war of heavy bombers using machine guns on surface and ground targets.

Guadalcanal had been a source of tense news because of the fierce fighting there—ground, sea, and air. Victory changed that to a brighter outlook in the Pacific and added a welcome badge of courage in American history. By December 1942, the long troublesome Japanese base at Munda was held at bay with U.S. B-17s and PBYs overhead by night and strafers by day. In one action, on 24 December, P-39s, F4Fs and SBDs caught Japanese Zeros in the process of launching missions. Twenty-four were destroyed by air and ground gunfighting.

Alaska's notoriously bad weather in the Aleutians put strafing to special utility. The extensive air-to-air combat of the South and Southwest Pacific was not repeated here due to that weather. As one P-40 pilot of 11AF in Alaska said back in RTU, "About the only way we could find enemy planes was when they were on the ground or water."

On one such mission, on 14 September 1942, twelve B-24s and 28 fighters took off from Adak at low level to bomb and strafe the Japanese base on Kiska. They attacked ships, submarines, aircraft, float planes, shore installations and gun positions. Strafing results included three subs and a 4-engine flying boat by P-39 cannon, and four Zeros and a twin-engine float plane by other fighters. Such attacks in combined bombing and strafing missions became normal operations against major Japanese bases.

Strong attacks of that nature by Pacific air forces against Rabaul inflicted major blows to Japanese shipping and aircraft. On 12 October 1943, one hundred thirteen B-25s, ninety B-24s, one hundred ten P-38s, and twelve RAF planes briefed for B-25 strafers to be first in, low-level, on airfields. Tactics included opening up long range with forward-firing cal-.50 machine guns on antiaircraft positions, then toggling 30-pound parafrags on enemy bomber dispersal and revetment areas. Only one B-25 was lost but numerous others had battle damage. Fifth AF reported 100 enemy planes destroyed and 51 severely damaged on the ground, plus 26 shot down in the air, and heavy destruction on airdromes.

On a similar mission on 18 October, bad weather turned back the B-24s and P-38s but most B-25 strafers got in low under clouds and destroyed some 40 enemy aircraft on the ground. Such operations on airfields and shipping up to mid–November neutralized Rabaul as a major threat to the landing beachhead on Bougainville. However, not all missions had only light losses. On 27 October, a force of eighty B-25s and eighty P-38s lost eight B-25s and nine P-38s with 45 pilots and crew members killed or missing in action.

Besides major enemy bases, hundreds of widespread separate airfields were attacked, including all fields on Bougainville. The B-25 strafers were again key players, using both parafrags and their multiple guns on AAA positions and aircraft, also gunning down labor parties caught in the open working to keep the fields in operation. The 5th Air Force Memorial Foundation, Inc., notes in its *A Proud Heritage* that "By November, 1943, it [5AF] had gained air superiority over New Guinea and New Britain, thus enabling Allied ground forces to begin the island-hopping trek back to the Philippines." The low-level work of that heritage includes the award of the Medal of Honor to Maj.

Example of cal-.50 machine guns in nose of a "strafer" light to medium bomber (U.S. Air Force).

Ralph Cheli. He led a mission of B-25s to strafe and parafrag an airfield near Wewak, New Guinea. With his plane already burning and doomed by fighter gunfire, he pressed on to take his mission through the attack before going down. Captured, he and other POWs were lost when the ship transporting them was sunk.

The first USAAF air strike in Europe was against German airfields in Holland. It was by the 15th Bomb Squadron, flying six A-20s borrowed from the RAF, on a joint low-level mission with RAF No. 226 Sq, 4 July 1942. Rumors circulated during the war that this entire mission was shot down but records show a less total disaster. American losses were two shot down and one severely damaged. RAF pilots reported the most intense flak ever experienced and there was some head-to-head gunfighting with it.

American Capt. Charles Kegelman had De Koor airdrome as his target. His plane took a hit in the right engine that knocked the prop off, started a fire, and damaged the wing. He lost altitude and bounced off the ground, but managed to fly on off. Observing a flak tower swinging its guns on his plane, he turned enough to align his nose guns on the tower, which he was flying below, and opened fire at close range. Fire from the tower ceased. Kegelman nursed his flying wreck of a plane back to base. He was awarded the Distinguished Service Cross. (The A-20s flew medium altitude bombing throughout

The Army Air Forces in World War II, vol. 41, cites this photograph of burning Japanese planes as an action in the early phases of "knockout" of enemy airpower (U.S. Air Force).

the war in Europe. Fighters took over in low-level strafing and gunfights with flak towers.)

The Allied landings in November 1942 and the early months of the campaign in Northwest Africa involved being strafed as well as strafing. Unit history of the USAAF 2nd Sq, 52nd Ftr Gp, flying Spitfires, notes their field at Bone, Algeria, being bombed and strafed nearly every day, and describes German Me 109s and FW 190s putting on some fancy flying shows as they beat up the field with strafing fire. Ju 88s also strafed but with less show. Some of this strafing came as pilots were climbing into cockpits and strapping in. The same unit history cites the American-flown Spits escorting P-39s on strafing missions and doing much strafing themselves in striking back.

One experience with the 79th in Italy ingrained graphically in the minds of all personnel the American strafing of German airfields. As the 79th made a number of leapfrog moves up the east coast of Italy in September and October of 1943, two stops were on fields in the Foggia area. These fields (Penny Post and Foggia #3) had been part of the huge complex of GAF airfields in that area. The scene of war aftermath on these fields was amazing. While that was a welcome sight of hurt on the enemy, there was more wonder on just what had gone on here. There were enemy aircraft after aircraft, now burned-out skeletons and bullet-riddled airframes, everywhere, plus huge amounts of shot-up ground equipment and spares, all of it totally gone from enemy use in the war.

LOCKHEED P-38

P-38, one of the USAAF top fighters, with cannon and machine guns compact in the nose (U.S. Air Force).

The story behind this was given as strafing by USAAF P-38s. One mission of 25 August 1943 by some 140 P-38s destroyed or damaged about 200 German aircraft on the ground here. On 18 September nearly 300 more were destroyed on Foggia airfields. An entry in *The Army Air Forces in World War II* (vol. 2) reads: "Increasing attempts by the GAF to achieve maximum dispersion by use of satellite 'strips' were countered by mass strafing and fighter-bomber attacks, a method which proved particularly effective against the Foggia and Gerbini complexes." This major victory in the air supremacy war was by and large preplanned missions to strafe enemy airfields, yet the massive destruction done was by the "time of fire" of cannon and machine guns of each plane, whose leaders and individual pilots had to "generalship" for themselves while over the widely dispersed fields and strips.

My first airfield strafing was also a preplanned mission—a multi-squadron effort with squadron formations of 16 planes, with the target of a Luftwaffe field at Pescara on the east coast of Italy. The majority of the enemy planes were dispersed, some parked down roadways close to stone walls and buildings on the outskirts of town and in surrounding villages. They were probably as well protected from a flat low-level attack as if in revetments. Thus our approach was from the sea at 9,000 feet descending down into the field, speed building to over 300 mph as formation sections and flights fanned out to hit designated dispersal areas. Only one pass was planned. The long steep run-in allowed pilots to pick out groups of parked planes early, start a series of shotgun bursts on them 3,000 to 4,000 feet out, then as range closed to fire on individual planes. Quick maneuver of aim was used to hit two or possibly three planes before pullout right on the deck.

Flak and auto-weapon fire was intense on flights flying over or near the field center, much less on those hitting wider dispersal areas. But our squadron had no losses. We claimed 18 GAF planes destroyed, mostly fighters, and 30 more damaged. Enemy planes had to burn or explode to be claimed as destroyed, and 18 of them doing that put off considerable smoke. Fueled and loaded aircraft were often "set off" with shotgun type strafing but that was more assured with close-in concentrated fire. Unfueled and unloaded planes were likely only damaged by shotgun strafing bursts but were often fully destroyed (if not always claimed) by pinpoint blasts. Numbers of these were seen on Foggia fields.

Strafing missions against airfields were more often preplanned (rather than going to look for targets of opportunity). Intelligence, general and specific, was used to the fullest in planning and tactics, where armed-recce, for example, created much of its own specific intelligence in the air. Group and squadron size missions were common against airfields, while most other strafing was smaller efforts, with four and eight planes the most common as the war wore on in Europe. Long-range operations in the Pacific were a different story on mission makeups. Of course, any element of surprise practical was used in mission planning and tactics—provided "goal of surprise" did not prevent or hinder the "goal of mission accomplishment." For example, on-the-deck surprise would have degraded target acquisition and shooting results at Pescara. However, to portray these characteristics as "standard" for airfield strafing in World War II without qualification would misrepresent the history.

I was not on another mission that strafed an airfield for six months, long after I had flown well over 100 missions. Had I gone home at the end of a normal tour (70 to 100 missions, per time frame, ETO and MTO), that one attack would have been my total combat in airfield strafing. I'm sure my views for life would have been dominated by that single experience. And if asked for those views, Pescara would have been the basis of my reply on tactics, passes, shooting, and the like. But since I did not go home then, quite a few more missions on airfields came along; and each case was not like the others enough to carry a label of "standard." One thing did fall under such a label though. Active enemy airfields were always well defended with auto-weapon firepower against strafers. Any mission of no losses was rare. At Pescara one veteran pilot, just two missions short of rotating home, felt that being scheduled to

Enemy aircraft. *Top:* This pilot nails an enemy plane out on an airfield. *Bottom:* This pilot kills one dispersed from its flying field. Streams of tracer rounds in enemy ground fire show in both photographs (gun camera, 86th Ftr Gp, World War II).

strafe an airfield so close to tour completion should be outlawed in war along with other inhumanities.

There were a few strafings that did not occur. In November 1943 the 79th moved to a short 3,000 foot PSI strip south of Termoli, called "Muddy Madna." Restricted from dispersal by coastline, surrounding hills, and a quagmire of mud, our four squadrons (85, 86, 87, and 99), plus a South African unit, were jammed together within several hundred feet of the strip. That included fueled and armed planes, fuel trucks, other vehicles, bombs and ammo, unit Hqs, flight line, mess and troop tents all intermingled. Enemy lines were only 13 miles to the north. On close support missions there we had several engagements with FW 190s, usually 8 to 12 aircraft, dogfighting with enemy fighters less than four minutes' flying time from our field. Friendly Spitfires gave air cover in the area and we had British auto-weapon AAA on the field (jammed in with the flying units)—but one mad dash by any of the enemy formations and even the wildest kind of strafing runs on Madna could have set off an inferno that would have dwarfed Wheeler Field, Hawaii, in 1941. Yet, the Germans never tried it, and we stayed in that situation for two months.

When we did move in mid-January 1944 it was to Naples on the west side of Italy, under the U.S. 12AF, flying from Capodichino (Capo), an ex-civilian aerodrome. It was a large grass field and we were not quite as cramped as at Madna but several other units shared the field and overall it was a fat target of hundreds of aircraft in one place.

Our initial assignment from Naples was low-altitude air cover of the Anzio invasion. The Germans put up substantial air opposition with their fighter and fighter-bomber attacks on our surface and ground forces. From D-Day, 22 January 44, we fought Me 109 and FW 190s, up to 30 or more at a time as they made attacks. This was almost daily at first, then at intervals over ships, beachhead, and up to and north of Rome on into April. Enemy night bombing of Naples, mainly the harbor, was common as were photo-recce flights, as we stayed there until June, reequipping with P-47s in April. But again the GAF did not try to strafe our crowded field—with one exception. That was at night by FW 190s. There were no bombs, just strafing. The FW 190s were aided some by the red glow of nearby Vesuvius in full eruption, and they also used aircraft lights, either landing or special equipment. Their low runs did substantial destruction and damage to aircraft, mostly to other units, enough so that we wondered if the Germans would continue this. But they didn't; there was only the one attack.

One mission of our P-47s on armed-recce well north of Rome returned with claims of two Me 109s destroyed by strafing in a field. Debriefing tried to tie that to some known GAF airfield, but no correlation could be found. The report was left as a field, not airfield. And, since the planes went up in flames, they were judged operational, not derelicts. Thus strafing enemy aircraft on the ground varied considerably from preplanned at times.

An issue of the *Jug Letter* of the P-47 Thunderbolt Pilots Association cited another example. In the ETO a P-47 mission out of the UK on armed-recce near Paris became suspicious of a field with lines across it. Making a low pass, what appeared to be a bush in an otherwise cleared field could be seen as a camouflaged airplane. Strafing fire sent it up in flames, and other planes

Part of "Capo" Airdrome, Naples, Italy, one of many crowded Allied fields (79th Ftr Gp, World War II).

were spotted under trees surrounding the field. Another pass destroyed two more German fighters. One P-47 was hit by ground fire and crash landed. The article cited an evasion saga by the pilot, who returned 30 years later to visit the town and people who cared for his wounds and hid him from the enemy. (That story was of pilot Ray Greenwood, age 22, later Col. Greenwood, Utah Air National Guard.)

The utility of strafing was evidenced in another way in that action. Once his fellow pilots saw Greenwood clear of his crashed P-47, they burned it with strafing fire to keep it out of enemy hands. Then while Greenwood hid 30 days in a French home, P-47s twice strafed German troops right in front of the house, once with bullets tearing through the roof into a room adjacent to the occupants. After that a trench in the backyard was used when strafers were overhead and as artillery fire preceded advance of, and rescue by, U.S. ground forces.

Preplanned missions could differ in type and degree of prior planning, also in plans once over an enemy airfield. In mid–June 1944 the 79th was based on Corsica flying missions over both northern Italy and southern France. On 26 July, late afternoon orders for a rush mission resulted in 14 planes from one squadron (85th, mission lead/attack/strafing) and 15 of another (87th, escort/cover) to strike the German airfield at Valence in the Rhône Valley

Certain models of the FW-190 were prime German fighter-bomber strafers (National Archives).

below Lyon, France. This was base of Ju 88/Ju 188 units that had been bombing USAAF medium bomber fields on Sardinia.

Pilots and aircraft were those quickly available, guns only; any bombs on planes were dumped to reduce drag. We needed all the range possible for the mission. It could not be flown with bombs. There was no common briefing, only field phone contact between the two squadron leaders. But we had common intelligence on a large grass airfield, dispersed parking and facilities mainly among scrub trees and some buildings. When airborne in the cover squadron on the 260-mile flight to target, my thoughts were less on strafing than on our anticipated gunfight with enemy fighters. Unit history records this action (in part) during the mission: "When the drome was reached 85 made several passes at the planes dispersed on the ground, and, when their ammo was practically expended, exchanged places with 87 allowing the 'Skeeters' [87 insignia was a mosquito] to do some fancy shooting." It goes on to cite the action as "A finest example of inter-squadron collaboration and mission success in the war." This is a factual account, but, as with most recorded history, it lacks pilot-eye image—and in this case one of the most epic and spectacular airfield-strafing missions of World War II.

Approaching at some 9,000 feet in good weather near dusk, the lead squadron made its planned descending run into the field. Flak came up in the full intensity predicted, but otherwise prior intelligence and plans were superseded by the current situation on the field.

The Germans were well along in marshaling planes for a major bombing mission. Fully fueled and loaded bombers, crews aboard, engines running, were all over—some already on the main field, others taxiing there, many in or leaving parking spots. Ground crews, vehicles, and equipment were in the open everywhere.

Most major airfield strafing created quite a pyrotechnic display. Perhaps this one topped them all. Tracers filled the sky, going both up and down, then in all directions as repeat passes were made. Enemy bombers erupted in great balls of fire and smoke, some exploded on being hit, others after burning awhile, and some wrecked themselves trying to avoid strafing fire.

From the view of the cover squadron above, the scene below could be registered only in peripheral vision while searching the skies for enemy fighters, which surely would be airborne to protect a mission launch of bombers. However, none appeared. Then as the squadrons switched roles, the scene below became one from within.

My flight of 3 planes first took on a dispersal area, as yet un-hit, outside the main inferno. In just seconds that was no longer so. The several engine-running and taxiing bombers there became part of that inferno. I did not count passes made anymore than I would count turns in a dogfight. In fact, firing runs were "turns" rather than "passes," with violent "stops" in mid-turn to hold guns on the next available bomber—probably eight or nine such turns, some 90 degrees, some 270, whatever it took. Other than the initial steep pass down into the fray, we never came up or out to set up a "pass."

Flak was shooting tops out of trees and roofs off buildings. Bombers exploding under or nearby were extra hazards. One fuel truck went up in a sheet of flame under my wing tip, but was no comparison as a ball of fire to that of a fuel storage facility going up. A grim reality of war was added as a P-47 crashed in flames on the field.

A main challenge in flying and shooting became smoke. Aiming and firing could no longer be done in the clear. There was no strong wind laying smoke down solid across the field and sharp flying managed to dodge between some smoke columns; but getting trapped and flying into and through some was inevitable. Once in the smoke it was so thick and black you wondered if your engine could run in such stuff. Smoke also hindered flights and planes staying in visual contact and affected reassembly for departure. Pilot decisions on free use of engine power to catch up, join and hold formation versus conserving fuel were part of the 150-mile trip out of enemy territory to the coast. Still no enemy fighters showed, and all planes, except the one loss, made it back to Corsica. A few did land on an RAF field short of home base.

Smoke played havoc with claims. After the first few runs no overall view of enemy aircraft destroyed was possible, nor could we see and correlate or

Enemy airfield. *Bottom:* This pass across an active airfield is shooting to add more "flamers" to aircraft already burning. *Top:* An auto-weapon shell explodes dead ahead, distorting this film, as the enemy plane just left of the white puff is accurately strafed (gun camera, 86th Ftr Gp, World War II).

confirm all individual results. Some 20 from early shooting were claimed as positive kills; everything beyond that was unspecified destruction. Most were Ju 88s/Ju 188s, plus a few other types including Do 217, Ju 52 and Me 109. Also claimed were several fuel truck and fuel storage fires. No figure was given for enemy aircrew and ground personnel killed or wounded.

One shame of this mission was that our planes were not equipped with

Smoke. Skirting columns of smoke and often flying into heavy thick fuel smoke was a distinct part of much airfield (and other) strafing. This pilot tangles with some on his run into a field (gun camera 86th Ftr Gp, World War II).

gun cameras to record the action. The point about the mission and pilots "being their own generals" needed no further recording. These bombers on the ground, getting set to attack Americans, were treated no differently than if they were already in the air to attack. They were attacked repeatedly, until our force was actually in jeopardy for fuel, just as they would have been in the air. Strafing didn't just stop this enemy force before it ever got in the air, it killed it forever in the war.

Hans Rudel, Germany's noted air-ground attack pilot of the Russian Front, who had some 2,500 missions as a dive-bomber and specialized strafer and tank killer with 37mm guns on Ju 87s and also flew FW 190 fighter-bombers, and wrote the book *Stuka Pilot*, had some words about U.S. fighters strafing on that front.

At Mielec, Poland, in July 1944, three squadrons of Stukas had just departed the GAF airfield there on missions against Russian ground forces—when USAAF P-38s, 82" Ftr Gp, swept in low strafing the field. The airborne Stukas left slim pickings on the ground for the P-38s but accompanying P-51 cover, 31[51] Ftr Gp, had a field day shooting them in the air. These P-38s and P-51s were on a mission over 600 miles from their Russian staging base near Kiev. Rudel reported another strafing attack by U.S. P-51s on his field in Hungary in early September 1944. This time 50 German planes were destroyed on the ground.

P-51 Fighters, primarily in bomber escort/screen role in Europe, were also enemy airfield strafers (U.S. Air Force).

The first half of August 1944 the 79th had a heavy dose of strafing airfields. Initially these were in the Po Valley of Italy, mainly the Verona area. Some missions had preplanned dual targets: first bomb a rail line or bridge on the Po and then move on to strafe an airfield. Then our effort shifted to airfields in southern France, mainly the Marseille area. On 13 August, P-38s (15AF) joined all P-47s (12AF) in mass strafing of enemy fields there.

The 79th had missions on Le Vollon, Istres-Le Tube, and La Jasse airfields, all on the flat delta of the Rhone. These operations earned the term "nasty." Relatively few enemy planes were found and destroyed, but lots of auto-weapon fire was. One squadron effort on 13 August used tactics of a low run on Le Vollen, and then they would do the same at La Jasse. One pilot was lost and one wounded over Le Vollon; one was lost and five planes battle-damaged over La Jasse. Claims were two enemy aircraft destroyed, two probable, five damaged—Ju 88s and Me 109s—plus shooting up airfield facilities, flak positions and a 400-foot ship in Berre Lagoon.

Intermingled with airfields was strafing of gun positions and radar sights on the French coast near Marseille. As on numerous past missions (such as the 88s of El Hamma, North Africa), strafing had the needed accuracy and close pilot observation to confirm results. Where possible, attacks from inland were preferred, despite the extra time spent over enemy territory. Any flying

More auto weapon "puffs" (also called "golf balls" and "marshmallows"). The photograph isn't first quality, but it is a rare gem in depicting strafing. Gun camera film usually shows only gunfire into a target, not the above and surrounding skies full of automatic weapon ground fire always present at enemy airfields and other hot targets. Pictured here is a seldom seen glimpse of what those deadly skies were like as pilots had to fly through them to get to targets (gun camera, 86th Ftr Gp, World War II).

low over the water, attacking or withdrawing, drew immediate violent enemy reaction of intense ground fire—88 and auto-weapon, probably the most accurate we encountered. That strafing rated a "tough" or even "brutal" title.

Of course this extensive strafing was in preparation for the Allied invasion of southern France on 15 August, which came off' with great success and no enemy air opposition, the latter a distinct change from Anzio. In this strafing, I was farther convinced that the most ill advised pass a leader could make was straight-line at very low-level over open flat land or water, especially over the runway or center of an enemy airfield—unless that was the only way to accomplish the mission. If surprise got all planes across before the enemy opened fire (which had not been the case on most fields), their gunners and flak towers had the altitude wired, and they only had to shoot out in front of the plane. Many fields also had "fixed" patterns of fire for low-flying planes, usually crisscross, which a pilot had to fly through on a pass across the field.

Fixed pattern or "barrage" fire was also encountered at higher altitudes over airfields and other key targets. In diving attacks the pilot had to go into and through it. Once in it nothing could be done, as maneuvers and flight path changes improved chances of not being hit, except the higher the speed the less time in it. On the other hand, in tracking fire, the inherent change in alti-

The people of Valence, France, who witnessed the 79th Fighter Group's strafing of the German airfield there, came out to say "welcome" and "thanks" when the 79th later occupied that field. A P-47 was separated from the active flight line for them to admire (79th Ftr Gp, World War II).

tudes, speeds, and directions of a diving or turning pass did compound the shooting challenges of enemy gunners. But if enough of those gunners were concentrating on the aircraft, or were real experts, then things could become worse than barrage fire. Some airfields had both. Major airfields were among targets that qualified for flak rating of "intense to unbearable."

I was never upset to get an airfield target of widely dispersed enemy planes instead of one with planes in the open on ramps near runways. We could get dispersed planes even if it took more maneuvers and passes, and do it with less time spent in the most intense flak patterns of the main field center. Out in dispersed areas the number of guns shooting at you at one time could be cut in half or more. But, of course, if the enemy planes were out in the field's center, that is where we went.

By 22 August 1944 the 79th was based in southern France on the Riviera, and then moved north to Valence on 1 September. On the ex–GAF field there, two things were apparent. The first was that our claims on strafing this field were well below actual destruction. The second was that engineer units had minimal work to make the field operational: just check for mines, no bomb craters to fill. Thus strafing alone had done the job on units here (as at Foggia and others), while leaving the field ready for our immediate use on arrival.

In mid–September I was back in Italy, now CO of 525th Sq, 86th Ftr Gp. Flying from Grosseto, then Pisa, our operations until February 1945 were in the Po Valley and up to Austria on the Brenner Pass supply line Germany to Italy, while also supporting the strong fighting by Allied ground forces to break through German lines in the northern Apennines. We were flying P-47Ds, the same as the 79th. Those in the 86th did have gun cameras, simple 16mm movie jobs, with two settings—"sunny" and "cloudy"—and were not famed for high quality photography.

Since July, GAF operations in Italy had been sporadic. We flew few pre-planned missions against airfields. Yet, our other operations in the valley had us flying near German fields such as Ghedi and Villafranca in the Verona area. Some strafing was done there, which was dirty work. The fields were well defended and there were few planes on them, those hard to burn or explode, making us suspicious they were not operational anyway. But a few active fighters were found and destroyed now and then, and a few Ju 52s were caught while attempting support flights.

Our armed-recce of these fields had a special policy. In my squadron it was never to wander or fly directly over them on the chance enemy planes might be spotted, but to go there only if such targets were seen from outside the field and then only if' they were observed as "active" or by other evidence known to be operational. Aircraft wrecks or even dummies arranged to entice us into flak traps seemed common on enemy fields in Italy at this stage of the war. Thus, leader "generalship" in the air was the heart of this airfield strafing.

Some of the preplanned attacks on known active fields were most notable. Capt. Richard C. Oldham, 525th Ftr Sq, 86thrtr Gp, was awarded the Distinguished Service Cross for one on 3 October 1944. He led eight P-47s against an enemy tactical airdrome where hostile planes that had recently attacked the Allied front lines were reported to be based. While aggressively diving through a barrage of accurate antiaircraft fire to strafe the enemy field, his plane received several direct hits that set his aircraft afire. He pressed on, leading his formation through the intense ground fire, and succeeded in destroying several enemy aircraft and strafed a number of antiaircraft battery positions before his plane crashed.

In the Pacific, when American fighters and fighter-bombers, both carrier and land based, joined strafer bombers in operations over the Philippines, Japanese air forces were duly devastated. Many enemy planes fell in air combat; many more were destroyed on the ground, some on water. This was perhaps

Opposite: Low-level pass: A pilot's view in on-the-deck strafing of an enemy airfield. In the lower frame he is firing into a parked aircraft dead ahead; in the middle and upper frames he is in a violent turn, wing tip almost dragging the ground, as he tries to put his guns on the Me 109 fighters ahead to the right (it's his decision if that is possible or if he has to make another pass) Some auto-weapon fire shows (gun camera, 86th Ftr Gp, World War II).

the most classic example of its scale in winning air superiority in an area or theater in the war. But such a beating in air warfare of a normal sense may have influenced the Japanese to expand air warfare in an abnormal sense—with the Kamikazes.

Yet, to say that strafing in the Philippines or elsewhere fell solely within operations of a certain type aircraft, or a specific role or mission, fails to portray the truly diverse nature of strafing in the war. One example follows, from *The Army Air Forces in World War II*, vol. 5, about Mindanao: "Having noted during the previous week a concentration of floatplanes at Caldera point and about twenty Betty bombers at Wolfe Field, Zamboanga, a Navy PB4Y of VB-101 based at Owi dropped down through the cumulus just after dawn on 1 October (1944) to destroy three floatplanes and damage five others at anchor. Not satisfied, the PB4Y swept east across Wolfe Field, strafing and firing three Bettys. To make sure of the destruction the PB4Y circled, repeated its pass on the Bettys, and then escaped unscathed." A Navy long-range patrol bomber, with a normal crew of 11 and with six turrets of two cal .50s each, making repeat machine-gun passes on a major Japanese floatplane base and airfield may be a special story, but it is just as much a part of strafing history as that of fighters and fighter-bombers in World War II.

Despite much hurt on their air forces, the enemy was not through strafing yet. In November and December 1944, USAAF B-29 bases on Saipan and Tinian in the Pacific were bombed and strafed, with low-flying fighters and twin-engine planes doing the most damage. In Europe on New Year's Day 1945, some 700 to 1,000 German planes hit Allied airfields in the Netherlands, Belgium, and a few in France, mainly by low-level strafing. Allied losses were 156 aircraft (36 USAAF), but those losses came at a very heavy loss to the Germans. Finally the GAF had made a determined low-level effort, but too late, against the massive Allied tactical air power on the continent. That air power in both Europe and the Pacific continued relentless strafing of enemy air power until the war's end.

· 6 ·

End of the Luftwaffe

The German Air Force was still a threat when two more USAAF fighter groups, the 27th and 86th, were transferred from the MTO to the ETO to add yet greater air support of the Allied push into Germany. The 86th was stationed near Nancy, France, from late February to early April 1945, and then moved into Germany at Gross Gerau, near Darmstadt. We were under the I TAF (1st Tactical Air Force). This was a provisional air force of several American 9AF and French air units, which provided air support for the 6th Army Group (U.S. 7th Army and French 1st Army) on the southern front. The U.S. 9AF covered American armies in the center. Our operations started out as intense support of ground forces in breakthrough of the Siegfried Line, then priority turned to strafing airfields. We were informed that the 6th Army Group specifically requested support to "keep the German Air Force off our backs in Germany." The following paragraph from *The Army Air Forces in World War II*, vol. 3, summarizes I TAF operations to fulfill that request:

> Following carefully formulated plans and aided by photographic intelligence reports, Allied fighters systematically patrolled and attacked active German airfields. Six airdromes in the Stuttgart area received constant attention from First Tactical Air Force planes beginning 26 March. In April when the Luftwaffe units pulled back to the southeast, Allied planes followed them and kept up the assault. Day by day, the enemy became more constricted and resorted to increasingly desperate measures such as attempting to hide planes in woods near airdromes and Autobahns. The futility of the GAF's last stand is indicated by First TAF's counter-air claims for the period 23 March to 8 May: in the air, 87 destroyed, 11 probable, 53 damaged; on the ground, 793 destroyed, 47 probable, 681 damaged. In the same period, the cost of the aerial offensive in support of the 6th Army Group was approximately 100 American aircraft of all types.

A summary of 9AF operations for the same period reads almost the same in attacks on the GAF, concluding with: "[T]he Ninth's fighter-bombers claimed over 1,400 planes destroyed on the ground during the last month of operations." The pilots of both 1TAF and 9AF who did that might like to see one addition to the history: "It was done by strafing."

One mission on a major airfield at Stuttgart brought on more awe of the

Air dogfight. All-out strafing of the German Air Force was not done without their fighting back in the air as well as with flak. We had substantial air kills too (gun camera, 86th Ftr Gp, World War II).

facility than the numerous planes on it or the intense flak encountered. A massive glass front semicircle stone terminal, plus hangars, large buildings and paved ramps, left no doubt the war had come to established "Fatherland" airdromes, not just to wartime strips. At the same time in Germany we encountered extremes in efforts to disperse and hide planes.

Down the autobahn (superhighways, which most of us had never seen the likes of back home) southeast of Stuttgart toward Munich was one stretch used as airfields. In some areas the regular 4-lane concrete was used as runway, in others the median had been filled in for a wider flying surface; holes in the median concrete held cut trees from adjacent forests to disguise use as runway.

Forests of this area added special challenges in strafing autobahn-based airplanes, most of which were fighters. Parked back under trees, often camouflaged, they were extremely difficult to spot. Some leaders actually flew down the autobahn below the treetops to look under the forest canopy. Others used keen eyes to pick out even the slightest interruption in the otherwise consistent canopy pattern, which was formed by German thoroughness in planting and maintaining forests in precise tree spacing. Interruptions in the canopy could be cut trees hiding taxiways and parking.

Once planes were found, each one (or that particular spot in the forest canopy) had to be kept in sight while maneuvering for a firing run. A common

Enemy bomber. Aircraft on open German fields allowed freedom in the type of passes to do this kind of damage (U.S. Air Force).

"pass" for low-level searchers was to pull up and off in a hard turn, roll near inverted, pull back down, and roll out on target. Shooting was often done while still near upside-down and during rollout. Higher flying searchers frequently made very steep firing maneuvers with violent pullouts.

One leader had a unique decision to make when he spotted a wrecked fighter on the autobahn. Was it a flying accident not removed quickly enough to avoid detection, or was it planted as a flak trap? That possibility had been discussed in briefings. Reasoning the Germans would not advertise they were flying off highways, our mission pounced on the area. We found and destroyed other fighters in the roadside forest, so it was a very productive decision.

Regardless of how enemy planes were spotted or the type firing run used, these forests came into play another way. The trees here, as in parts of northern Italy, Austria and southern France, were taller than others in much of the ETO and MTO; these were 90 to 100 feet or more. That height cut into gun bore sight distance and reduced pullout clearance drastically. This applied to all strafing in such forests—aircraft, trucks, trains, armor, troops, etc. The fact I had earlier moved bore sight distance out to 900 feet for the Alps helped here.

Still, flying into trees was common. Some were remarkable cases, such as a plane mashing down into treetops and cutting a swath in the forest and still flying up and back to base. Hitting trees and surviving added to the P-47's

Other planes, like this Me 262 jet amid tall trees, put special shooting demands on pilots (U.S. Air Force).

reputation of ruggedness to withstand battle damage of all types. But of course not all such damage was survived. Tall trees were not totally bad for strafers. Enemy gunners had to find or make open positions in order to see and fire on aircraft. Less view of us reduced the fire encountered. At the same time, a cut site amid trees was easier for us to spot and turn on.

As our efforts against airfields moved farther south and east, many were in the Munich area. Terrain was flatter and less forested, more farmland and open space. These fields were congested with planes, Finding them was no problem. Many were on ramps or bunched on grass. Others were widely dispersed but not always hidden. Flak was intense, especially on fields with Me 262 jets. Open terrain, along with flak towers and rooftop positions, gave enemy gunners excellent views and fields of fire against us.

Our squadron policies on tactics emphasized a couple of points in carrying out the military mission and duty. First was that extreme aggressiveness in combat was best for both accomplishment and survival (timid war fighting will get you killed). Second was that although weather might at times prevent

Opposite: German plane in tree line. *Bottom:* This pilot is firing from a tight turn into an opening in the forest to nail a fighter. *Center:* Instantly rolling out in his pull up. *Top:* Pulling high "Gs" to clear the trees (gun camera, 86th Ftr Gp, World War II).

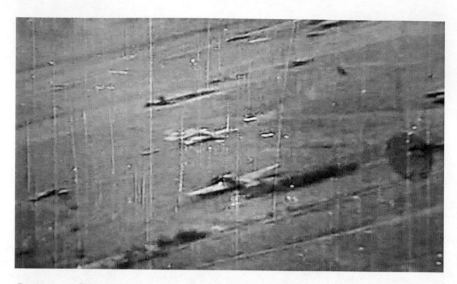

German airfield. Objective of max total kills: get as many as possible on each pass on fields like this (gun camera, 86th Ftr Gp, World War II).

us from completing a task, the enemy would not be allowed to. Beyond that we had no SOP (standard operating procedure) for strafing airfields. Each field and mission, each time, place, situation, etc., got its own evaluation and tactics, even if we had a dozen a day in the same area.

All tactics were constantly discussed and evaluated mission by mission all day and each night. At times this went beyond military experiences. A prewar dove hunter explained his choice spot on one farm was under a big tree between two cornfields. His reason: doves were hard to hit flying in the clear above the fields and he used too many shells; but they were easy to hit when skimming around the tree flying field to field and he saved money on shells. Dove hunting did not become a foundation of tactics but my experience in combat did correlate that the more rounds fired up did not always mean the most danger to you.

These airfield missions in Germany had the overall objective of destroying the GAF. Thus our job was to get as many planes as possible on each mission. Some missions were scheduled against particular airfields, others had objectives of "go to Augsburg (or Munich) complex of fields and destroy planes." The precautionary "don'ts" of our voluntary armed-recce of airfields in northern Italy were reversed. We went after planes on every field, made repeat passes when productive and used all ammo. In cases of enemy planes clearly in the open we made some flat low-level runs spreading fire through them instead of our normal diving pinpoint shooting.

One pilot quote from Italy 1943 follows: "Ain't no airplane fast enough to strafe in—much less a P-40." And he was strafing trucks, not airfields. High

Airplanes in a courtyard? In approach to an airfield, this pilot (and his camera) sees what appear to be two airplanes in a barracks courtyard. First thought: are they fake or display rather than active? Decision here: press on to destroy combat planes on the field ahead, check this later (gun camera, 86th Ftr Gp, World War II).

speed had great pilot appeal against airfields in reduced exposure time. The P-47s and P-51s had top rated speeds of around 430 mph but could greatly exceed that in dives—up to their Mach limits of .70 and .72 or about 530 and 550 mph at sea level. Some initial low passes were well over 400, but our squadron held to about that or under for best control and shooting. Repeat hard maneuvering passes were slower, down with most other strafing, 300 to 350 ballpark.

Gun camera photos with this text, all from action in the Augsburg and Munich areas, record widely varied strafing runs on airfields.

In the bottom photograph, this near vertical pass is being done by a cover flight on switch with a strafing flight below, in a dive from their patrol location rather than taking time to position for a particular type run, which would give the enemy a lull in being strafed. We pilots did not want that or any delay in the swapping of flights. Airborne enemy fighters were still a threat and in April 1945 the 86th destroyed 11 and damaged 10 in air battles while destroying 145 and damaging 198 on the ground as the month's contribution to 1 TAF totals. The center photograph shows the overall most used and most effective method of shooting, a 15–30 degree dive; film shows the pilot in position to manipulate short bursts into several planes on this run. The top photograph is of on-the-deck strafing in a repeat maneuvering run, not a flat fly through. At times this

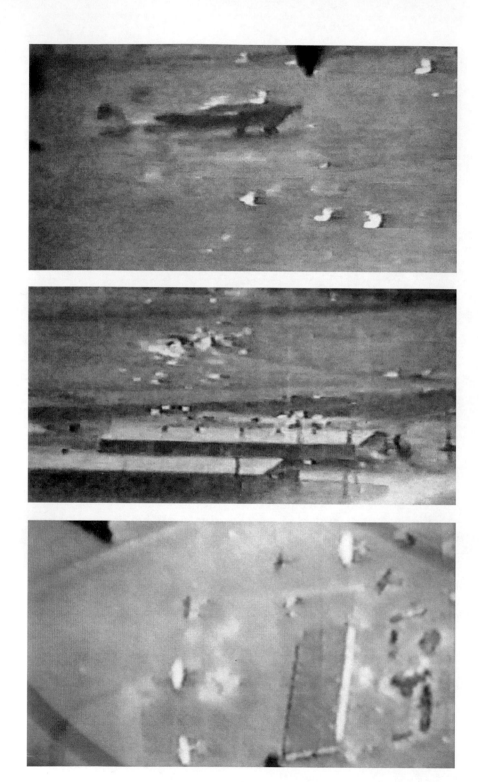

low pilots could readily put their guns squarely on a plane up ahead, but often it was a contest of determination versus judgment on whether it could be done by maximum hard maneuver without high speed stall and losing control. Being ever so close to a kill but needing one bit more to get it could reverse who gets killed. Combat film is its own record, and probably the best history, of varied maneuvers, runs and shooting—and of pilots being their own generals.

A second Distinguished Unit Citation was awarded the 86th for results on 20 April 1945 of a peak day in strafing kills that included a number of Me 262 jets. Other groups receiving the same award included the 78th Ftr Gp for destroying numerous aircraft on five fields near Prague and Pilsen on 16 April, and the 355th Ftr Gp for strafing airfields in a snowstorm on 5 April.

The 78th and 355th were 8AF units, evidence that all fighters in the ETO had part in destroying the GAF. According to 8AF P-51 pilots after the war, they probably used more low-level run-ins and larger formations as means of concentrating fire on enemy planes than our frequent "swanning" tactics from above. Yet, record of one 8AF group CO being lost on the sixth pass on an airfield shows no one format applied to their strafing, either.

The fighters of the MTO were in on destruction of the Luftwaffe too. Lt. Raymond Knight, 350th Ftr Gp, 12AF, received the Medal of Honor (Posthumous) in this action. On 21 April 1945, he led two missions on airfields north of the Po River, Italy. Multiple strafing passes destroyed numerous planes, 13 by Lt. Knight while being hit several times by flak. On a mission next morning, he and his flight had destroyed three bombers with gunfire when his plane was severely damaged by flak. Flying almost to home base at Pisa, the plane crashed and Lt. Knight was killed.

If recording on paper how air forces, groups, mission leaders, and pilots went about this entire air-to-ground gunfighting in each case is complicated—and it is—the end result is not. When the German Air Force was finally destroyed, it was with gunfighting—by strafing and strafers.

From the 86th base in Germany another aspect of earlier strafing hurt on the GAF evolved from a non-airfield scene in the town of Gross Gerau. On a rail overpass was a destroyed locomotive, with a full freight train behind. On the highway below were two burned-out skeletons of trucks. How this came to be was known to us. A flight of P-47s spotted the train and trucks. The leader pounced first on the trucks, which could take cover quickly to escape, but the train could not. With both trucks "flamed" by strafing, the locomotive was hit as rapidly as possible and destroyed, maybe with the crew still aboard.

Opposite: **German airfields. Each mission used tactics for max kills.** *Bottom:* **A steep pass as a cover flight swaps with a strafing flight and opens fire on the way down.** *Center:* **This pilot in a shallow dive picks out and kills a plane.** *Top:* **Down on-the-deck point blank work. Action of these frames is described in the text (gun camera, 86th Ftr Gp, World War II).**

German Air Force equipment, personnel and support workers were often taken out when trains and trucks were strafed too, such as the trucks in a cloud of smoke and debris on the highway through this village (gun camera, 86th Ftr Gp, World War II).

These boxcars were not strafed; ammo was saved for more locomotives. A claim of one locomotive and two trucks in a small town would hardly be thought of as much of an impact on the Luftwaffe. But examination showed every boxcar on the train contained GAF equipment and supplies. And it was learned locally that the trucks were taking workers to an aircraft parts factory and repair facility in Darmstadt. Thirty of those workers were killed and others badly injured. We also learned that the field we were now flying from had previously been the home of the GAF 53rd Fighter Wing (JG53), who evacuated it on 17 March 1945 after being strafed by eighteen P-47s on 16 March.

Japanese air forces on the home islands came under USAAF fighter machine gunfire in April 1945 when the first all-fighter missions from Iwo Jima were also strafing. Examples included P-51s strafing Atsugi Airfield near Tokyo with 84 planes destroyed or damaged. Enemy airfields received prime attention for strafing during the heavy fighting on Okinawa and continued with extensive P-51 and P-47N machine-gunning of airfields and other home island targets.

We could summarize quite a record of strafing's role in counter air victories

While airfield strafing remained deadly throughout, in the end, duty and sacrifice by brave men left the bulk of the German Air Force like this, a feat done overwhelmingly by strafing (U.S. Air Force).

in World War II, including the British in North Africa, the Japanese at Hawaii and the Philippines, and the U.S. in Alaska, the Mediterranean, the Pacific, CBI (China, Burma, India), and Europe. Numerous other specific entries in official histories could be noted, such as "Our ground forces advanced through Germany with little or no opposition by the German Air Force."

Strafers of the European war in that history hold quite dear such memories as being told after VE-Day that U.S. ground forces extended "thanks for keeping the Luftwaffe off our backs" (message for the 86th Ftr Gp from U.S. 7th Army). Surely such memories exist from all theaters.

However, certainly the ultimate remembrance is of those who gave their lives in this destruction of enemy air forces. Our unit losses had been relative low during the extensive airfield strafing in intense enemy auto-weapon fire. But we did lose an experienced pilot on one of the last missions flown against a GAF airfield when on a very low pass his plane was hit and burst into flames, then immediately crashed into a hangar. The victories were not without sacrifice.

· 7 ·

Gunfights
Enemy Support Forces

During World War II one "fact" of service life in the Navy often stated to friends and families by sailors in training was: "If it moves, salute it—if it doesn't, paint it." That "wisdom," with slight modification, can better outline the gunfighting of this chapter than official terms for various air operations: If it moves, strafe it—if it doesn't (but it can), strafe it too. Never mind what it is, military or civilian, as long as it is enemy and can support combat forces, regardless of where found from homeland source to "in hand" of troops in battle. Never mind what it is doing, or might be able to do—delivering or returning, moving or hiding, dispersed or in hubs and parks. Just as strafers successfully coped with dispersed enemy aircraft, strafers played an enormous role in coping with all "underway" elements of enemy support: hunt, strafe, destroy, and kill. Before the war this was another aspect of strafing I had no reason to appreciate, certainly not in the scope of varied operations shown in the following two examples.

In the Battle of the Atlantic, German aircraft combined with U-boats and surface raiders against Allied shipping. Various bombers were employed, plus the FW 200, a 4-engine civilian airliner converted to long-range maritime patrol. While the FW 200 bombed too, the German crews reportedly had a distinct attraction for using their eight or more cannon and machine guns to strafe merchant vessels far out at sea. (My younger brother, Bob, who was a radio operator with the U.S. Merchant Marines, on runs to Murmansk/Archangelsk, Russia, had firsthand experience with such strafing, along with U-boats, mines, and the like.)

The following quote from *The Army Air Forces in World War II*, vol. 4, is about "hunting" much closer to ground fighting, this in the Pacific, Bougainville, November 1943:

As the fighters moved up to their station over the beaches, frequently they were ordered to make careful searches of trails, rivers, paths, always on the alert for any signs of movement in the dense green jungle below them. They strafed along the

Piva, Jaba, and Torokina Rivers, the trails between them, and the barge hideouts along the coast and in river mouths, sometimes enjoying a field day at the enemy's expense.... [T]he longer-legged P-38s did the same all around the island; canoes, huts, small groups of Japanese, all were targets for the strafers.

(My older brother, Jack, U.S. Army, had firsthand experience with this type of strafing support in his service with a division in the Pacific.)

Other examples of "hunter-killers" against shipping and other watercraft and its degree of impact include Guadalcanal in December 1942. The Japanese ordered a force of some 50,000 Asian war-wise reenforcements into the battle. The goal was to reverse the situation of beleaguered Japanese troops there, then retake the island. A month later the plan was abandoned. The enemy was forced to evacuate with the total loss of Guadalcanal. A Japanese captain said after the war that the Army high command strongly wanted to retake the island but bringing in the additional troops was too difficult. He cited mainly the U.S. dive-bombers and strafing planes that were able to locate and destroy the transports and landing barges, which the Japanese tried to hide during daylight. *The Army Air Forces in World War II*, vol. 5 records this "hunting" on return to Luzon, Philippines: "As the American forces undertook to clear the port of Manila, remnants of Japanese units sought safety across the bay on Bataan and at Corregidor. Heavy barge traffic, noted by fighters on 11 February (1945), was vigorously strafed by 348th Group planes during the following four days, with claims of 2,000 enemy soldiers killed."

By VJ-Day the public was well aware of U.S. success in both sea and air warfare against enemy shipping and warships in both the Pacific and the Atlantic. They probably had vaguer background on strafing of watercraft in the land mass fighting of Asia and Europe.

When I joined the 79th Group in 1943 some of the hairiest war stories of veteran pilots were about missions on watercraft in the Messina Strait as Axis forces withdrew from Sicily to Italy in a mass of ships, ferries, and barges protected by a mass of flak. From then to VE-Day my experience involved strafing all of the following on water (plus the freighters previously noted): Barges, from animal-pulled and some powered types in Italy and France to large towed and self-propelled versions on the Rhine, Danube and other waterways in Germany. A few impressive passenger vessels on the Danube were also hit, and some we reported as speedboats on big Lake Garda in northern Italy. One of my missions machine-gunned a large ferry or excursion ship on that lake, literally blowing chunks off upper decks before it burst into flame and became an inferno from the waterline up.

Almost all of this strafing was "add on" armed recce after having accomplished another primary mission, such as rail cut, voluntary decisions of leaders to hunt other targets. Spotting barges and boats was quite easy when they were underway in open water, even on canals. But as always when fighter-bombers showed up, the enemy worked hard to make all "movers" difficult to find. Extensive camouflage and hiding schemes were encountered, such as complete covers on barges to blend with the water surface, slips cut into fields with covers to match crops growing there, and cut trees mounted onboard to blend with forests along riverbanks. Enemy vessels in coastal waters were attacked mainly by air units of coastal patrol commands, but we had a few scheduled missions on ports and were called in at times on certain coastal targets, for air rescue cover, and other operations.

Shooting barges and small boats on inland waterways was almost all diving passes. Seldom could a flat pass be effective. Barge cargos did in a few cases explode, but often they carried coal, lumber, etc. To assure destruction of the barge itself, passes had to be pressed in to bore sight range with full impact on engine room, fuel supply, and other critical components.

Strafing fast boats when underway was definitely more like air dogfighting than ground attack. Their speed required substantial "lead" in aim. They were hard to match in maneuver and fully as difficult to hit as an enemy fighter, and the strafer had several restrictions not present in most air fights. He could not turn with and get on a boat's tail, nor could he ever come up on or pass under one. In fact, he better never forget that the best flying for proper aim would easily crash him into the water.

Waterways themselves received attention. Extensive systems of dams, water levels, and locks of moving gates were involved. Many of these, especially those with control buildings, operator stations and guard shacks, were shot up by strafers. So were the floating elements of pontoon bridges, which the Germans relied heavily on to cross rivers of the Po Valley. At times fighter-bombers caught pontoon bridges still operating in daylight, bombed them, and then strafed the blown apart sections and pontoons floating downriver. More often disassembled bridges were targets in daylight. Pontoons and sections hidden along the banks, camouflaged in some way, were sought out and strafed.

Most vessels strafed were straightforward transportation. German E-boats or similar vessels in coastal waters were definite military targets. A few craft, such as on Lake Garda, raised questions as to just what they were. But we reasoned two things: one, with German fuel supply shortages, any powerboats being used must be of value to their war effort, two, operators and others onboard most coastal and inland waterway vessels were extremely vulnerable to strafing fire. Killing them took more enemy manpower out of the war. Thus they were strafed.

In literature citing history's "great weapons of war," among such arms as crossbows, machine guns, and atomic bombs is also found "railroads." Every major country involved in World War II had extensive rail systems supporting the war. Germany's war planning included manufacture of 5,000 extra locomotives and associated rolling stock and facilities. Tremendous expansion of American rail service occurred at home, and military railroad units were organized and equipped, trained (by Southern) and sent overseas. In North Africa,

The barge at this waterway dam or lock is hit with a burst of accurate fire. Control facilities, personnel and guards were shot up too (gun camera, 86th Ftr Gp, World War II).

German planes quickly strafed our military trains. In turn, antiaircraft guns and crews were put aboard. Yet, my fighter training in early 1943 did not mention that, or hint that the enemy would logically do the same; nor did it forecast that some of the roughest air gunfighting of the war would be between airplanes and trains.

However, strafing trains was one thing I had thought about back then. I had completed training as a fireman on steam locomotives (Atlantic Coast Line) in fall of 1941. It was hard work but I loved the hours I spent on fast citrus-hauling freight trains out of Florida. Once I began flying fighters and encountering ground gunnery I realized that crews of "locos" (in pilot lingo) would be targets of strafing. A few weeks after entering combat I was strafing them.

In the MTO, the farther north Allied ground forces advanced the thicker rail traffic and targets became for fighter-bombers, peaking in northern Italy and on into Germany. Also, pilots of P-47s (radius of 250–280 miles) in that role versus about 150 for earlier P-40s could reach farther into enemy rail systems. A pilot of the MTO in 1943 and early 1944 had far less railroad strafing than one of late 1944 on to the war's end. The ETO and CBI may have had less pronounced change as the war progressed, but in the Pacific once fighters were operating over Japan rail targets were certainly most plentiful.

Of course, fighter-bombers were not the only fighters that strafed trains. In the ETO, 8AF fighters, mainly P-51s, turned loose on rail targets in late 1944 claimed some 600 locomotives shot up in a single week. In Europe during P-61 night attack operations combined with 20mm fire in early 1945, the 422nd Sq. was credited with hitting nearly 1,000 locos and rolling stock.

Trains underway were far from the only railroad targets strafed. Locomotives anywhere anytime were high priority. Certain cargos on trains underway and in yards were prime targets, including troops, vehicles, armor, field guns on flatcars, huge railway guns, rail line work and repair equipment, etc. Other users of rails were strafed: motorcars, streetcars, trolleys, hand-pumped rail inspection cars, or anything else on the tracks.

Power stations of electric rail lines were planned targets by both bombing and strafing to force enemy reliance on steam locomotives. In turn, water and coal towers for the latter were strafed. So were shops, yard offices/facilities, depots/stations, switch/signal posts, guard shacks and, of course, the people found anywhere near anything "railroad."

The most common "road" equipment was "rolling stock," a wealth of it found on trains and in yards, sidings, and shops throughout rail systems. Historians and writers normally lump everything pulled by locomotives into the term "rolling stock." Yet, most pilots never did. At debriefings (and in bar talk) we reported shooting "cars," whether on trains or in yards and sidings, generally as "freight" but often more specific as "box," "flat," "tank," etc. Certain other wording is found in literature that varies from most pilot talk on strafing rail-

A "blown" locomotive. Solid hits set off a classic example of a loco "blowing," sending smoke and steam high in the air (gun camera, 86th Ftr Gp, World War II).

road targets. One case is the phrase, "They strafed the locomotive to stop the train," often adding "so they could strafe it." While that sequence did happen at times, the quote by itself infers "standard" practice. Also it leaves the strafing of locos and cars combined in a single thought. This can lead far astray from the real or "inside" story.

First, my unit, and others I am familiar with, strafed locos underway or otherwise with objective and tactics to totally destroy them on the spot—and very likely kill the crews at the same time. The train stopped as a result. As further text of specific actions show, although we may have also strafed the train quite often we did not, but rather saved ammo for more locos. Second, pilot and crew shooting challenges and techniques for both results and best survival on locos versus cars involved different considerations, whether on a train together or separate. They were often associated targets, but not similar targets.

Locomotives, while varying in size and weight from large mainline freight and passenger types to small local and yard switch engines, were "iron" horses. Whether steam or electric, they were relatively "hard" targets. To be claimed destroyed, a steam loco had to "blow," or rupture in a cloud of steam (at times with parts flying oft) or derail and wreck. An electric loco had to erupt in a display of fire, sparks, and smoke, with parts flying in order to be claimed. Only close-in pinpoint shooting achieved those results. Sprayed bullets never did.

Strafing locos gave pilots graphic proof of the impact force of all guns hitting together, both in power to penetrate and to "blow" such a mass of metal—and in cases (usually smaller types) actually knock them off the tracks and generate wrecks of underway locos and trains. On the other hand, a single round sprayed or otherwise hitting a freight car, or string of them, on a train or in yards could set off fire or explosion, a common occurrence. A few examples follow.

[Citation, Air Medal, 2nd Lt. Frederick F. English, 27th Ftr Gp, P-47, France, 9 September 1944]

> Flying at minimum altitude owing to heavy cloud cover at 4,000 feet, Lt. English, despite intense antiaircraft fire, pressed home a determined attack against a locomotive and fifteen freight cars near the town of Colmar. One of the cars exploded causing Lt. English's aircraft to flip over on its back while a direct hit by 20mm fire exploded in an ammunition bay badly damaging one wing. Regaining control of his crippled plane, Lt. English, with superior flying skill, flew it back to a friendly field and managed to land it safely despite great difficulty.

A photograph in *Impact* (USAAF intelligence magazine sent to combat units in World War II) showed the aftermath of one explosion in France where a train had been strafed that left a train-long crater some 300 feet wide and 30 to 50 feet deep, with nothing showing of train, rail line or roadbed. Pilots of the 27th Ftr Gp, including flight leader Lt. Calvin K. Ellis, set off an explosion with their P-47s in rail yards at Ingolstadt, Germany in April 1945 that obliterated much of the yards and numerous surrounding buildings.

Locomotives and freight cars on trains and in rail yards simply posed conflicting shooting decisions for pilots. Locos demanded close-in full force impact. Freight cars were the opposite; more could be destroyed by spreading

The locomotives are destroyed. Now it is the mission leader's decision to stay and strafe the train or recce for more locos. Often it was the latter (U.S. Air Force).

bullets among them than by zeroing in on single cars—and doing it from longer range might prevent the plane being blown out of the air. But tank cars for fuel and chemicals were often zeroed on to start fires. As a result, many units reversed the sequence of "shooting the loco to stop the train" and instead fired a few initial rounds of "sampling" fire from longer range (the entire train might explode) before pressing on in to kill the loco. For rail yards, "sampling" bursts on the cars from 3,000 or more feet out during the run in was common (and in a case like the Ingolstadt explosion it was fortunate they did).

Other complexities were involved. Often intermingled with boxcars were flatcars carrying army tanks and other "hard" targets that took close in shooting to "hurt" and thus were not similar targets to the boxcars around them. A bit of "sampling" fire from well out often preceded pressing in close on the "hard" cargos.

Then there were the flak cars, the rolling auto-weapon defenses on railroads. Early in the war most of these carried field-type 20mm or 37mm guns and crews. Later, more special designs were encountered such as armor or concrete-protected, quad-barrel 20mm, some power-driven turret versions, two or more sets of guns per train. It is a sure bet that pilots who strafed a German train with flak cars in it, especially late-war versions, made debriefing reports that stressed one hell of a "gunfight" far more than "shooting" of either the loco or the train cars, as later specific actions will attest in detail.

Strafing box cars and other rail cars often had spectacular results. Here is an oil/fuel fire with black smoke cloud to the right of an adjacent train; sometimes there is a terrific explosion (gun camera, 86th Ftr Gp, World War II).

Varied operational and flying situations put yet more pilot and crew decision factors into the strafing of railroads even within the same theater and the same time frame of the war. In the MTO in fall and winter 1944-45, our fighter-bombers operated in a classic situation for strafing railroads. Battle lines across Italy held in the northern Apennines despite strong attempts to break through by the Allies and equal defense and counterattacks by the Germans. In the Po Valley just to the north was one of the world's foremost rail systems, a major network of dual-track routes interconnected with numerous single-track lines. Allied air dominance forced the enemy to primarily night and bad weather movement but the level of ground fighting could not be supported without some enemy day and good weather traffic too, both rail and road. Thus "movers" were frequent targets. The situation in the ETO that winter was much the same as U.S. fighter-bombers roamed into Germany over an even denser rail system.

In months of flying over the Po Valley pilots became so familiar with the geography and with rail lines, roads and waterways that they could have flown without maps; but of course they always had them and the maps were always religiously updated. Many missions to bomb a rail line were much the same. But pilots knew that after each such rail cut they could expect to go on armed-recce and strafe targets of opportunity, which they did not expect to be the same.

Main rail routes were seldom without auto-weapon flak along the lines, always intense in hubs and cities along with heavy flak, and trains on dual lines were almost sure to carry flak cars. Our recce policy was much the same as for airfields: Look for active locos/trains, which could be seen from a mile or more away. Low "grubbing" in efforts to find inactive and hidden locos in intense flak favored the enemy to do the most hurting. Strafing locos on main lines was tough business but underway trains there were judged important to the enemy and leaders gave eagle-eye attention for "movers" there.

Full-fledged shootouts were expected, but there were rare exceptions. In one case, during the 86th Gp's, the first mission in January 1945, four P-47s, airborne after a stand-down due to a major snowstorm over the valley, sighted a speeding passenger train—a big engine and some 12 cars on the Milan to Bologna line—only a few miles short of getting under protection of storm clouds still over the eastern valley. The engine was strafed, blown and destroyed, and the train slid a couple of miles to a stop. Unexpected was the lack of flak cars or other auto-weapon fire. People poured from all train cars, but went no farther and jammed into a mass along each side of the train. It dawned on amazed pilots above, already in return strafing passes, that those people were bogged down in heavy snow.

Receiving only individual weapon fire from the ground, a "gunnery pattern" was set up and each pilot expended all ammo in repeat passes on these people—now identified as troops. Passes were lengthwise down the train, slowly "walked" fire (controlled by diving runs, gradually reducing dive angle) to keep dense impact patterns moving along the target. Uniquely, this was one case where a normal "bugaboo" of gun harmonization in strafing down a train could be converted to very effective use. With a pilot firing along the train from 2,000 feet out (about double bore sight distance) bullets from each set of wing guns crossed over and impacted some 18 to 20 feet apart. With aim kept directly along a train, bullets missed it just wide on each side, not a desired result normally. But here those just wide impacts went directly into the massed troops on both sides of the train. Then as range closed and bullet impacts converged, pilot aim was switched to troops on one side or into the cars and troops still inside.

At debriefing pilots estimated over 500 troops outside the train, an unknown number inside, 8,544 rounds of API ammo fired, one loco destroyed, 12 cars damaged. It was assumed the train was caught in the open because the storm had moved east faster than the enemy expected, or the train was slowed in the storm, causing loss of its bad weather protection. Not reported was that it would have been better if pilots could not have seen these strafing results so up-close and clear (at least that was my feeling as mission leader).

As opposed to "main lines," armed-recce of connecting and local lines normally took on a different character. It often was a search for layover and hidden locos in addition to active ones. The tremendous numbers of freight cars seen in yards and sidings throughout the Po Valley led to personal conviction there were more locos around them somewhere than we were seeing on normal operations. We tried some closer looking, searching mainly side or connecting lines. This was low recce, down to and less than 1,000 feet. From familiarity with the valley we could avoid known intense auto-weapon areas. However, no low recce over German territory on any scale would ever completely avoid such fire. Missions of four P-47s in elements of two, spread apart, could maneuver so both elements rarely came under concentrated fire; and when fired on, one element could turn on the enemy gunners.

We looked for locos in places they were not usually seen on railroads back home while parked or laying-over. We searched little used spurs and special ones run into villages, buildings, under covers, etc. Also, we modified the reasoning that tracks were sole trail to locos. Those tracks might be camouflaged, have "remove-replace" links, etc. An extra note was made to not think "parallel only." On a single rail line out through the countryside and villages the entire system is generally parallel to the line—including the small yards, sidings and locos and cars on them. A loco on a disguised spur, parked unparallel, particularly at 90 degrees, to the rest of the system might go unnoticed simply because it was "out of parallel." We hit tank cars too, which were critical cargos and prime fire starters.

In operation we seldom ran into more than one or two auto-weapon positions together, surprisingly few at times, and were very successful in knocking out those encountered. Claims of locos destroyed took a sharp increase as hidden ones often "blew" as readily as underway counterparts. This was achieved without any real change in our losses, but with considerably more minor battle damage to planes from small arms on the low recce.

A program of bad-weather loco-busting missions was added, officially termed "Specials." These were flown only after normal fighter-bomber operations were halted due to bad weather in the Po Valley; however, this did not apply to any and all bad weather, only to one type. The pancake-flat valley floor was at times 100 percent blanketed by an equally flat layer of low stratus clouds that obscured all targets to pilots above who were flying in clear skies and unlimited visibility. On a mission in the valley in November 1944, this particular weather developed as we continued to recce and strafe, now under a level ceiling of some 2,000 feet. On return to base, we climbed through the stratus layer—no turbulence and plane-to-plane formation visibility OK in the clouds—breaking out at 3,500 feet above level cloud tops with mountains in view and weather good at home base.

Armed with this experience I requested commanders up the line to let us try a "special" mission: the next time that same weather halted normal operations, to deliberately takeoff, penetrate the cloud layer and strafe locos while the enemy rail system was in full operation under protection of bad weather. The commanders approved one. It was flown with four planes, guns only, with

Underway single locomotive. This leader aims for the crew, firing into the cab. Other pilots of his flight will hit the boiler/firebox to destroy the locomotive (U.S. Air Force).

the outcome of 10 locos hit and no loss or damage to us. This success and reenforcement to command that I knew the valley well enough (headings and distances between all valley features) from the in-view mountains to avoid cities and radar flak while above the overcast, and to let down in areas free of flak and auto-weapons, resulted in approval of a set of procedures to fly more.

In essence these were purely voluntary for mission and pilots; when specified weather conditions existed, I could ask to lead a "Special" consisting of 4 planes, guns only, and 3 other pilots from the volunteer list, which was every pilot in the squadron. Personal approval was required in turn by the group CO, Col. Earl E. Bates, or Col, George T. Lee, then by the XXII TAC CG, Brig. Gen. B.W. Chidlaw. Every request was approved. Nine missions were flown during the winter, most in December. Results were almost identical on each: 10 active or underway locos destroyed. We strafed no rail cars or other targets and we had no losses on these missions. (Besides appearing in unit records, accounts of these "Specials" are found in *Dear Mom and Dad* by Glenn C. Moore and other references.)

In the bulk of loco strafing tactics, flights and elements operated together. All four pilots of a flight (or in some cases an element of two) followed through in individual runs on a loco, each firing a short burst of less than two seconds, up to 200 rounds, for a total of 700 to 800 rounds into the engine. The rea-

On the "road." Our "Special" missions caught the enemy rail system in full operation, as we were not expected to be flying under low overcast. Pinpoint shooting got maximum kills per mission (gun camera, 86th Ftr Gp, U.S. Air Force).

soning of this tactic was to insure so many hits that no strafed loco could ever be repaired. With this procedure, up to 13 locos were destroyed on some 4-plane missions.

Some variations in tactics were involved. The "Specials" used the above procedure but attacked by elements. And strafing was usually broken off after 10 locos were strafed. Enemy aircraft—if seldom encountered on regular missions in the Po Valley when the sky was full of Allied fighter-bombers—were considered a prime threat on the "Specials." Only four U.S. planes were up there. Enemy fighters had the solid cloud cover to fly under, shift from base to base, etc., without worry of being swarmed over by Allied planes. In fact, there was nothing to keep them from doing just that to our four planes. Counters to that threat were to shift attack areas between missions, keep one element "eyes up" while the other strafed, save a bit of ammo (which the pilots who strafed 10 locos did), and remember that we could quickly get into the clouds if need be.

Direction of strafing runs on locos was more critical than on trucks and barges. Ninety degrees from the side, shallow dive, firing for maximum bullet penetration into boiler/firebox of steam locos and main guts of electrics was the desired run. These side runs worked well from most recce patterns. However, if roll-in position or speed of a moving loco and train caused firing at more than 45 degrees off of straight in 90 degrees, then effectiveness was lost. Too many bullets ricocheted off sides of the engine. Runs had to be planned or adjusted to prevent this. If we were not able to fire from the side then firing squarely into the front or rear was next best, often through the crew cab. Also, out of four pilots making runs, one often was designated to hit the crew compartment anyway.

Strafing railroads brought extra obstructions into play, including widespread wires and supports of electric lines. But more varied in threat were numerous other poles and towers along tracks, sidings, and in and around yards. These were inconsistent in height, some quite tall, and often not easily seen in haze and smoke. With locos demanding close-in shooting, close encounters with obstructions were common and collision not always avoidable.

While mission results and unit claim reports (as well as most pilot talk) stressed "kills" of locomotives and rail cars, there was always one other object of "kills." That was enemy troops and rail workers of all kinds. Most of those were inherent in kills of locos and troop trains, which our tactics always aimed to maximize. However, mission leaders on armed-recce also caught workers in the open on tracks and at yard and repair facilities. This is not a pleasant subject to discuss; but it is war and is a case where some deliberate spraying of bullets into an area could be more effective than pinpoint shooting. I well knew how key the yardmasters and others in the buildings in the yard were to railroads.

Rail yards had numerous buildings, water tanks, towers and other structures that posed extra hazards to low passes, hazards that often had auto-weapon guns atop (gun camera, 86th Ftr Gp, World War II).

Strafing of railroads in the war certainly was not limited to major industrial areas of the world. The CBI may have had the distinction of a most successful job of it. Allied air attacks inflicted such destruction and damage on rail systems and equipment in parts of China that the Japanese gave up trying to operate them and turned to full reliance on trucks for support of their armies. Strafing railroads was not limited to any one category of unit, pilot and crew, aircraft, or mission. The famed low-level strategic bombing attack on the Ploesti, Romania, oil fields and refineries on 1 August 1943 by USAAF B-24 heavy bombers was one example. Publications of the 8AF Historical Society today contain a number of personal accounts by gunners on those B-24s who fired their cal-.50 machine guns point-blank from altitudes of 200–300 feet in gunfights with the enemy below, including flak car gunners on trains.

When the 86th Group moved from the MTO to the ETO in February 1945, first based near Nancy, France, our gunfighting with railroads was mainly in southern Germany on systems through Mannheim, Stuttgart, Ulm, Augsburg, Munich, and on to Austria. But eventually it involved an absolute maze of tracks over the entire country. This denser population and rail network meant fewer long stretches of open tracks to recce, more sidings and yards closer together and more junctions, hubs, and the like. Night and bad weather rail operations alone would not meet Germany's needs in support of war against the Russians on the east and the Allies on the west and south. Trains had to move in daytime and good weather too. We had far less need to grub-out hidden locos and could concentrate on active traffic almost anywhere, even surprisingly close to battle lines.

A steam "cloud" from a well "blown" loco, but obstructions such as poles could be hidden by the steam (gun camera, 86th Ftr Gp, World War II).

Roundhouses have long been a source of interest and lore in American railroading (as well as a source of a few jokes by railroaders such as "Run into the roundhouse, Nellie, he can't corner you there"). Whether Nellie was in mind or not, roundhouses were one place to find locos in bunches. While German roundhouses could vary from classic American versions, they equally bunched locos together and were prime targets, gaining a strong niche in strafing lore as well as in that of railroading. A roundhouse often meant multiple-pass tough strafing in much auto-weapon fire. The same was true when we found "bunched" locos on underway trains, four to six or so being dead-headed or moved to repair facilities.

Overall tactics of strafing locos in Germany was much the same as for Italy and France. However, the story on flak cars was a bit different. In the Po Valley we had a fair idea which trains were sure to have flak cars (those on mainlines and Brenner Pass lines), and which trains would not (those on local and connecting lines). No such differences showed in Germany. All were considered "flak car" trains until proven otherwise.

Crews on strafing passes in various situations could and did encounter a mismatch of firepower in the enemy's favor, cases where they had more guns to bear on strafers than we could put on them. This was known in advance to leaders of small missions in decisions to strafe warships, columns of armor, multiple flak towers, or other targets. With flak cars on trains this was a variable. In some cases they could outgun strafers, in others not. Some early-war

German railroad shops and version of a roundhouse. These were almost sure to have locomotives present. Two mainline locos to the left of the building are the target here (gun camera, 86th Ftr Gp, World War II).

flak cars were disguised as boxcars. Fake sides dropped so troops could open fire on already committed strafers. Later-war versions seemed to forego all disguise or surprise in favor of being fully ready for action. The most frequent location of a single flak car on a German train was close behind the engine—first to third car—but often with another further back. However, trains had been encountered (mostly near Verona, Italy) with as many, or more, flak cars as regular cars. These were dubbed "flak trains," viewed in purpose as flak traps rather than transportation.

Pilot identification of flak cars could not be assured from most recce altitudes and distances out unless they had already opened fire. The flak cars often resembled flatcars carrying heavy equipment. To fly close enough for positive eyeball detection put strafers well within the effective range of enemy 20mm and larger guns. But, enemy trains could not be given "free passage" and left unstrafed due to the threat posed by flak cars. There was no decision to be made about that. They were strafed, relentlessly. The decisions involved were on tactics of doing it. These tactics in my unit reiterated the premise and frame of mind that we "fought" trains rather than "attacked" or "shot" them; therefore, we were to approach them with all-out aggression. Options and details, which were continuously discussed and reviewed, fell on mission leaders in the air but with the following policy.

When fired upon by flak cars, pilots immediately turned into, concentrated fire on, and killed the gun and gunners and did not give enemy gunners time or opportunity to transfer and hold fire on each attacking plane. Against a normal enemy train configuration of one or two flak cars, that might be done and also the loco hit on the same pass by close-interval runs of near line abreast

Flak cars. When taking on these tough foes, accurate shooting had top priority; and instead of short bursts to save ammo, the maximum rounds possible were quickly pumped into enemy gunners (gun camera, 86th Ftr Gp, World War II).

attacks (best from 90 degrees to the track). In one example for a 4-plane flight, the flight and element leaders (No. 1 and 3) would concentrate fire on the flak cars, while the wingmen (No. 2 and 4) hit the engine. With 8-plane and larger missions, coordinated maneuvers might further divide attention of enemy gunners. But in cases of unexpected flak cars, limited maneuver room in valleys, or other factors the rule was to go all out to kill the flak first, then the loco. In all cases, passes and shooting had to be unyielding and accurate. Against most enemy flak-car trains these tactics were generally effective, but they required deadly flat out gunfighting.

In other situations flak cars on trains were augmented by additional auto-weapon positions in the area, those of general defenses, mobile guns of military units, etc. Now, besides more enemy guns, many of them were in unknown locations, all of which could not be quickly found and engaged. Flying around in intense ground fire trying to find each gun and then attack it would qualify as suicide. In these situations strafers simply had to ride out that fire in their pass, which was no different from bomber crews on a bomb run in intense flak.

In the extensive Allied bombing and strafing of enemy rail systems, repair of lines, facilities, and equipment was their main means of the enemy staying in operation. Such repair work was extensive and determined. Work trains and railroad cranes or wreckers capable of lifting locos, cars, bridge sections, and other components were the primary "rolling stock" elements in this effort. In fact, the cranes or wreckers probably were the single most needed item of equipment in the German transportation system. When strafers found one of these, or most any work or repair train, they were certain to encounter both

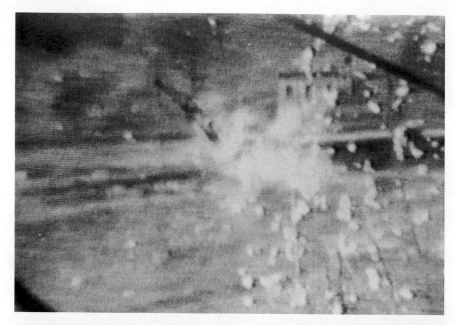

A railroad wrecker. This pass in intense ground fire is on one of these important machines used to keep rail lines open. The wreckers were always well defended. Its boom shows to the left of strafing impacts on the wrecker cab (just below the building in the background). Details of this gunfight are in the text (gun camera, 86th Ftr Gp, World War II).

flak cars and nearby mobile auto-weapon flak. Accompanying gun camera footage shows one such gunfight, with the pilot holding steady aim and fire on a crane or wrecker in intense enemy fire. Railroad work trains were very tough targets.

With railroads documented as one of the greatest weapons of war, World War II established strafing and strafers as being railroad's greatest enemy in war, the great destroyer and killer of road equipment and crews. Trucks are seldom cited as great weapons of war. Yet, they were the most familiar single piece of ground mobile equipment to U.S. military personnel in World War II, mainly the 2- and ½ ton "6 × 6." They were used in post/base housekeeping, training, transportation and supply systems, and combat units both at home and overseas. The Jeep was much publicized but far more troops rode in trucks.

Ships and trains played huge roles in moving combat forces and the tools and supplies of war, but in the land campaigns each mile closer to the fighting meant the more the job fell to trucks such as the enormous fleet of trucks (6 × 6s and larger) dubbed "Red Ball Express" that rushed supplies forward in the Allied push across France and into Germany. Then distribution on to combat units was all by trucks, weapon carriers, jeeps, and other vehicles, and in numerous situations by pack animal and men on foot.

Air supply had key roles in the war. One famed example was flying the Hump in the CBI. Yet, the need for trucks there was evidenced by the efforts to build and keep open the Burma and Lido/Stilwell roads. The Alcan Highway to Alaska was another case. As well as being supported by trucks, most units in ETO, MTO and CBI moved by land vehicle. For example, our fighter group moved over a dozen times to new bases while I was there. Each time, each squadron had enough trucks and other vehicles and trailers to load everything it possessed—troops, tents, parts, supplies, etc.—into their own vehicles and move themselves, with all their specialized trucks and vehicles—refueling, crash, shop, ambulance, water, jeeps and staff cars—going along too.

Enemy trucks and other vehicles were in much the same situation. They were not limited to any one role or place either. They were present in air forces, ground units, transportation and supply, in government, industry, and general home front uses. This chapter deals mainly with them while in support roles of combat forces and in civilian uses. There was much dependence on trucks from the beginning; as rail systems were bombed and strafed, trucks became ever more important in such roles.

American pilots in fighter-bomber operations over land mass theaters strafed more trucks than any other target, except for troops, and did so from earliest days to war's end, from front lines to deep into enemy territory, from single vehicles to columns and truck parks. A truck was one of the least complex and inexpensive moving machines strafed. That fact, along with their commonplace status put trucks far down any list of "prized" targets, well below airplanes, locos, and boats. Trucks were at the bottom of interest to war cor-

respondents, and probably the same was true in news back home. Also, official claim reports cited enemy trucks and vehicles as M/T (motor transport). That term never caught on for great public use in war lingo, nor did it have gloried legend and lore from the past that mules and elephants did.

Some literature contains the observation that an enemy truck was not worth one plane and pilot. If that is intended to imply that we used that belief in our decisions about strafing trucks, then it is grossly wrong. Millions of feet of combat film, official records, and testimony by our pilots and the enemy confirm that single trucks were strafed religiously and relentlessly all during the war. Obviously if single enemy trucks were not strafed (as not being worth risking a plane and pilot) then the enemy could operate them individually all over any theater almost totally unhindered in their mission. That certainly never happened. Instead, strafers left single trucks as bullet-ridden burned-out hulks all over those theaters.

If the contention that an enemy truck is not worth one of our planes and pilots is intended to mean we were wrong in strafing all those single trucks, then the public should know a bit more about the matter. We did not strafe trucks because of what they were or what they cost. We strafed them because of what they did and what they carried. Their cargos included troops, ammo, weapons and other vital needs of enemy combat units to use against our ground forces. It could also be flak ammo to use against us. Or how about a tractor pulling an 88mm flak/artillery gun? They were all strafed, whether singles or in bunches, to keep those cargos from being used against Allied forces.

In some respects the "killing" of trucks was the simplest of shooting. Direction of bullet impacts was not critical. Engine, fuel, and driver were usually close together. API ammo tore through everything. Most trucks quickly burst into flames, and numerous trucks exploded. Seldom was a short burst of accurate gunfire by more than one plane needed to do that. Yet, normally we kept integrity of flights and elements by pilots following through with short pinpoint bursts. And above all, once a truck or vehicle was sighted we went in quickly, directly, to get there before the driver could take cover and before people could escape. The objective was not just to stop a truck or vehicle from reaching the front on this trip, it was to destroy it and all cargo and kill occupants so they were totally out of the war.

Also highly significant, was the fact that trucks were not tightly tied to fixed bases. They needed no facilities comparable to airfields, rail lines or yards, or waterways and ports. While primarily using roads, they were not restricted to them. At any given time the majority of enemy trucks were not centralized anywhere. They were spread all over enemy territory. Certainly supply depots

Opposite: Trucks. Strafing of three single trucks in different locations—each hit accurately with a short burst, each burned or destroyed: "time of fire" put to perfect use (gun camera, 86th Ftr Gp, World War II).

Double perfect shooting: a precise short burst on one vehicle, then immediate reaim and similar destruction of a second vehicle on the same pass (gun camera, 86th Ftr Gp, World War II).

and dumps did "bunch" some trucks, as did motor pools and parks; but these in themselves were largely mobile too. They were just a bit more prized catch.

As widespread movers and hiders, single vehicles or small convoys, enemy trucks had only one real threat from the skies above. That was strafers, mainly fighter-bombers. Only roaming strafers (with time of fire, plus accuracy of their guns) sought out and killed widespread trucks and vehicles on large-scale continuing basis. Enemy trucks and other vehicles in occupied countries did have some threat from partisans, freedom fighters, and others, but for air interdiction, it was only strafers.

While of low news value as targets, the "doing" of killing trucks and vehicles with machine guns and cannon from the air is far from the bottom of the story and heritage of strafing and strafers or in the history of war.

Overall, pilots and crews were involved in more dogged pursuit of the foe while killing M/T than any other support target. An earlier chapter mentioned my initial strafing of trucks in southern Italy and touched on the fact they could be hidden easier than trains, ships, etc., and, more important, they could change themselves quickly from active traffic on roads to hiders under nearby trees, among buildings, or other structures. Tactics of armed-recce covered earlier remained the foundation against M/T, as did pinpoint shooting, but situations and enemy defenses changed greatly by time and place during the war.

As German armies held across Italy, Gustav Line, in the winter of 1943-44, strafing trucks involved gunfights ranging from shooting "sitting ducks" to near reversal of pilots being the "ducks."

In early January 1944, RAF Spitfires and U.S. P-40s caught snowbound enemy transport spread about on road and rails on the east side of Italy in the Chieti area. When the shooting was over there were destroyed 57 vehicles and 2 locos; damaged 200 vehicles and 5 locos, which somewhat of a "turkey shoot" in pass after pass, with little or no enemy ground fire.

The first couple of days after the Anzio landings, when we had ammo remaining after patrols and dogfights with enemy fighters over the beachhead, we found and destroyed trucks relatively easily on the west coastal road between Rome/Anzio and the Gustav Line as we returned to base at Naples. Several days later this was quite rough strafing in intense auto-weapon fire. Such defenses developed on all road links with Anzio, extending well north of Rome. Most notorious was the Liri Valley, the main enemy route between Rome/Anzio and Cassino, the pivotal point on the Gustav Line. As weeks and months went by this became one of the most intensely defended supply lines against air attack in history. Along with auto-weapon fire, 88mm flak was so intense on fighter-bombers that going to higher altitude approaches was not a salvation. Flying lengthwise in the valley was talked of as suicide. Attacks were mostly made by entering from the side of the valley and doing the job with as little up and down the road flying as possible, then going out the side. In the urgently needed air attacks against enemy movement to support Allied breakout of the Gustav Line and Anzio in May and June 1944 was some of the most deadly fighter-bomber flying and fighting of the war.

Northern Italy's Po Valley in winter of 1944-45 was a classic situation against trucks just as for trains. Some were easy sightings and some tough grubbing, some meager and some rough defenses. Long stretches of open roads, much farmland and few trees other than those lining roads made vehicles of all kinds quite vulnerable once they were underway; and they were likely to be spotted anywhere pilots might be flying in the valley at any time on any type mission. A prized hit was a tanker fuel truck that went up in a big ball of fire.

Some pilots wondered how enemy vehicle drivers felt about survival as they left one city or town for the next one in daylight and good weather. Those drivers probably rested hopes for safe arrival mainly on the huge size of the valley. Our planes could not cover every mile of all roads all the time. Pilots searching for those drivers had interest in the size of the valley too, with relief that enemy guns could not be as thick everywhere in this vast one as in the smaller Liri Valley.

However, the Po Valley did have numerous villages and a wealth of farm-

"Grubbing." *Bottom:* This pilot spots a truck between buildings in the left center of this photograph. *Top:* His pinpoint shooting kills it (gun camera, 86th Ftr Gp, World War II).

houses and buildings spread throughout. Most of those, except for the very northernmost, appeared to be heavy stone structures. Trucks parked among or against such buildings were often hard to spot, and then demanded attack from a certain direction to fire through narrow openings between buildings or in steep runs down on them.

Pilots became so familiar with both road systems and rail lines that true "hot-spots" were well known, and our policies minimized armed-recce exposure to them. Often rail and road targets were intermingled, with us making a firing pass on a truck, then one on a loco, or vice versa. However, a main decision on tactics was to get both where practical, usually truck first then loco, but without risking losing the loco. On mainline trains, especially the Brenner Pass route, all ammo was put on those locos along with prime cargos such as troops and armor.

Greater attention was needed to prevent restrafing already destroyed trucks than was needed for locos. Except for the last few weeks of the war, the enemy did not leave derelict locos on useable lines and sidings blocking tracks. They were moved to out-of-the-way places and many probably salvaged as scrap. But derelict trucks and vehicles were left where destroyed all over each theater, just pushed aside on roadways. Thus active traffic and destroyed hulks were in the system together. In the Po Valley, units and pilots actually kept tabs on locations of destroyed locos and trucks, but the latter were far more numerous and difficult to keep up with. Some recce was low enough for pilots to distinguish between usable vehicles and old wreckage.

In France and particularly southern Germany trucks had increased cover to dash into—more trees, forests, villages and buildings—along roads. These came into play on vehicles spotted on highways and open roads. But often the combination of a village with tree-lined streets and buildings and homes with well-treed yards were the nearest hiding spots for enemy trucks when our planes came overhead. At times they were spotted hiding there as well as caught in the process of ducking there. Beyond being an intact truck, further identity meant little. It was strafed whether military, commercial, or local garbage or delivery. Disliked by almost all pilots was that this hiding put targets so close to civilians.

Varied hiding spots also caused hard maneuvering passes to get clear shots and put obstructions of trees and buildings into pass pullouts. Several gun camera photos in this book show near misses of such items, and a few impending hits too, as trucks were being strafed on the close-in shooting demanded to assure kills of vehicles and cargos. A pilot could never waver in concentration, and few pilots finished a tour without having one or more trucks explode in their face or under them.

Rarely would a truck be envisioned by the public as calling for great skill and cunning by pilots to shoot and kill. Yet, that could be the case. Accompanying gun camera stills show one case of that quite well. In the lower photo

the pilot is attacking a moving truck from about 90 degrees to direction of travel. If this target had been an enemy plane in the air, a curve of pursuit pass "leading" in aim would be normal in that it would not matter much if the plane slid a bit beyond and below the target or high-speed stalled some in the turn. But a curve of pursuit pass on a moving truck (as on a boat on water) could cause all of that and send the aircraft into the ground.

This pilot avoided making a curve of pursuit run. He made an immediate violent maneuver before closing farther—a snap to left, snap back to the right— to set his pass more from the rear of the truck as shown in the upper photos. From there his final tracking and firing were in a less severe turn with a flatter dive angle than his original pass would have been. Now he had a decent shot at the target with far less risk of flying into the ground. (His rapid maneuver was what changed the orientation of farm crop rows between the lower and upper photos during a single pass.)

The enemy had quite a bit to say about air attacks on their support forces. Field Marshal Kesselring, the German commander in chief in Italy, noted in his memoirs that he had divisions well below strength in men and equipment, with an ever-growing toll inflicted by Allied Air Forces, "which ravaged the transportation system and destroyed so many replacements before they could reach the front." Of key note, he did not say reinforcements were "prevented" from getting there; he said they were "destroyed" before getting there—a characteristic of strafing. Much of it was on trucks, including single trucks. That's what strafing them was about.

Another enemy statement is found in the *War Diary of the* 7th *German Army High Command*, printed in *Impact* in 1945, and reads in part: "1. Rail transport is impossible because the trains are observed and attacked in short order: under those circumstances, the expenditure of fuel and wear and tear on material in bringing up Panzer units is high." Significant here is that this army did not say the rail system had been knocked out of operation; they said that moving trains did not get where they were going. That was the work of strafers killing "movers."

Certainly strafers were not fighting alone against enemy transport. "Transportation" was one of the major categories of strategic bombing objectives. Medium and light bombers had paramount goals against rail systems and bridges, such as systematic cutting of rails and all bridges on the Seine River and other routes inland from Normandy in support of Operation Overlord. Similar bombing was done in Operation Strangle in Italy. Bombing had a

Opposite: Moving target. This is a single pass on a fast moving vehicle (perhaps 80 kph or so) and is an example of flying the airplane correctly to put the guns in position to do the job. The patterns of the snow-covered fields show that a violent aircraft maneuver was made between bottom and middle photographs. This is explained in the text (gun camera, 86th Ftr Gp, World War II).

Vehicle "flamers" were left all over theaters worldwide. Relentless shooting of the "movers" took thousands of vehicles of all types and their cargos and drivers, crews and passengers out of the war on the spot and hurt the enemy immeasurably (79th Ftr Gp, World War II).

definite effect. It disrupted and delayed traffic, caused use of ferries, pontoons and fords, and caused traffic jams. The latter gave strafers some field days.

Bombing and strafing were used on a wealth of targets other than traffic support. They included supply, ammo, bomb, and fuel dumps, warehouses, communications, power plants, and other facilities that helped move stuff to combat forces. Strafers actually had numerous missions here and some spectacular results.

Yet, whether in mainland Europe and Asia or islands of the Pacific, whether industrial area or rice paddy or jungle, the "killing" of moving elements (equipment, operators, cargos, passengers) out in the support and supply systems was where strafers' and the "time of fire" of their guns filled a gap against enemy transport and movement that no other air power could do.

Evidence abounds that this was something the enemy did not expect— the massive destruction and killing of far-flung, underway, and hiding elements of his transport and vital cargos; but it happened and they attest it hurt them badly.

Opposite: **Strafers were by far the top foe and killer of "movers" on rails and water and relentlessly took them out of the war immediately, to the great detriment of the enemy (U.S. Air Force).**

· 8 ·

Brenner Pass

Concurrent with our operations in the flat Po Valley our group flew a major effort in total opposite terrain. The main enemy supply line between Germany and their forces in Italy was the historic Brenner Pass route through the Alps. Medium bombers, mainly B-25s, were a primary interdiction effort against this route, but they struggled to operate high enough to clear some of the mountain peaks. The intensely defended route (reported as close to 1,000 flak guns), along with massive flak in the entire Verona area of the Po Valley, made their bomb runs very deadly. Heavy bombers flew missions against the route at times, but at the expense of their primary strategic bombing effort.

In October 1944, 12AF fighter-bomber units were moved as far forward as possible. The 86th and 350th groups were scheduled to move to Pisa, only 10 miles or so from the front lines. My squadron was the first unit moved there, followed in a month by the rest of the 86th Group. From this and other bases near the front, P-47s could fly missions as far north as Austria, and our orders were to interdict train movement in the Brenner Pass route. We were deadly familiar with Verona at the southern end, and now the towns on north up the route of Rovereto, Trento, Bolzano, Bressano, and the pass itself would become equally so.

Operating as a separate squadron, we set our flying procedures and tactics for the task. We had operated in mountains before, but not amid peaks of over 12,000 feet and valleys 10,000 feet deep. Some pilots asked if we had reconnaissance photos of the valley. I could say "No" while thinking it was probably best we didn't. We could expect missions of bombing rail lines and facilities and, of course, strafing, both added on to bombing and planned "loco busting" missions. Range of our planes allowed carrying bombs to a target and then having fuel remaining for effective armed-recce strafing on the lower route from Bolzano south to Verona. We could carry bombs farther north without planned add-on strafing, but missions on up to the pass and Austria would be pure strafing—on power stations when needed but mainly on "killing locos."

I had already asked my armament officer to look into changing our gun bore sight distance from 750 feet out to 900 feet. This would now be partic-

Rail tracks and yards in valleys caused more passes down them than across them. Bullet impacts and steam from hit locos blended with deep snow and showed less to pilots and on gun camera film (gun camera, 86th Ftr Gp, World War II).

ularly valuable for strafing in the Alps. The armament section took on the extra work to get our planes set at 900 feet.

When airborne on our first missions, we flew out and returned over the peaks west of the route and right over the middle of Lake Garda. This was to avoid as much flak as possible while "going and coming." That was continued for most all missions and of course was contingent on weather. We set firm policy against flying in clouds and mountains at the same time. Pilots had to have enough clear view ahead when among peaks and in valleys to safely reverse course if necessary. We would not give our German foes the benefit of our flying an entire mission into a mountain. Thus when weather blanked that ability to see ahead, alternate attacks were made on rails in the Lake Garda area or Po Valley (and this accounts for our familiarity with boat traffic on that lake).

Operating in deep valleys among high peaks squeezed us closer to rail lines and forced extremely hard maneuvering runs, aiming, firing and pullouts. Much strafing was steep, shooting down into locos head on or from behind. The 900-foot bore sight let pilots put concentrated fire on locos a bit farther out but still not all runs could be pressed in to even that greater distance and a successful pullout made. Every pass was pilot judgment to get in as close as possible for effective fire on the target and still pull out to miss obstructions or mountainsides. Our 900 foot bore sight instead of 750 did help in these split-second decisions.

Enemy fire came down from mountainsides and peaks as well as up from valley floors. From our very first missions, flak cars were encountered on almost all trains and the mountains often restricted our maneuver to cope with them.

The mountains added other hazards, including cables. Although the problem occurred worldwide, the cables of the Alps might have been the most notorious both in number and size. The many steel cables could rarely if ever be seen in time to avoid them. The larger ones were usually rather high above valley floors. (The diameter of one was about 2 inches, which was determined from the width of a cut in a P-47 wing from leading edge to bomb pylon/rack that fortunately broke the cable and stopped the cut there.) Our tactic to cope with the bigger cables was to descend steep into valleys for minimum time among them, then, when possible, to stay and operate below them without flying into something. We simply flew and strafed among the lower cables.

Climbing up out of valleys was also a pure gamble. The P-47 could not hold both steep climb and good speed for the thousands of feet from valley floors to clearance of peaks; and we were among cables and almost surely in enemy fire throughout. We usually kept speed up in intense flak rather than trying to lessen exposure time to cables. A number of pilots, this writer included, flew flak- and cable-damaged aircraft up through those long climb outs.

We modified several operating policies and procedures of the Po Valley for missions in the "canyon" as pilots commonly called the Brenner route. One was to increase "Bingo" fuel. That is the predetermined amount of aircraft fuel remaining in a target area required to safely return to home base. When that fuel level was reached, action was normally broken off and a course set for home. This fuel increase was to cover extra fuel used in max-power climb-outs from valley floors. Also, when possible, only the latest models of our P-47s were scheduled for the valley. These aircraft had engine water injection systems that gave an additional 300 horsepower for up to ten minutes. This aided climb-outs, especially with battle-damaged aircraft. I had used the full supply of water injection in my case of climb-out with some cut-off wing.

Normally we took off, went west out to sea, climbed to planned altitude, then entered enemy territory across unpopulated spots on the coastline and over the Apennines into the Po Valley. We usually avoided flak in the process this way. For Brenner missions we took off and went straight north, then did an immediate climb over Pisa, the nearby Apennines and enemy front lines, all while still climbing, and doing so lower than we liked, and with more risk from both the enemy and just flying the heavy-loaded airplanes. However, this saved considerable fuel over the normal departure, and we wanted that extra fuel for best mission results and survival when far north in the Alps.

When flying over mountains going out and back on missions, it might seem prudent to stay well above all peaks. But we did not do that in the Alps on Brenner missions for a definite reason. Experience showed that doing so over or near the "valley" put planes in more line-of-sight of gunners, or radar and drew much more heavy flak than flying lower where peaks could block some view. One early flight at altitudes above 20,000 feet to the pass received some heavy flak fire almost all the way. Returning lower among the peaks received far less.

We also anticipated enemy fighter opposition on these missions, especially on the far north of the route, both from known German fighter bases in the Udine area and in Austria and Southern Germany. Going and coming west of the valley, farther away from Udine, and flying down among the higher peaks could help avoid being surprised by enemy fighters. As always, full alertness in looking for and being ready to dogfight enemy counterparts was ingrained in all missions. But enemy fighters did not show (or didn't find us) except for a few fleeting clashes that were in the Verona area in the south.

Assigned specific targets to bomb or strafe were, of course, hit exactly where ordered. Tactics were set for that target and situation of enemy defenses and the valley terrain at that point. For armed-recce in search of targets to strafe, a main objective became to find spots in the valley where the greatest lengths of rail line could be seen from the "rim" on entering the valley. At places the valley was open for flying, in others it was very tight. At places the rail lines were much hidden with curves, twists, rocks and trees. Best results were obtained when we could see the most track on arrival. More trains were seen that way and in time for the most effective passes to be made. We also got a better look at the makeup of the mountain trains—how many engines and where—and the same for flak cars and prize cargos. Last-second sightings at lower altitude in backgrounds of deep snow, while often flying from sunlight into deep shadows, gave less chance to see train makeup (and played havoc with gun camera film quality too). Also, the automatic impulse to fly a hard turn to get "on target" had to be controlled to prevent flying into a mountain. The pilot had to judge if it was possible to maneuver and shoot.

Most missions were eight aircraft or more; but tight sky in most of the valley and intense flak almost everywhere made it unwise to put that many planes on armed-recce strafing together or to fly cover over the valley in the flak. Most strafing was done by separating into four-ship flights on different segments of track.

Our results from the valley reflected more strafing of "trains" than "locos" and "cars" on Po Valley missions. That was due both to challenges of flying and shooting in the valley, and to multiple locomotives, flak cars, and key targets on trains, such as troops, armor, and tank cars, that warranted strafing the whole thing and with repeat passes where possible. Tank cars were a prime target in destroying trains. One mission of my squadron strafed a train with

Low passes. Where it was possible to make them in valleys, violent twisting and turning flying and shooting was required, far removed from a pilot handbook version of ground gunnery (gun camera, 86th Ftr Gp, World War II).

four locos and some 50 cars loaded with trucks, tanks, guns and other types of motor vehicles. In the strafing they reported that one tank car burst into flame but the other only put out smoke. Then six cars caught fire and exploded, and additional cars began to burn and explode on through the train, destroying both railcars and much war-fighting equipment.

Rail yards and facilities of major support points on the route, including the main towns and the Brenner Pass, had some of the more distinct valley floors. There we had a bit wider sky for maneuver. Active trains were almost sure to be seen. But so was the most intense enemy flak—and likely more cables—to the extent that these areas got equal or even higher ratings of "tough" than Mother Earth's hazards of tighter valleys. Overall, veteran pilots judged strafing on this route of the famed peacetime "Rome-Berlin Express" to be "up top" with the war's roughest air-ground gunfighting, actually done in terrain and conditions where aircraft normally would not be flown. Some pilots did muse "are we really doing this?"

While doing it, the 86th Group received orders on another Brenner Pass route task one night. That was to suppress flak for the B-25s that were still bombing marshalling yards and power stations in sections of the route but were suffering heavy losses—and to do it starting tomorrow morning. Without orders of how to do it, each squadron proposed their plan to the group. My plan was to do it by strafing, not prior to, but along with, the B-25 mission. The plan approved, we flew our P-47s as escort with the B-25s. When they began their bomb run (usually about 12,000 feet altitude), we started a long

Rail support facilities (gun camera, 86th Ftr Gp, World War II).

Flak suppression. Some strafing passes were made "up" instead of "down" when enemy guns were spotted on a mountainside such as this (gun camera, 86th Ftr Gp, World War II).

shallow dive into the target area, pulling ahead of the B-25s. That had us looking down for 88mm and larger flak guns, the main threat to the B-25s, which when sighted we immediately strafed. As the B-25s bombed, we flew clear of the target and bomb impacts, but stayed in the area and continued to look for and strafe enemy guns as the B-25s withdrew. This worked out OK. We destroyed guns and killed enemy crews both before and after bomb drop. The B-25s reported it to be a definite help to them. We, and other units, continued flying flak suppression when called on until we moved to the ETO in February 1945.

We had long viewed most strafing in the war as more the nature of "dogfighting" than ground attack. This flak suppression "under the bombers" was perhaps epic in that respect. Initial strafing passes on flak positions could be made diving into them, but once down low, performing repeat runs and shooting was max performance fighter flying. Guns were sighted as we flew close by or just over them, guns fully manned and firing at our bombers above. Max "G" turns were made to get our guns on them as soon as possible. If it took a fraction of a second more to do so than a pilot had to safely clear obstruc-

Hard flying put strafing bursts into active German flak guns, often in open positions, as with this crew on a heavy gun (National Archives).

tions, more often than not the gamble was taken to get the target. Treetops were flown through. Cables were hit. Some 88s were up on mountainsides, others in valleys. Sighting a position up above caused a strafing run "up" at a target instead of "down" on one, and that was something never mentioned back in training. Auto-weapons, 20mm and 37mm, were thick too, and their fire was directed on us. But blasting enemy gunners off their guns from point-blank range as the B-25s bombed was the payoff. Fortunately our pilot losses did not go sky-high. Glen Moore noted in his book that our pilot losses in the Brenner Pass were surprisingly low in comparison to other fighter squadrons operating there.

A member of today's 86th Group Association made a remembrance tour in recent years to Verona and the Brenner Pass route. An elderly lady living there told him of a conversation she had with a German officer back during the war. The officer, commander of the flak units in the area, told her that U.S. P-47s were killing off his gun crews at a tremendous rate. He had lost many good men, he said.

Our results of loco kills per missions in the Brenner Pass route were not as high as on some missions in the Po Valley, but they were substantial and very significant. Numbers of them were multiple kills, and almost all were mainline engines in full trains, many hit with crews still aboard. We had strafed several troop trains and trains carrying armor. We had set off fires and explosions on main lines and in yards. We had played a part in keeping electric trains out of service and had killed steam jobs, all of which can be included in German field marshal Kesserling's lament that "replacements did not arrive, they were destroyed by strafers."

· 9 ·

Gunfights
Enemy Ground and Surface Forces

This chapter is about strafing elements of enemy combat forces, ground and sea, in battle from front lines and beachheads to far out at sea, on the move, at rest areas, or in posts and ports. Coverage of the topic is not directed toward any one air role or task or category of target. Actions range from close air support to attacks far in the rear: covering targets of troops, artillery, armor, vehicles, antiaircraft guns, warships, submarines, and more. Strafing and strafers were in all of this and more. The gunfighting, usually versus a well-armed enemy on the ground, is the subject here.

One example in the Philippines (from *The Army Air Forces in World War II*, vol. 5) was a long-range fighter sweep from Mororai to immobilize the Japanese garrison on Mindanao in connection with the Leyte landings. The fighters' shooting covered quite a bit of "garrison": "[O]n 16 October (1944) fifteen P-38s of the 35th and 80th Squadrons flew to Cagayan on the north-central Mindanao coast, where they fired three vessels in the harbor, strafed and put to flight a troop of mounted cavalry, strafed a Sally bomber and a staff car at Cagayan airdrome, and then swept down the highway to Valencia destroying fifty to sixty military vehicles along the road."

Strafing has not been commonly associated with attack of warships at sea, even though newsreels during the war showed some B-25 gun and cannon attacks on Japanese vessels. There definitely was a lot more. At the Battle of Midway at 0130 hours, 4 June 1942, four U.S. Navy PBYs found Japanese transport by radar. They torpedoed one transport and strafed the column of transports, causing some casualties. At 0130 this obviously was a night operation. In Alaska on 14 September 1942, twelve USAAF B-24s and 28 fighters flew a mission from Adak at low level to bomb and strafe at Kiska. Among claims were three enemy subs, blasted with 37mm fire from P-39s, plus six aircraft including Zeros and a 4-engine flying boat. On 29 September, P-39s strafed two more submarines.

At Guadalcanal, on the night of 29 January 1943, an American naval task

Enemy ship. Terrible film, but a prime surface target. The underway enemy vessel can be discerned putting out a distinct wake as this pilot pulls the trigger to fire on it (gun camera, 86th Ftr Gp, World War II).

force covering transport ships bringing more Army units to the island had flares dropped on the force. The destroyer *Waller* and cruiser *Wichita* were strafed by Japanese planes in a case of enemy night strafing. In the Mediterranean in August 1943, Capt. Paul Striegel and Lt. James Griswald flying USAAF A-36s of the 86th Ftr-Bm Gp, sank an enemy "light cruiser or destroyer." Striegel scored direct bomb hits; both pilots heavily strafed the combat ship. That same month, three P-40 pilots of the 325th Ftr Gp repeatedly strafed an Axis submarine with their cal-.50 guns. It was claimed damaged but later confirmed and credited as sunk.

About Bougainville, November 1943, this entry on Japanese barges and shipping is found in *The Army Air Forces in World War II*, vol. 4. "They were hunted down relentlessly and P-39s did well at it but most successful of all were the B-25s of the 42" Bombardment Group—hunting down Japanese surface vessels all around Bougainville, bombing and strafing them from minimum altitudes."

These are a mere smattering of examples and they are not against the most heavily antiaircraft-gunned ships—cruisers, battleships, and carriers. The best reflection on strafing heavier warships that I have run across over the years is a well-quoted one by a U.S. Navy pilot (whose name I could not determine) in the Pacific: "Strafing a cruiser is like looking into a furnace." This pilot is said to have gone on to add a message for posterity on tactics of strafing a cruiser: "Getting in close" was essential for effective results. A "furnace" was addressing just the firepower of the ship, rather than the entire defenses likely to be faced, including enemy fighters and antiaircraft guns of accompanying ships.

Records confirm that submarines, transports, and various auxiliary vessels were sunk or burned by automatic-weapon fire from aircraft. It would not be expected that cruisers, battleships, and large carriers would be destroyed by such gunfire. But pilots could expect that much equipment topside on those monsters could be disabled, such as radar, fire control, communications, scout or other onboard aircraft, etc., and antiaircraft gunners and other personnel hit. (A less-tough breed, a jeep carrier, would appear to be a prime target for strafing, vulnerable to being burned or sunk, planes destroyed and casualties realized.)

Records do reflect that pilots and crews, from fighter to heavy bomb and long-range patrol, used bombs on enemy warships as first choice. But they strafed these ships, too, either in addition or when guns were the only armament available, rather than leave an enemy warship unattacked or underattacked. Graphic evidence of such strafing is found in one source of great exposure to the public (if an unlikely source of scholarly research). That is the movie *Midway*. Opening lines contain small print to the effect that "This production contains extensive actual combat film." Viewers can easily identify that "real war" film as it appears and see that it is gun camera footage of U.S. Navy aircraft firing machine guns into Japanese planes in the air and into Japanese warships and combat vessels on the water. It is photographic evidence that can support "like a furnace" and "getting in close" with concentrated gunfire "on target." If such film does not show each warship explode or sink from strafing fire, it clearly shows the determination and courage of the pilots and crews putting it there.

One role in which aircraft guns were key weapons used on enemy forces was Air-Sea Rescue. Downed airmen at sea were picked up by surface vessels, submarines, and sea and float planes, and amphibians. Among the famed aircraft involved were the American "Cat" (Navy PBY, AAF OA-1) and British "Walrus." Numerous rescues are legend. Often told was one from the MTO of a "Duck Butt" that landed offshore of Genoa, Italy, taxied (or motored) into the harbor entrance, picked a downed airman out of the water, then taxied back out to sea while gunners onboard shot it out with enemy positions on shore. Plane and crew survived but with aircraft damage and wounded crew members.

Pilots of my unit were involved in a few rescue operations in coastal waters in the MTO. Those involved flying cover while the rescue plane or vessel was en route and during pickup. Any enemy vessel that made an effort to approach the downed pilot was strafed. The English Channel and the Pacific had extensive air-sea rescue operations and strafing support. One example was an epic Pacific rescue on 21–22 October 1944, in enemy controlled waters west of New Guinea. Seven P-47 pilots, 58th Ftr Gp, flying from Noernfoor on a late-day strike to Ambon, were forced to ditch their planes in Darnier Straits.

Before daylight next morning the rescue was underway, including several "Cats" with P-38 and P-47 cover. During the day all seven pilots were rescued. One AAF "Cat" pilot, Victor Kregel (later col., USAF, now retired), in recent years described the action of his pickups, one from water and three from shore, while coping with miles of shallow coral during landing, taxi, and takeoff and even extending the wheels in the water during taxi as a "bumper" against coral. He included the following on strafing (from *58th Fighter Association Newsletter*, January 1994): "During another shore pick up ... the Lightnings [P-38s] found a pilot on the beach near the tail of a Jug [P-47] sticking up out of the water. After we had landed and rescue seemed assured, the P-38 leader called me and suggested they blast the Jug tail so other missions would not report a downed aircraft." With OK from Kregel, the protruding tail was shot to bits with gunfire, and strafing recorded one more niche in its history of great utility.

Strafing was involved in rescue of downed airmen inland in enemy territory too; however, except for rare cases, there was no quick pickup (as this was before wide use of helicopters and pilot emergency radios). About the best that could be done from the air to help the downed pilot was to give him some unmolested time to exit a crash-landed plane and hide his parachute, then himself. Yet, situations and options of doing that were varied and complex.

Long-range missions had no extra fuel to remain overhead. Also, some cases of doing so could be detrimental. Survival of a wounded pilot or one in Alps snow might depend on being reached quickly by someone on the ground, even the enemy. In Germany, strafing the immediate area, possibly killing women and children would not have improved his status. Intelligence suggested the best survival bet in certain areas was through capture by the German military. Leaders in the air had to call the shots in each case. Whatever the leader's decision, invariably aircraft guns were the armament available. In one category they made the difference, and that was when an airman down in an occupied country was seen to be physically capable of movement. One pilot bailed out and was seen running toward bulrushes on a riverbank. Mission pilots immediately strafed two German vehicles in the area. The downed airman made it to cover, evaded capture, and was hidden by an Italian family the rest of the war. But a more common action by mission pilots was not to fly cover directly overhead the downed airman (which would bring enemy attention to that location) but to roam out several miles around him. If enemy vehicles or troops hit roads toward the downed airmen, they could be strafed. However, that normally did not happen. With strafers above, the enemy was not prone to jump out into the open. Strafing and strafers kept the enemy at bay without the enemy firing a shot.

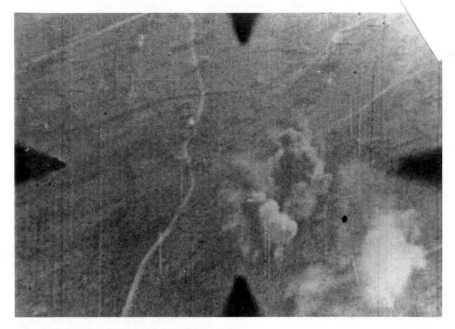

Battlefield positions—strafing in a dive-bomb run on enemy positions as bomb bursts of preceding runs show below, a tactic used by some units but banned in most cases by others (gun camera, 86th Ftr Gp, World War II).

Strafing played a big part in efforts to suppress enemy antiaircraft defenses. This ranged from planned suppression for bombing (as in the prior chapter) to combat resupply and airborne operations to forms of self-suppression by various units. Another example of "preplanned" was a risky airborne operation in the Philippines. In addition to B-25s, over thirty A-20s were sent in to bomb and strafe antiaircraft positions on Corregidor and Caballo islands just ahead of the U.S. parachute jump into a tricky pinpoint drop zone on "Topside," the high point of Corregidor, in initial phases of retaking it from the Japanese.

In fighter-bomber operations some units strafed at times in dive and glide bomb runs, usually in the earliest stages after roll in, then turned their attention to the bombing. Against densely defended large targets such as a city marshaling yard, military post or port, this fire could hit and inflict hurt on a number of things, including flak guns (if mainly by chance). Perhaps it was just tempting, or a kind of satisfaction, to some pilots, especially so in cases like the 79th Ftr Gp, which bombed an aircraft carrier in the port of Genoa amid worlds of flak. (The 79th is credited with a carrier destroyed or sunk, according to *The Falcon*, the 79th combat history).

Groups had varying policy on strafing in bomb runs on various targets. Some restricted it on rail cuts in open country as wasting ammo and even pro-

Enemy rear line positions—strafing an enemy position just across the road from this building complex. Big guns, flak and artillery, were often found in city parks, soccer fields, etc. (gun camera, 86th Ftr Gp, World War II).

hibited it as possible distraction from the bombing task, but it was used in some bomb runs and thus is part of the history.

A memorable case of strafing enemy flak was just prior to the invasion of southern France. Some of the 88mm gun, fire control, and radar positions on that coast were quite open, others well bunkered. Some automatic weapon positions, especially quad-barrel 20mm, were turret mounted in concrete bunkers, with crews well protected. Enemy fire was extremely accurate, both 88 and auto-weapon, especially out to sea. One early mission exited out to sea as 88 rounds exploded and hit waves all around them; auto-weapon tracers blanketed the planes and churned water under them. We lost a pilot. Where it was possible to see and fire on 88s from inland we attacked from there rather than from the water. Many of us rated this among the toughest flak suppression done.

Mention of enemy armor can lead to more thought of "weapon effects" on tanks than the flying and fighting of pilots and crews in combat. That was particularly true in the 1980s and early 1990s as much literature and discussion was addressed to weapon effects regarding Soviet tanks in Cold War days.

If asked for my views on choice of weapons for preplanned attacks on tanks in World War II, my answer would have been a P-47 with combination of firebombs and the aircraft guns. Firebombs of two types were used. One was napalm in drop tanks, normally released in low flat or very shallow dive attacks. The other was incendiary compound in thin-skin versions of GP bomb casings, which had the trajectory of GP bomb but no high explosive blast;

thus it could be dropped quite low, too, in dive/glide/skip bomb runs. Some American fighter units had rockets (2.75- and 5-inch). Those units might rate rockets as prime choices too. In all cases the aircraft guns remained a full co-choice. They were used in follow-up attacks to kill escaping tank crews, accompany infantry, and support trucks; but mainly their time of fire was there to attack yet more tanks. If the choice of only one weapon had to be made, the guns were always the top pick.

These choices of multiple weapons were used in many attacks in World War II; but to give them status as primary or basic in the story of pilots and crews who attacked tanks in World War II would leave the history grossly flawed and incomplete. Pilots and crews went after tanks relentlessly with whatever munitions and armament they had—and in so many cases all they had was the guns. Firebombs and rockets did not enter combat until mid to late 1944. All prior fighting was without them. Preplanned or anticipated missions were only one part of the effort against armor. More attacks came other ways: general armed-recce, diversions from other tasks, and spotting tanks while attacking other targets such as artillery. Attack of tanks was not limited to any one role or situation. It ranged from battlefield to hundreds of miles beyond. A few cases from my experience can highlight widely varied operations.

Back in 1943 1 had strafed a few tanks on guns-only armed-recce as the Germans withdrew to "winter lines." We had also bombed and strafed a few tanks in battlefield situations at those lines. The largest collection of tanks for me in that era of the war was recorded in the 79th Group's *Falcon* as "The last target on the 9th (January, 1944) was a fighter show by twelve aircraft (P-40s) of 85 and 87 squadrons on snow bound tanks near Pescocostanzo." Those tanks, 16 in number, were 30 miles behind the lines on a mountain road. A previous armed-recce mission expecting to find trucks had spotted and strafed the tanks. Then this mission was quickly launched, about half with GP bombs and others with guns only. The tanks were bombed and then repeatedly strafed. Claims were several tanks severely damaged and disabled, and all apparently abandoned for the moment. Pilot opinion was that these tanks were being moved from one area of the front to another.

At Anzio, 79th Group pilots flew low-altitude fighter air patrol over the beachhead, with only guns for armament. When relieved on patrol, any ammo remaining after air fights with enemy fighters and fighter-bombers was used to strafe trucks and tanks in enemy territory on return to base. The most tanks and closest together in any one place were, by far in my experience, in southern France. We had only guns on the mission (covered later in enemy mass movements).

In the ETO in February and March 1945, the 86th Group had notable success using firebombs along with strafing in support of ground forces in hard fighting at the Siegfried Line, some in battle, some en route to it. Numerous

tanks were also hit by strafing alone. The same was true in support of the
Allied push through Germany. In both the MTO and ETO we found trains
loaded with tanks or other armor. In a few cases we had bombs, most often
only guns. Either way, with bombing or without, we made repeated machine-
gun runs. Some pilots strafed more tanks that were chained down on flatcars
than they strafed on the battlefield.

Certainly some theaters brought more armor into open play for air attack
than others: North Africa offensives more than winter-line stalemates of Italy;
China land campaigns more than some Pacific island hopping; and beyond
doubt the Allied pushes in France were heavy with armor clashes. In theaters
of greatest armor operations, naturally our fighter-bomber units anticipated
more tanks as targets. Yet, evidence is strong that this anticipation did not
result in more reliance on heavy external loads of bombs and less on aircraft
machine guns. In fact the trend may have been the other way around.

This entry on USAAF fighter-bomber support of U.S. Army tank-led
columns in dashes across France in 1944 is found in *The U.S. Army Air Forces
in World War II*, vol. 3:

> The form which such actions took had become somewhat stereotyped since St.-
> Lo, as mission after mission took off for armed recce or ACC. The only marked
> variants on the established themes now exhibited were that fuel tanks often
> replaced bombs on wing shackles and that the tremendous firepower of the P-47
> was more than ever conspicuous. The concentrated streams of projectiles dis-
> charged by its eight 50 [-cal.] machine guns tore through thin-skinned vehicles
> and, by ricochet from roads into the soft underbellies of tanks or by direct pene-
> tration of the air vents in their afterdecks, could even put panzers out of action.
> Since incendiary bullets were used, gasoline fires often resulted.

As far as tactics go, obviously more than one class and type of enemy
tanks were faced. Japanese tanks had generally less tonnage than German.
Some early war versions were far less armored than late war tanks. The most
common German tanks, Pz Kw III and IV, had combat weights of about 25
tons. The more notorious Pz Kw V Panther and Pz Kw VI Tigers had gross
weights from about 45 tons up to 70. A Tiger II had roof armor almost twice
as thick as the front/bow armor of the earlier Pz Kw IV.

Two things were basic in techniques of strafing tanks. One, specific aim
points were demanded. Shooting into the main armor would not work, and
the heavier the tank the more critical the aim point. Two, whatever aim point
was selected, the full-power impact of all guns hitting there together and
"square" (not angled) was required.

The preceding quote from *The Army Air Forces in World War II* cited two
techniques: ricocheting rounds off roadways into the underbelly, and firing
into rear deck louvers (or similar air intake systems). A third, not mentioned,
was to aim on the tank track/bogie wheel system. All three techniques had
merit but varied in opportunity and effectiveness of use.

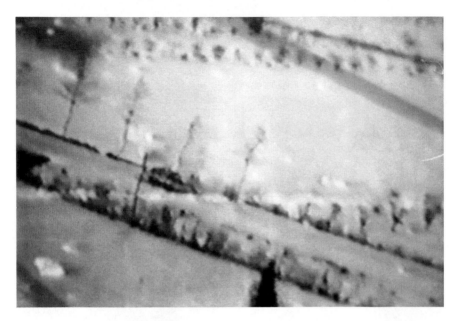

Armor. Killing armor of all types demanded concentrated accurate hits, often with specific aim points. This pilot is lining up to fire on what appears to be a half-track vehicle while flying through a stream of auto-weapon fire (the line of white puffs across the photograph) (gun camera, 86th Ftr Gp, World War II).

Ricochet into underbelly catches attention for ingenuity; and some units had success with it, mainly on roadways of France. However, many tanks were found in desert, fields, mud, or dug-in where the method would not work. Some tanks in columns were too close together for this. There were doubts of it working on the belly armor of Tigers. Some pilots, including me, did not consider it necessary on most tanks. We could get them with other techniques. Aim for tracks/bogie wheels with solid accurate fire could immobilize the tank and was a frequent choice on a side pass. But terrain or a dug-in tank often blocked a direct line of fire, and a few carried armor to protect tracts. Aim for upper rear deck and intake/louver system offered a direct line of fire in the greatest number of situations—shooting down into it. Most pilots, and I strongly felt so, believed this was the best bet by far in most cases. When it was successful, which was regularly on lighter tanks and occasionally on some of the monsters, the tank normally burned or exploded and was destroyed, often with its crew. However, these aim points were small and still very "hard" targets. They took expert shooting. It has been stressed (and overly stressed) that "getting close" was essential for best accuracy and max-power impact. Another reason was that a pilot had to be close in order to clearly see such an aim point and precisely fly the "pipper" on it.

The realities of war did not always allow pilots to do such close-in, precise

aiming and shooting. Situations of terrain, obstructions, bad visibility, and other factors at times demanded firing farther out. In these cases, pilots fired as close in as they could and hit as hard as possible from top, side, or rear. Even this set some tanks on fire.

Decision on, and the "doing" of, strafing tanks was not about weighing capabilities of cal-.50 API bullets against tank armor. This was based on what we pilots believed at the time. And we strongly believed we could hurt and kill tanks with machine guns, and for good reason. First, tanks (especially of commanders) had exposed communications antennas and signal gear and air cleaning systems (on German tanks), and they often carried external cargo, spares, etc., all subject to destruction by machine-gun fire. From experience we knew good gunfire bursts tear off tracks, and in louvers cause eruption of fire or explosion. In later stages of the war, numerous German tanks burst into flame with less than perfect shooting, particularly those well behind the lines. We wondered if shortages of fuel and our killing of trucks supporting tanks caused the Germans' desperate measure of carrying Jerry cans of fuel externally on tanks.

Quite significant was the fact that enemy tanks overall did not ignore U.S. "strafers" as if immune to our gunfire. We saw tanks take cover just as quickly and religiously as trucks when we came overhead. Enemy tank crews in rear areas were seen to abandon their armor and run for forests. They went to great effort to hide when not in action or motion.

It is true that in some cases we put accurate bursts into tanks in a pyrotechnic flash of power as a hundred or more API rounds smashed into armor and yet the tank was still there, with no gaping damage or destruction. But we also saw some then run off roads into gullies and trees. Some hit this way were noted on missions of following days in that area to be sitting there still just where hit. We did wonder what that strafing was like for the German crews.

As the war progressed the enemy produced an ever-higher percentage of armor other than tanks—tank destroyers, self-propelled guns, and others as well as wrecker/recovery versions. All of these generally had lighter or less complete armor and had more exposed equipment, such as hydraulic/winch systems, which strafing could play havoc with in addition to the armor being an easier kill of the basic vehicle and crews. Then, too, enemy panzer, motorized, and infantry divisions had numerous lighter-armored vehicles such as halftracks. Good strafing destroyed these about as quickly and easily as regular trucks. Various other vehicles were part of armor operations including command cars, jeeps, and trucks. Killing these and personnel hurt the armor effectiveness too.

Opposite: **Tactics on medium and heavy tanks—often a steep pass firing down into thinner roof armor and into louvers of engine intake and exhaust systems. Two targets here are on the white road to the right of the buildings (gun camera, 86th Ftr Gp, World War II).**

Armor under fire. Concentrated impact of Cal .50 API rounds on armor put on a pyrotechnic show. Some tanks caught fire and lighter armored vehicles often "blew" in fire and smoke (gun camera, 86th Ftr Gp, World War II).

The story of strafing tanks is further reflected in reports such as the following regarding the Allied crossing of the Moselle River in France, 8–11 September 1944 (from *The U.S. Army Air Forces in World War II*, vol. 3): "[F]ighter-bombers hit at targets indicated by ground in the immediate front of American units and on their flanks, tank concentrations being their favorite assignment.

In one attack on such an objective a unit of the 406th Group (P-47s) made forty individual passes at fifteen tanks near Arry on 10 September and was confident that all had been immobilized or destroyed."

Some Allied and enemy air forces employed specialized "tank killer" aircraft. The Germans put 37mm cannon on Stukas (two Flak 18/36 guns, one under each wing) for antitank operations on the Russian front. German pilot Hans Rudel credited these aircraft with a key role in his unit's large claims of Russian tanks destroyed. British Typhoons and Russian Stormoviks were others noted as armed with cannon for killing tanks. These are a definite part of strafing history.

The USAAF stuck with its regular fighters and fighter-bombers. While bombs and rockets as well as guns were involved, the record seems clear that the guns were overwhelmingly the most used armament by American pilots and crews against tanks in World War II and were our main tank killers. It was not easy strafing but was high in pilot and crew satisfaction, both in direct results observed and with effectiveness of cal-50 guns/AP1 ammo as armament.

Of course, in postwar years more about results of that strafing became known. For one thing, because of it the Germans incorporated thicker roof armor in tank production lines, which increased manufacturing materials and

Exact cause of this kill is unknown, but apparent machine gun hits show on armor above the track system (U.S. Air Force).

A kaput flak panzer. Our strafing of armor caused the Germans to divert tank chassis to make these, which we then destroyed in gunfights (U.S. Air Force).

process and slowed delivery; and the extra weight hurt mobility and caused early wear-out of suspension systems. Also, armored automatic-weapon flak vehicles were produced and assigned to accompany tank formations. A substantial number of tank chassis (mainly Pz Kw IV) were diverted to build these vehicles, called flak panzers. Tank chassis were a critical element in the level of German tank production. Besides killing tanks in the field, strafing indirectly kept many tanks out of the war because they never existed. The flak panzers that replaced them were of no comparable value in ground battle as tanks. While formidable firepower foes to strafers, we could destroy flak panzers with strafing fire much easier than we could tanks.

Opposite to the satisfaction of gunfighting, enemy armor was a category of target that went back much further in history and tradition in war than tanks. These were four-legged "troops." One of my early encounters with these targets was a mission in southern Italy in January 1944. We found enemy M/T (motor transport) stuck in snow in the Avezzano area. Claims were 15 trucks destroyed by strafing, plus follow-up passes on men and mules that had been working to free the vehicles. Mules and donkeys were regularly used to supply front-line units by both sides in the mountains of Italy. Often these animals (and men on foot) were the only means of getting critical items such as ammo and food to the front in snow and mud that made vehicle use impossible. They

Strafing flak panzers. Here smoke and fire from a heavy impact pattern totally obscure this target (gun camera, 86th Ftr Gp, World War II).

were used extensively in other theaters too. Many missions in particularly close work behind the battle lines included attacks on these animals. While fully realizing their great value to the enemy and his war effort and the military need to attack where they were present, most pilots didn't relish it at all; in fact they hated it. Strafing could do the job, but we had rather not see the results so up-close.

As the Germans lost more and more fuel trucks and other fuel haulers to our strafers (and the fuel supplies with them), they were forced to use animal-power replacements—mules, oxen, and especially horses—to pull carts and wagons, inoperative vehicles, guns, and other items. HDV and HDC (horse-drawn vehicle and conveyance) were standard items among strafing claims in MTO and ETO in 1944–45. They were found and strafed while mixed in with other vehicles and armor, and in groups or singles on their own. Strafing horses was perhaps a yet more hated task, and gun camera film hints that some pilots seemed to put their utmost skill toward "surgical" shooting on these targets—destroying the conveyance and occupants and cargo but not the horse, apparently succeeding in some cases, which strafing's good accuracy could do by holding the total impact pattern to a small area (inside 20 feet or even less). That small diameter could lessen collateral damage in many other cases too, such as vehicles beside houses. Then in one case in southern France, a mission received a last-minute target to strafe a corral where the Germans were holding a large number of horses they had rounded up for military duty. That was the only time I even remotely ever entertained an idea of not hitting an assigned target, and just to go hit something else belonging to the enemy. But we didn't do that, we went to the corral. If it were possible to wish away certain events as never having happened, missions on corrals would be high on certain pilots' wish lists.

As everyone in military service knew, staff cars and command vehicles were not assigned to ordinary soldiers, but only to high-ranking commanders and staff officers. Thus when spotted from the air these vehicles of the enemy were pounced on immediately by strafers. This shooting resulted in some dire consequences, both indirect and direct, to enemy officers, up to supreme commanders of theaters. An example of indirect is found in memoirs of German field marshal Albert Kesselring. In Italy he could oversee little of his command personally because it was too great a risk to fly or travel by road in the daytime with Allied aircraft above. Forced to do most travel in his command vehicle after dark, one night his driver crashed into the barrel of a big gun (which was forced to move at night too) seriously injuring the field marshal.

A famous case of direct strafing (found in numerous references) of a top enemy officer is that of Field Marshal Erwin Rommel, commander of German forces facing the Normandy beachhead, who risked daylight road travel on 17 July 1944. Returning from a tour of the front, his staff car was spotted by USAAF fighter-bombers. Rommel's driver desperately tried to reach and turn

Horse drawn vehicle. A faint photograph, but it shows a pilot's gunfire hitting the vehicle and not the horse (gun camera, 86th Ftr Gp, World War II).

Horse drawn vehicle and staff car. This pilot singles out the staff car and kills it by making a last second aim adjustment. Pullout will be a high "G" close call (gun camera, 86th Ftr Gp, World War II).

off into a tree-lined side road, but he was too late. Strafing fire killed the driver, wounded an accompanying officer, and inflicted severe face and head wounds, including multiple fractures of the skull, on Rommel. The enemy was denied the service of one of their best at a time and place of critical need. The strafing tactic of "get there quick" during armed-recce paid off quite "highly" this time.

The mention of "close air support" (or "direct air support" in World War II terms) often turns thoughts to concepts, roles and missions, and command and control. World War II saw developments in those areas that have endured ever since. A major milestone was U.S. Army Field Manual 100-20, in which air power and land power became "coequal and independent forces" under a supreme commander or theater commander. The tactical air roles in support of ground forces were listed as (1) Air Superiority, (2) Interdiction, (3) Close Air Support. During the war, developments in Close Air Support included colocation of air and ground command elements, communication nets for request of air support, direct radio contact between ground units in combat and pilots above, and use of pilots as FACs (Forward Air Controllers) for that contact. Navy and Marine and joint operations involved similar advances. To pursue doctrine further goes astray of goals in this book, but developments in close air support operations did affect the story of the gunfighting itself in tactics and "generalship" of pilots in the air.

Before late 1943 a mission leader was usually "on his own" to identify and attack a target that had been pre-briefed by coordinates and description. Contact with ground forces was really no different than World War I, such as colored panels or smoke to mark friendly positions. By 1944 (with exceptions) leaders in the air had a partner on the ground or onboard a ship offshore for assignment and confirmation of targets and to verify location of friendly forces. The nature of the ground action often changed the nature of the air support. Periods of major battles against heavily defended enemy lines and positions— such as the Gustav and Siegfried lines, Iwo Jima and Okinawa—set up different air-ground gunfighting experiences than periods of mobile and fast-moving ground actions such as Allied pushes in France, Germany, and some situations in China. Major invasions and landings had special experiences. A few examples of varied gunfighting follow.

Some close support was not for ground forces but was rather in support of air units. In the invasion of North Africa, American-flown Spitfires of the U.S. 31st Ftr Gp flew into Tafarui Airport, Oran area, on 9 November 1942. Just after landing they came under 75mm shellfire from French Foreign Legion forces still loyal to the Vichy government. Pilots took to the air to stop this. They found and silenced the French guns by strafing with the four cal-.303 machine guns and two 20mm cannon in their Spits. They also destroyed several French tanks (which were observed to have external fuel tanks) and lorries advancing on the airport. Besides protecting themselves, the 31st received commendation from American ground forces for stopping a French attack. Such

French resistance lasted only a few days. Vichy French forces joined Free French, all Allies thereafter (story from *31' Fighter Officers Association Newsletter*, October 1992).

When FACs were introduced into Italy in fall 1943, policy decreed that air support was not to replace artillery. Air would strike targets that artillery could not handle or had been unsuccessful on. Thus emphasis was on use of GP (high explosive) bombs against bunkers, dug-in positions, stone buildings, etc. However, it did not take more than the initial missions for this controller system to pump in repeat strafing passes over and above the bombing—just as pilots had done before the days of FACs. Steep strafing runs on the enemy in battle positions always had good potential to kill troops, hit equipment, and explode ammo.

As in all strafing, pilots making one pass often saw nearby targets other than the one being attacked, such as another gun position, tank, or troops. Reporting them to the FAC for repeat attacks created a form of "ground coordinated armed-recce." The time of fire of the guns simply allowed more targets to be hit on each mission than with bombs alone. In late 1944 in Italy, 12AF rotated fighter squadron commanders on short tours in the front lines as sort of super FACs to establish a system where the entire process of target request, approval and control of strikes was conducted on the spot at the front. In this, there was a strong continuation of bombing, plus napalm after October 1944, and with even greater expansion of "add on" strafing.

Returning to specific examples, I thank Glenn Moore, captain and flight leader, 525th Ftr Sq, for two typical if different ones (and some later quotes) from his book, *Dear Mom and Dad, Don't Worry—I'm OK*, and his daughters Ann and Gena for consenting to their use.

In one, the mission never attacked a close support target, but got a "well done" from the FAC. Flight leader Moore reported in to an FAC: "We have two 500 lb GPs [bombs] each, ready to strafe too. Do you have a target for us?" The FAC replied: "Patrol over my position; look for artillery flashes from ridge to north. We have troops advancing; the enemy probably will not fire with you on patrol." Thirty minutes later, Moore came back on: "We have seen no flashes, still have bombs and guns; do you have something to use them on?" FAC: "We have had no incoming fire, troop advance went well, no specific target at the moment, proceed on your mission briefing [to an alternate interdiction target], thanks."

The other example involved a mission at Neustadt, Germany. The FAC reported our ground forces had received 88mm fire from a grove of trees outside of town and requested the P-47s to look for muzzle flashes there. Capt. Moore, the mission leader, went down alone on a low slow recce pass. No guns were spotted, but in an adjacent field some 200 enemy troops were seen lying in ditches along a road. Reporting this to the FAC, the reply was in expletives on what to do, but paraphrased for sensitive ears, it meant "Kill them." Four strafing runs were made by Moore's flight, two planes firing on each side of the road on each run. The enemy troops had no cover and none to run to. They were literally shot to pieces. On Moore's order—"That's enough"—one unidentified pilot uttered, "Thank God." The second flight was sent in to strafe the suspected gun positions in the grove of trees. On return to base, 96 bullet holes were found in the belly of Moore's plane, surely received in the low pass to search for enemy guns.

Strafing of enemy ground forces has often been depicted in movies as low-level runs on the enemy with great or total surprise. Almost all close air support missions in World War II were totally lacking in the element of surprise. Missions often flew over targets, even circling several times while already under enemy fire, deliberately giving up surprise in favor of assuring and confirming proper target and location of the nearest friendly troops before attacking.

In mobile ground situations, close air support might well fill in for artillery, which would not be present in force at the head of advancing columns. The American air-ground teams of France were a prime case. Pilot FACs in lead element tanks had direct contact with fighter-bombers above. In one well publicized example, the FAC asked, "We think there is an enemy tank directly ahead of us, blocked from our view by tree line—do you see it?" P-47 flight leader: "Yes, but it's awfully close to you—can you pull back a bit before we hit it?" FAC: "Roger, Wilco" ("understand, will comply"). After the pull-back, the air attack was made, the enemy tank was knocked out, and friendly tanks proceeded onward. Strafing's accuracy and time of fire fit well in this very close air support.

My squadron's experience with air support in Germany involved rapid change from one ground situation to another. From heavy "in position" battle by the U.S. 3rd and 7th Armies at Saarbrucken, we switched to rapid tank and infantry thrusts into and through Bavaria by the U.S. 7th and French 1st Armies, but the latter was interspersed with major fights at points, usually a city. At Heilbronn, for example, strong enemy resistance for several days put city buildings and streets into our gun-sight view during strafing runs instead of battle "fields" or "lines."

In rapid friendly ground force advances, much close air support was called in to hit less formidable "spot" enemy defenses, usually at a road junction or village. At times the mere arrival of P-47s over the enemy position resulted in the end of resistance, often by surrender. If they tried to make a fighting withdrawal, they became open targets for our guns. When they continued to fight, on the FACs request for us to attack a village we often carried incendiary cluster "sticks" on this close support and used them to start fires; then we stayed overhead prepared to strafe troops evacuating structures. When armed only with guns, we started the fires with the guns and then stood by with saved ammo. Almost always the FAC reported, "Good work, enemy resistance ended, our forces moving on."

Strafing among man-made obstacles. *Top:* Battlefield smoke obscures this village, except for the church steeple on the left. *Bottom:* Target ahead, a smoke stack on the right (gun camera, 86th Ftr Gp, World War II).

Enemy resistance in villages (top) and buildings (bottom) was often overcome just by strafers being overhead or by strafing to start fires and burn out troops (gun camera, 86th Ftr Gp, World War II).

In the war against Japan, close air support covered a wide range of aircraft operating in varied ground and island-hopping campaigns. Two examples can highlight extremes in their scope.

In March 1945 in the Philippines, two P-61s of the 520th Night Fighter Squadron, in close support of friendly guerrilla operations, tore up a concentration of Japanese troops with 20mm cannon fire. In April 1945 in China, Allied air support against the Japanese offensive toward Chihking, which controlled the vital Hsiang Valley, is summarized in *The Army Air Forces in World War II*, vol. 5: "The .50-caliber machine gun proved to be the most important single weapon used in support of the Chinese ground forces. The 5th Fighter Group (CACW) alone fired 1,800,000 rounds a month during the nearly two months of battle. For the most part, Japanese troops occupied hilltop positions; to strafe effectively, the fighters fired their guns during a 90 degree dive and did not pull-out until a relatively short distance from the foxholes." Air support also included bomb and napalm on caves, bunkers and tanks, which, combined with the strafing, smashed the Japanese offensive and gained a Chinese victory viewed as the turning point in the war in China. Following it the Japanese started a withdrawal in south China.

While strafing was used in about every type of planned air-ground operation, perhaps even greater evidence of its flexibility was its being "thrown into the breach" without ties to any specific air role or task. This often occurred in critical situations.

At Guadalcanal in the harrowing days of October 1942, the Japanese put 5 or 6 transport ships offshore in daylight, not more than 10 to 12 miles from the American Henderson Field. U.S. forces on Henderson had very few flyable aircraft, but everything that could fly was put up to oppose the enemy landing. This included Marine F-4Fs, which strafed and killed enemy troops both on decks and while they were being landed. As other planes were made flyable, Marine SBDs and AAF P-39s/P-400s joined the fight. A few planes bombed, all strafed. By late afternoon, three enemy transports were burned or disabled. The others withdrew. Considerable numbers of troops had landed but far fewer than if there had been no strafing. At times during this brazen landing, aircraft guns were the only armament or weapons available to counter it.

Days of crisis for the beachheads' survived after the invasions of Salerno and Anzio are well known. Less known and perhaps the most desperate of all was a leap-frog operation on the east coast of Italy in early October 1943 from *The Army Air Forces in World War II*, vol. 3:

> On the 1st and 2nd, 160 U.S. P-40s paved the way for a[n] Eighth Army landing at Termoli on the Adriatic by bombing and strafing troops and vehicles on roads north and west of town. On the day of the landing (3 October) and the day after, despite bad weather, fighter-bombers with some help from B-25s inflicted severe punishment on enemy traffic. Fighters and fighter-bombers then went all-out to help the Eighth hold the beachhead against a series of hard enemy counterattacks.

Three army trucks. These are in battlefield support just behind the lines. This leader destroys the first truck and its cargo or troops aboard. His flight will kill the others (gun camera, 86th Ftr Gp, World War II).

On the two most critical days, the 5th and 6th, Spitfires and P-40s of the RAF and U.S. 57th and 79th Fighter Groups flew approximately 950 sorties over the battle area. They broke up the main enemy concentration, struck hard against road movement, especially around Isernia, flew direct-support missions over the battle line, and protected the ground troops against a few Luftwaffe raids. Without their efforts it is doubtful the beachhead could have been saved.

The war album of the 79th Ftr Gp, *The Falcon*, has an entry for 1 October 1943 that goes hand-in-hand with the above history: "Our program accelerated to a solid sheet of strafing."

In my personal experience in those missions, we used some bombs, especially frags, but with or without bombs, every round of ammo was fired on every mission. The weather was very bad. We lost two pilots attempting dive-bomb runs with GP bombs. They crashed into hilltops. Just as in World War I, strafers could still operate under low ceilings and this was done to the max. Targets of tanks, guns, and troops were strafed, but the most common was trucks being used by the enemy to mass for counterattacks.

At Anzio the German's major effort to throw the Allies back into the sea, 16–19 February 1944, the previously cited USAAF history reports the following: "General Devers [deputy MTO commander] said that close air support on the 17th disrupted the enemy's plan to launch a large-scale attack and that the German assault when it did come was stopped by 'combined artillery and air action.'" On the 17th MTO aircraft of all kinds were thrown into the crisis at the beachhead, many hundreds of sorties in relatively good weather. The following day the weather was bad and only about 100 sorties got in, mainly fighter-bombers at low level strafing, dodging snowstorms earlier, rain squalls later, in poor visibility, taking enemy flak, and flying among incoming and outgoing artillery fire. A sample of mission results reveals that P-47s in the 79th Group exploded an 88mm gun position, silenced three machine-gun nests, destroyed two armored cars, and shot up six tanks, and two platoons of troops in the open.

Another aspect of aircraft gun utility was evidenced at Anzio. It was the last invasion where the Germans put up strong air opposition. The low-altitude patrol protection against the Luftwaffe over Anzio was by fighter-bombers— in early days P-40s, and in later ones P-47s, primarily of the 79th Ftr Gp. All four squadrons were heavily engaged in air battles with attacking FW 190s and Me 109s and all scored impressive records of air kills. The pilots involved like to believe this was one reason the Germans did not put up air opposition over Normandy and southern France.

During periods of strong ground action at Anzio, we flew missions of combination tasks such as takeoff with bombs to bomb enemy positions oppo-site the beachhead, then to join air patrol over it and fight enemy aircraft. At

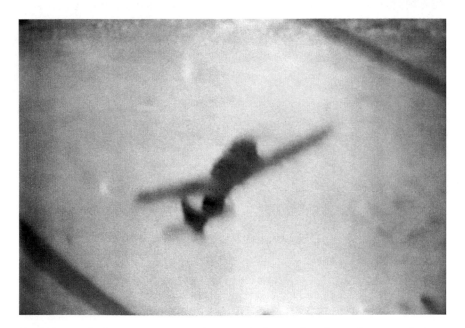

Enemy aircraft. At times pilots had fights with these and tanks on the same missions (gun camera, 86th Ftr Gp, World War II).

times we even went to strafe enemy targets. In one case a mission on patrol was quickly diverted to strafe tanks, making a bold daylight attack. All aircraft when returning to base with ammo remaining flew back over enemy territory and strafed targets of opportunity. Pilots scored kills of enemy aircraft and tanks, guns, trucks, troops, and so forth on the same mission. While both air and ground gunfighting occurred on numerous missions all through the war, Anzio was our most extensive case of it, as we switched almost from round to round fired until all ammo was gone on each mission—a lot of air shooting, but a lot more strafing and both playing a special part in saving the beach-head.

In postwar comments of German ground commanders, two words were prominent and often used together: "counterattack" and "impossible." One example (from *Impact*, 1945) by General von Vietinghoff, commander of the Tenth Army and later supreme commander in Southwest (Italy) recounts that "On the Italian and the Western Front, all freedom of movement for reserves and tanks was denied during daylight hours [and nights were very short during summer in Europe]. Thus counterattacks were impossible." Of course the Germans did mount a strong offensive in the Ardennes in late 1944 during the Battle of the Bulge, which was aided by a prolonged period of bad weather; and our ground forces certainly fought hard and won against many attacks and counterattacks in both the MTO and ETO. But from the German command view, obviously the kind of counterattacks they wanted and needed for end success could not be assembled and launched.

As in World War I, this war had "mass kills" inflicted on large enemy combat commands when the latter made (or were forced into) open operations and movements in daylight. Representative of a smaller-scale kill, in North Africa on 21 January 1943, P-38s strafed the retreating Africa Korps in southern Tunisia on the Gabes-Medenine-Ben Gardane road, destroying 65 vehicles. A truly massive kill occurred in Italy, generated by the Allied breakout of Cassino and Anzio and retreat of German armies to new defensive lines in the northern Appennines. In a six-week period, from 12 May to 22 June, some 5,000 enemy vehicles were destroyed and another 5,000 damaged. A typical day's claim for one fighter-bomber group (in this case, the 86th) was two hundred seventeen M/T destroyed, 245 damaged. Among the largest such kills was the Falaise-Argentan Pocket, or Gap, in France, August 1944. RAF tactical air, mainly Typhoons, and USAAF 9AF, mainly P-47s, joined in a literal slaughter of German forces squeezed into the tightening pocket. A good feel for the scope of destruction is found in the report of one German panzer division on its efforts to escape. With only limited tanks remaining, the division tried to go out at night as the gap closed; but already air-destroyed wreckage was so thick on and about the roads that even tanks could not push their way through it. With no other choice, individual and small groups of tanks tried to filter out across open countryside but few were successful.

Along with large claims in these operations, another characteristic of "mass kills" was the part that air attack, mainly strafing, played in setting them up. *The Army Air Forces in World War II*, vol. 3, notes the following on the breakout of Cassino and Anzio: "But it is certain that the collapse of enemy transport, especially the breakdown of local distribution immediately behind the front, greatly accelerated the Allied breakthrough as well as the pace of the advance on Rome which followed, a fact which the ground forces fully recognized and appreciated."

Again, the significance of strafing trucks is highlighted. Trucks were the backbone of that local distribution. And strafers were the overwhelming killers of trucks. Typical of pre–Falaise Pocket Allied kills was the one by the 405th Ftr Gp which sent mission after mission against three miles of enemy forces on a road. Friendly ground forces reported over 100 tanks, 250 vehicles, and 11 guns destroyed there by air attack and some artillery fire. Another mass kill that summer was in the German retreat north following the Allied invasion of southern France. It was perhaps the "most in smallest area" of the war, often called "strafing's greatest victory," and it was known to pilots as "The Road to Montelimar." It is covered in chapter 10 in detail from the pilot's gunsight view on the initial shots in that major event.

Other mass kills were the result of the Battle of the Bulge. The first came when weather broke and fighter-bombers got into the action. More followed in January 1945 as the Germans withdrew from such places as the Clerf-Dasburg-Vianden area, where the havoc wrought by fighter-bombers of XIX TAC among the stalled columns was reported as far surpassing the destruction in the Falaise Gap.

Another slaughter was in March 1945 in front of the U.S. Third and Seventh Armies. As Saarbrucken fell on 20 March German defenses west of the Rhine River caved in, resulting in a mass fallback or flight to the Rhine. Several "field days" of strafing action ensued for our fighter-bombers, including my group, from attacking trapped enemy forces in the Saar-Palatinate "Triangle."

At the time, Gilbert Burns was a first lieutenant, veteran leader (105 missions flown) in the 313th Squadron, 50th Fighter Group, flying P-47s from Toul, France. Gil has been kind enough to provide an account of the strafing of a German division at Frankenstein (near Kaiserslautern):

> It was on March 20, I was flying my plane "0" or "Ginny." Our intelligence got the call to send someone pronto. When we arrived on the scene we could not believe our eyes, [as] trucks, vehicles, tanks, everything, stretched for miles. There were already 47s there, I guess two flights, eight planes. So we were second to get there. Our planes were clean, no bombs, they just loaded the fifties and got us into the air. We threw the rulebook out, forgot the top cover and just strafed. Don't remember if there was flak, if there was, we, just ignored it, too busy strafing.... I emptied my guns. When we finished, we flew back to Toul at *full throttle*. The only mission that ever happened (normally flew back at cruise

A view of the slaughter from a strafing "frenzy," this one in Germany on the west side of the Rhine in the Kaiserslautern area (U.S. Air Force).

power).... We got back fast to tell intelligence what was going on, and we knew we'd be reloaded to return.

Returning the second time I had napalm. When we arrived on the scene, again we could not believe our eyes. The word was out and other groups had joined in and there were planes everywhere, darting here and there, a feeding frenzy ... killing, devouring, destroying. I spotted an intersection in the road that was jammed with tanks and trucks. I came in low with the napalm and when the target disappeared under the nose, I counted three seconds and released (normal technique). The tanks (napalm) landed squarely in the middle of the intersection, a direct hit ... again we emptied out guns. We had two problems. First, the gun barrels kept overheating and started to spray. We hated to take it slow and cool, the targets were too inviting. Second, there were so many planes, there were close calls, coming too close to one another.

This vivid account is typical of experiences by numerous P-47 pilots in the German retreat at the "triangle." The same is true for tactics (or lack of them) in this and some other big kills. A complete story of strafing and strafers cannot leave out "frenzies" in the overall tactics used—or the fact that the time of fire of the guns was what made a "frenzy" possible. But at the same time, the story must remember the heavy American P-47 pilot losses during the breakout from Cassino/Anzio, and on the Road to Montelimar as well as the

From entire enemy field armies down to single dispatch riders, enemy ground forces did not get where they were going. As one German commander made clear, his reinforcements never arrived because they were "destroyed" on the way, much like the ones burning and sending up a towering column of black smoke pictured here (79th Ftr Gp, World War II).

"generalship" decisions of leaders on tactics during those operations in some of the bloodiest strafing gunfights of the war. These were anything but "easy targets."

In February 1945 Field Marshal Model issued an order regarding Allied strafers to all German ground forces on the Western Front. *The Army Air Forces in World War II*, vol. 3 calls this order "interesting testimony to the effectiveness of the [U.S.] fighter-bombers." It read:

> TO ALL DRIVERS AND PASSENGERS
> WHOEVER CAMOUFLAGES LIVES LONGER
> CARBINE AND MARCH DISCIPLINE VERSUS STRAFING
> The Anglo-American ground attack aircraft are the modern highwaymen. They are searching not only for columns of traffic, they are hunting down every gasoline truck, every truck with ammunition.
> Our fighters and anti-aircraft have had considerable success during the days of the great winter battles. But fighters and anti-aircraft cannot be everywhere....
> EVERY SOLDIER CAN AND MUST JOIN IN THE FIGHT AGAINST GROUND ATTACKERS! ... SPECIAL FAVORS WILL BE SHOWN SUCCESSFUL GUNNERS AND UNITS. EACH SOLDIER WHO KNOCKS DOWN AN ENEMY STRAFER WITH HIS INFANTRY WEAPON RECEIVES 10 DAYS SPECIAL FURLOUGH! UNITS WHICH HAVE BEEN PARTICULARLY SUCCESSFUL IN SHOOTING DOWN ENEMY GROUND-ATTACKING AIRCRAFT WITH INFANTRY WEAPONS WILL RECEIVE SPECIAL RATION ALLOTMENTS!
> Therefore: SEEK COVER FIRST,
> Then: FIRE AWAY!

This order from a top field commander was intriguing in terminology as well as message. Model did not use their official terms for "air power," "tactical air," or "fighter-bomber," nor their common nickname or acronym for "fighter-bomber," which was "JABO." Instead, he used the terms "strafing," "strafers," and "ground attackers" to describe the problem and what to shoot at. They specifically were what he wanted shot down. Also, Model's words reflected that attack on columns of traffic had been expected, but the dogged gunning down of individual vehicles had not been expected. Emphasis in the order on the latter would reflect that situation was hurting more than was expected. In fact, it was the reason for the order: the work of our strafers.

Down at the foot-soldier level that problem apparently was equally well recognized and assessed. One German soldier commented: "Hell, my unit could not even send out a dispatch rider on a motorcycle and expect him to arrive at destination—too many strafers around." That seems about the same as saying that our strafing and strafers largely paralyzed his unit by killing anything and everything that moved, which would indeed cripple their ability to attack and counterattack, which is one more reason that pilot Glenn Moore said the Browning cal-.50 aircraft machine gun was the fighter-bomber pilot's superior weapon of the war, his most valuable. Many other pilots, this writer included, fully agree.

· 10 ·

The Rhone Valley

Probably the least publicized strafing "mass kill" of enemy forces in the war is the one in France's Rhône Valley in the summer of 1944, some 13 days after the invasion of southern France. For example, *The Army Air Forces in World War II*, vol. 3, has only a small entry:

> On the 25th of August, Saville [XII TAC commander] reported that in the previous two days around 400 M/T had been destroyed: for the period 23–29 August, XII TAC claimed the destruction of 1,400 M/T, 30 locomotives, and 263 rail cars. The heaviest toll was along Highway 7 in the bottleneck between Montelimar and Valence where U.S. Seventh Army on 31 August reported 2,000 destroyed vehicles within a thirty mile stretch.

Official histories rarely give a full story of those doing the fighting. Certainly that is the case above. In this chapter the warrior's story is addressed as well as additional postwar findings on it and I'm sure readers will agree that this definitely was not a sitting duck or turkey shoot.

It was late afternoon, 28 August 1944. At the 79th Ftr Gp's air strip, San Raphael, in southern France, combat flying in the 87th Sq was finished for the day. Ops and Flight Line were buttoning up. Two other pilots and I were sitting outside Ops briefly before going to quarters. This day was perhaps the best one to date in my 13 months overseas. Our flying had gone well since we moved into France shortly after the invasion. Our quarters were villas on the coast. We had more fresh food and a party was scheduled that night with a unit of French freedom fighters—perhaps a wee feel of serenity in a war day. If so, it changed when a clerk ran out shouting, "Captain Colgan, Group wants a mission right now—to 'go take a look up the Rhone Valley north of the Bomb Line.'"

Three fueled P-47s were quickly "unwrapped." They had no bombs or other external stores, but the guns were always loaded and charged. The three available pilots made up the lead (Red) flight: Capt. Bill Colgan (me), leader; F/O Russel Jennings, wingman; and Lt. Phil Bagian, element. We took off in just minutes, briefed only with the exact words above. A second flight of four would be put together to follow. A grease pencil route of Red Flight was left on a map for the second (White) flight.

The hope in this mission was to strafe and set off fuel and ammo fires and explosions in tankers and vehicles among the armor at the spearhead of this huge column we found in the Rhône Valley—and to block and stall it there (U.S. Air Force).

What Red Flight saw in the Rhône Valley was the hulk of the German Nineteenth Army jammed together on some 33 miles of Highway 7—tanks, guns, trucks, other vehicles, horse-drawn wagons two and three abreast, infantry on foot alongside—making an attempt to retreat north and avoid being cut off and trapped in southern France by advancing Allied forces. We flew alongside this enormous column its entire length, rear to front, noting several things about it other than size and makeup. It was intact, no fires or breaks or gaps; obviously it had not been attacked up to this time. Even with our P-47s in view, above and just east of the column, it did not break up or take cover. As we approached the spearhead near the town of Montelimar we saw just what we knew would be there—a mass of armor, assuredly accompanied by a mass of automatic-weapon flak. Naturally the Germans did not want this army slowed or stopped in a narrow valley, which had few side roads out, by either French resistance forces or by U.S. strafers.

About then White Flight, leader, Lt. John Boone, checked in by radio. They were about 15 minutes behind us. I first instructed them to relay the sighting "of a massive solid enemy column extending over 30 miles beyond the Bomb Line" back to anyone they could reach by radio. We had been unable to contact any agency or other aircraft. Then I ordered White Flight to take a course for Montelimar and to attack the column some three or four miles behind the spearhead and destroy as many vehicles and start as many fires as possible at one point to block the road there. And I advised them that Red Flight was "going in" now on attack at the spearhead.

With hopes that fuel trucks or other vehicles carrying fuel could be set afire among the armor and block the road there too, and that fires could serve as beacons to lead following air attacks on the column after oncoming darkness, three P-47s took on the strong point of an entire enemy army in a strafing gunfight.

Before my wings were even vertical on roll-in from the east to strafe, an explosive round hit the right wing. Once I regained my senses, I could see a huge hole in that gun bay area, two guns blown completely out of the plane, the other two mangled and askew with the bent barrel of one pointing directly at me in the cockpit. I watched the linked ammo supply slither out over the trailing edge of the wing. Yet, the plane still flew OK. I continued the pass and was hit by more enemy ground fire, including a solid shell impact felt throughout the plane.

In a P-47 when the pilot pulled the gun trigger, all eight guns fired. He had no option of firing fewer guns, and all guns were charged when loaded. The pilot had no way to clear them. Thus, the gun pointing at me had a round in the chamber. When I pulled the trigger it would fire if it still had electrical contact. Perhaps the bent barrel could stop a round but then the gun would likely explode. However, when I fired it did not fire at me or explode, and I pulled out just above the enemy column, clearly seeing the types of armor and the small German black and white insignia on them, as well as some likely fuel haulers. Red 2 and 3 followed and pressed their passes in close too. Neither called that he was hit, but the odds of no damage to their planes were slim indeed. Once on the far side, I made an immediate decision to come back on a second pass, which was deemed needed and also was the quickest route to get to and behind close-by hills on the east side of the river and out of the enemy fire. All three planes made the second pass firing down to point-blank range. My four guns in the left wing fired fine throughout.

We had good solid strafing impacts, and fires erupted among the armor, enough for potential block and stall of the column. But we were wiped out by more hits from enemy fire in the process. No. 3 went down. No. 2 called that he was severely hit. My plane, in addiction to some power loss, now was on fire in the engine compartment. I was able to undertake a shaky turn to attempt to join No. 2 but before I could do so he crashed. White Flight radioed they were coming to our aid. I ordered them, "Negative, stay where you are and put every round of your ammo on vehicles there."

I unstrapped from the cockpit seat. If the plane exploded while I was trying to get as far away from the enemy column as possible, I might be blown

Artist's depiction of my battle-damaged P-47 on our initial pass on the column spearhead (Charcoal by Glen and Susan Palmer).

out, and probably too low for a parachute to open. I pulled the turbo charger control to "OFF." This diverted engine exhaust overboard rather than into the turbo system. Fire and smoke lessened, and gave me hope for the oil burning in turbo exhaust, not a fuel fire. The engine continued to run although my plane and engine took more enemy hits when I turned back toward the enemy column. Unable to do other than limp along barely flying I headed home.

Without engine power to climb high enough to go on a direct route over mountains, I had to cross low and slow over German positions while following valleys home. A barrage of 88s engulfed my plane, all explosions were heard, the plane was further riddled and I was almost thrown out of the cockpit. I knew the next enemy rounds would be the end. But minutes went by and they never came. The engine ran without oil all the way to home base and quit only when power was pulled off on approach to landing, which was a gamble with such damage, but was successful. The plane was scrapped on the spot after landing.

In debriefing, Red Flight's main report was loss of two pilots and three planes. It was a one-person report, thus unconfirmed on results, which were not fully observed anyway, and these planes had no gun cameras. White Flight made a normal mission report in which results were some 65 vehicles destroyed amid numerous fires, with no losses, but all planes had battle damage from small arms fire. There was hardly reason for celebration over the outcome of this mission, for Red Flight a loss of three planes and two fine pilots with no confirmed results. However, following days began to put a much different light on what the results actually were in the end.

The 79th moved from San Raphael to Valence Airfield during 1–2 September 1944. The ground movement was up Highway 7 passing the scene of the Red and White flight strafing on the 28th. An entry in the 79th unit history has these words from ground personnel on that trip:

> As we traveled up the Rhone Valley the destructive power of fighter-bombers became apparent with a grim clarity that none of us had ever fully realized. For a distance of roughly 30 miles, centered on the little town of Montelimar, was a shambles that may well have had no counterpart in this war. Here had been created a bottleneck of traffic, lined bumper to bumper, that had been ceaselessly attacked for days on end. Vehicles of every description were blocking each other until all fell victims to Allied air power. There were great diesel busses such as once were used for passengers on the streets of Berlin, there were tanks and horse-drawn carts, there was in actuality everything that could move on wheels, and all were now abandoned in flight. Only the odor of decaying bodies, animal and human, remained to connect this spectacle with the part it had once played for the Wehrmacht [German military forces]. The debris had been cleared from the road to the ditches alongside by a bulldozer which was still thus occupied as we hurried northward.

Group personnel on this trip estimated the number of destroyed vehicles at over 5,000. They also noted the road surface was intact and usable immediately on removal of wreckage, not full of bomb craters. And they quickly tied this scene to the mission of Red and White fights on the 28th. Those pilots were first to attack this enemy army. They set up the entire slaughter. These 33 miles are the true results of their mission and their strafing, an action which became known by pilots as the "Road to Montelimar."

After the 79th had been on Valence for several days, Red Flight's No. 3, Lt. Bagian, hobbled into the 87th Sq area. He had survived the crash of his plane. Although badly injured, he further survived an ordeal of hiding in a vineyard as German troops walked north past his position. Time after time they searched the area around his crashed plane and also fired machine pistols into vineyards, including the one where he hid. Somehow he was not hit, and once the German troops (a good part of an entire army) passed on north, French farmers came looking for him, took him in, dressed his injuries and made him a tree-limb crutch. When American ground troops arrived, he was taken to a field hospital, from which he engineered his own release and hitched a ride by vehicle to an airfield, then he continued by plane back to our unit.

Besides our great relief and thankfulness over Bagian's safe, if battered, return, he added a new aspect on Red Flight's part in the mission of 28 August. Of course there was a report made on his downed pilot escape and evasion ordeal. And he confirmed my previous one-man report on combat actions prior

Above: Remains of the German Nineteenth Army, some 33 miles of wreckage and carnage in the Rhone Valley: the end result of what our mission started (U.S. Air Force).

to his crash. His account agreed with mine in sightings, decisions and actions. Both of us were glad to see that information go into squadron reports and, it was assumed, to group and up the line. Bagian also noted important facts on results from his flying and shooting. Some of these were published in later years. One example is in *Une Mission de Guerre, 28 Aout 1944, Mission 2375, 79th Fighter Group (Colgan, Bagian, Jennings)*, by the French organization Association Rhodanienne Pour Le Souvenir Arden (ARSA), which is summarized here from a Bagian statement to them:

> We took our first pass from the east, but after that I zig-zagged back and forth across the road, shooting what was in front of me at the moment. My shooting got less across and more lengthwise as I went. I was cutting across the road when a quad 20mm gun set up on the east side of the road hit me good. The engine immediately ran rough; I used my energy to pull up in a climbing turn and rolled back in toward the gun that got me, now heading about east. My propeller was only wind milling. Then the engine seized. I fired non stop at the gun until my guns either burned out or ran out of ammo. I still had enough airspeed to pull around a hill on the east side of the road and picked out a field to belly-in. There was a line of tall poplars at the near side of the field though, and I didn't have enough speed to get over them. Rather than stall and crash, I flew through them. The plane survived that well, but lost flying speed. It dropped hard onto the ground and did not slide much at all. The engine broke off and bounced 50 or 60 yards ahead and to the left. I dove out onto the left wing and rolled to the ground beside the fuselage. The plane was already burning. I ditched my unused parachute, and unable to walk, I crawled to a vineyard several yards away.

From there his account deals in specifics of his escape and evasion.

With Bagian's report confirming mine, in addition to unit personnel witnessing the miles of destruction and carnage on the "road to Montelimar," the squadron's previous view of the mission as "questionable" was totally erased. At about the time of Bagian's return, military search for Jennings' crash site confirmed that he had been killed in action, and the mission would always carry that hard-felt loss.

Discussion in the unit on the flying and fighting of that mission was now greatly expanded. For example, Bagian said he had lost contact with Colgan and Jennings after the first pass and had gone all out to get as much effective shooting as possible into as many tanks and vehicles as possible—and was doing great at it until shot to hell himself. My passes had not been just straight-away runs either, especially on the second pass. I had jogged in aim on one and then two other apparent fuel trucks. I reported seeing definite destructive hits and fires from my shooting plus other smoking and burning vehicles that obviously were the work of Jennings and Bagian. Thus, while we had no chance to go back and get a good look to make specific claims, our unit now had a confirmed two-pilot report of the strafing done at the spearhead by Red Flight and the knowledge that their shooting had inflicted substantial damage

This mission and mass "kill" on the German Nineteenth Army has received some additional public exposure in recent years. Being featured in my

Vehicles, cargoes, and equipment of the German Nineteenth Army burning in the town of Montelimar (U.S. Air Force).

book *WWII Fighter-Bomber Pilot*, it was featured in *World War II* magazine of November 2002, in the article "P-47 Thunderbolt Strike on the Road to Montelimar" (by my son, Bill Colgan, Jr.). The French association ARSA, mentioned above, especially through the efforts of Andre Besson, has completed a full investigation and report of this mission in their work on American pilots and plane crashes in France during the war. They have examined unit and service records on it. They found (as I have) that records at XII TAC (command of air operations in southern France, under 12^{m} Air Force in Italy) have very scant coverage of this and almost all missions of late August 1944. For this one, their records show only that seven P-47 of 79th Fighter Group on armed-recce on the west side of the Rhone destroyed some 60 vehicles and lost two aircraft with two pilots missing, which is the wrong side of the river with no grid location given. As ARSA noted, "Let them be pardoned for it." The battle situation in southern France was then fast moving, and 12^{m} Air Force had its TAC personnel split between Italy and France, operating two different campaigns.

In USAAF missing aircrew reports, those of Bagian and Jennings varied and were found misleading in locations. ARSA efforts (my input to them was insistence that both sites were close to Montelimar, east/southeast, Bagian nearest the river and Highway 7 and Jennings several miles further east southeast) brought forth witnesses from that area who had seen the crash of a P-47 on 28 August 1944, including a man who had taken a photo of the crashed plane. That snapshot showed the aircraft tail number. It was Bagian's plane. The location was near La Bâtie-Rolland, east of Montelimar.

Other witnesses were located who had seen the crash of another American aircraft on 28 August 1944. One witness specified a single-engine machine that "had just strafed the Montelimar area." The pilot's body was near the aircraft and he was buried at the crash site by local monks. That was near Taulignan, southeast of Bagian's crash. It was confirmed to be the crash site of F/0 Jennings. His body was later removed to a military cemetery and after the war to his hometown of St. Charles, Illinois.

The officers and representatives of the Association Rhodanienne Pour le Souvenir Aerien and the Association Nationale des Anciens Combatants et Ami(e)s de la Resistence (ANACR) plus many French people deserve our heartfelt gratitude for their research on American crash sites and contributions to the history and heritage of our pilots and aircrews. Many honors have been bestowed by French towns and communities as well. In 2002 the town of La Bâtie-Rolland, based on ARSA reports, made Lt. Philip Bagian "Citizen of Honor of the town, *for his bravery during World War II.*" An earlier memorial to F/0 Russell Keith Jennings (ANACR efforts mainly by Philippe Biolley), resulted in a stone monument in his honor placed at Taulignan in 2008 with relatives of Jennings present at the ceremony.

In the case of *28 August 1944, Mission 2375, 79th Fighter Group (Colgan, Bagian, Jennings)*, ARSA and ANACR not only contributed to its history and memory they also produced the facts to finally make a full mission report, which was not made in August 1944 because Red Flight did not return to make it.

· 11 ·

Mindoro Beachhead

As noted throughout past chapters, my combat service in World War II was in the79th and 86th fighter groups. In the Korean War, I served in the 58th Fighter-Bomber Group and a later chapter will include more on that. But some war fighting by the 58th in World War II is perhaps an ultimate example of strafing being an "ace in the hole, saving the day." This action is also irrefutable evidence that puts straight numerous misconceptions on strafing, such as a few mentioned back in the introduction of this book. What happened here certainly is not "strategy," nor is it just "another name for close air support?" But it would fit with the lady's comment there that the word strafing sounds "nasty." *The Story of the 58th Fighter Group of World War II*, a book written by A.J. Kupferer, a pilot of that group, has been praised as an outstanding unit history. The following paragraphs are my summary from an extensive account in that book (all excerpts used are material identified as unit records):

In the Philippines in December 1944, American forces landed on Mindoro Island on the 15th, an invasion Washington had concerns over as being too risky. It was nearly 300 miles from Leyte, site of initial U.S. landings in the Philippines, and almost under the nose of main Japanese forces on Luzon. On the 22nd the 58th Fighter Group started moving its personnel and P-47 planes onto the Mindoro beachhead, to a newly scraped strip called Hill Field. By the 26th two squadrons were in place. Throughout they were under Japanese air attack, taking cover during the night and coping with bomb craters and a soft, rough, very dusty field and enemy planes during flying operations.

At 1600 hours on the 26th a U.S. patrol plane sighted a Japanese naval task force 100 miles west steaming at 28 knots toward the beachhead. Reported as a battleship, one heavy cruiser, and six destroyers, they were suspected of carrying troops on decks. The nearest Allied naval force of comparable size to counter this threat could not arrive before afternoon on the 27th. While the beachhead braced for attack, all air units were alerted to strike the task force. They were the only means of engaging the enemy en route.

At the 58th Fighter Group, Colonel Gwen C. Atkinson, the commanding

The P-47Ds of my unit were the same models flown by the 58th Fighter Group on Mindoro Beachhead and were key strafers in both Europe and the Pacific.

officer, had volunteered to get airborne as soon as possible. Headquarters replied to stand by ready to go and Atkinson assembled all pilots. With 32 planes available he had squadron commanders and flight leaders select 31 experienced pilots; he would fly the 32nd.

As planes were made ready, a stark reality was faced: there were no bombs on the field nor any close enough to be brought in before the enemy force arrived. The only weapons available were the aircraft guns. Advised of that fact, headquarters' orders came down to launch anyway and attack the task force with or without bombs. For the 58th, that meant without—guns only, strafing. Also the orders directed not to return to Mindoro, which was expected to come under attack, but to land at Tacloban, Leyte. And by now the mission would be flown at night. These are a few extracts from Colonel Atkinson's report of events before takeoff:

> I knew little of the plans of Headquarters ... numbers or types of planes that would support us.... I did realize that the situation must be extremely serious ... [and it was] vital that everything we had—even fighter planes without bombs—be thrown into the fight.... The chosen 31 pilots were called together and given the picture or as much of it as I knew.... Making strafing passes on anything larger than a destroyer is damned risky at any time. At night, when you cannot see to keep protective formation; it's a one way ticket.
>
> I knew that I could not order any of those pilots out on that mission.... An

With no bombs available, the guns were always there. Shown is ammo being loaded into the trays of each of the four guns in the wings of a P-47 fighter (photograph published in the *Jug Letter*, P-47 Thunderbolt Pilots Association, reputed to have been taken by Max L. Campbell, ETO).

order was not necessary. There was no dramatic volunteering. No man said a word. They just looked at me and I looked at them. We understood....

Colonel Jasper Durham, Deputy Group Commander was preparing for the possibility that the Nips might land ground forces.... While listening to Durham give his orders, I thought of calling Headquarters and telling them flatly that I would not accept the mission ... we had never refused a mission, but when I thought of the odds against any of my 31 pilots coming through alive I felt like turning that one down.

But I didn't. You never do.... I knew that none of us could face each other afterward if we refused to go, and that I would rather die than to fail when the need was greatest. What was 32 compared to thousands.

Excerpts follow from Colonel Atkinson's report covering takeoff and action in the air:

[T]here was a red alert. Nip planes were headed for us. We hurriedly got into our planes and took off.... The Nip planes arrived and began bombing and strafing the strip before all of us were off. The last few had to take off between attacks by the Nips, and between two of our planes that had cracked up on the soft runway and were burning.

After a brief search we found the task force fifteen miles up the coast and five miles offshore. The ships were dark blobs on the water marked by phosphorescent wakes....

I knew we could do no formation fighting in the darkness. Our best chance lay in each man fighting his own fight.... There was a grave danger of our running into each other, so I ordered that all passes be made from west to east, so we would all be going in the same direction.... Picking a ship I went down on a first pass.

As I opened fire I was spotted by my tracers—there had been no time to remove them—and every ship opened up on me. It was as if a volcano had erupted to blast open the night.... [W]ith fire like that turned on us I didn't expect any of us to come out of that fight.

The official reports say there was no battleship, but I saw, or thought I saw—a battleship, two cruisers and five destroyers....

There were bombers and fighters of other outfits up there with us.... I saw none of them ... saw none of my own planes ... every pilot was alone. I kept diving, strafing, pulling up and climbing to dive again ... held my fire until I could see the superstructure of a ship ... do all the damage possible. I strafed all the ships.... The big baby was long enough and wide enough and had enough firepower for a battleship. Passing over it was like passing too close over a blast furnace.

I made nine strafing passes in all before my ammunition gave out, last gun to run dry was outboard right wing.... [M]y last pass it was the only gun firing ... was put-putting like a toy rifle. I missed the buck of my plane that comes when all guns cut loose....

I forgot the gas gauges and kept strafing until that last gun went out. Then I headed for Leyte ... 300 miles away. The weather was bad ... enough gas for about two hours.... After an hour and 40 minutes flying on instruments through thick weather, I came over the island ... little hope of finding the airfield in that muck.... My savior was the ground controller at the Leyte strip ... his instructions ... suddenly a searchlight filtering through ... a hole appeared ... the airstrip. I had just enough gas for four minutes flying time when I set the plane down.

A few excerpts from the report on thoughts by Colonel Atkinson after the mission follow:

We lost five pilots in the hell that was thrown at us that night ... a lot of good men. Others landed all over the Philippines, and it was days before we got back together again. One was seriously wounded; another was hit and had to bail out.... Others ran out of gas and jumped.

Our pilots fought a better than good fight, they took all the Japs could give ... the job you set out to do was done. The Japs never landed a man on Mindoro that night. Their shelling was brief and inaccurate, no major threat to beachhead survival. Final reports of the battle showed both of the heavy ships badly damaged two of the destroyers sunk and a third damaged. A captured Jap naval officer had said that the shelling was so poor because all range finders and automatic aiming devices for the ships guns had been shot out.

Fighter pilots of the 58th didn't do all of that (other planes, some surface forces/PT boats were involved).... But we helped, and we are proud of that.

The above is only one of the pilot reports; many others involved even greater ordeals.

The first planes got off at 2030, the last ones not until 2300. Crews and pilots heroically struggled to get this done—in darkness. Planes bogged down or stuck had to be pulled out by tow vehicles and trucks; planes crashed; people hit the ground during each Japanese bombing and strafing attack, then got

The Philippines

After strafing the task force, pilots faced flying some three hundred miles to the east through terrible night weather to land at Tacloban Field.

right back to the job. Most reports cited similar action in the air over the task force: using wakes to line up on ships, holding fire until close in, making pass after pass, and awesome display of firepower from all ships, especially the big ones. Some pilots mentioned when pulling off attacks, and out of ack-ack range, turning on wing lights hoping to avoid collision with other planes, then lights off for the next attack, tracers whizzing past coming up from ships, some coming from Japanese planes in the melee.

Some pilots made it to successful landing on Leyte. Some short on fuel landed back on Mindoro and managed to get fuel into their planes and take off again for Leyte. Many experienced serious problems and challenges en route that included battle-damaged planes, driving rainstorms on arrival, forced bailout. Remarkable survival and rescue were involved. But also there are those without reports—those who went down in the action and never made it back at all. The battered and crippled enemy task force came close enough to do some shelling, without major damage or casualties, then quickly withdrew. Japanese prisoners also noted that in addition to shot-up fire control equipment another reason for this was that many sailors were killed and wounded on the ships.

The unit history lists the following pilots of the 58th in this action:

The 311th Squadron: Major Odren, commander; Captains Benner, Ellis, and Jander; 1st Lts. Bordon, Borunda, Crepeau, Evans, Foster, Itzkowitz, Johnson, Marston, and O'Leary; Lts. Benson and McDonald; Colonel Atkinson.

The 69th Squadron: Major Self, commander; Captains Bosenbark and Jackson; 1st Lts. Bridgeford, Emrich, Foulkes, Linton, Lewis, Maika, Martin, and Nacht; Lts. Campbell, Ellenberger, Girard, and Gregg.

Fourteen planes were lost, two in crashes on take off. Ten failed to return (five pilots were rescued and five missing in action—Bordon, Bridgeford, Emrich, Foulks, Girard). Two planes which made it down safely on a Leyte strip were later hit by a landing B-25.

The U.S. Army Air Forces in World War II, vol. 5, reports that Brig. Gen. W.C. Dunckel, the Army commander of beachhead forces, thought that without a doubt the airmen had saved the beachhead from serious losses. The author quoted from a letter by Dunckel to the 5th Air Force: "The action of our air units on that night will stand forever ... as one of the most gallant deeds to be established in the tradition of American fighting men." This action also forms a very proud chapter in the history of strafing and strafers as part of, and contributors to, that tradition.

· 12 ·

Trail of Gun Smoke

Earlier chapters have mentioned a wide variety of targets that were strafed, but far from all. Claims of the 79th Ftr Gp included seven large railway guns. 86th Ftr Gp mission reports cite a cement mixer, airport terminal, and an observation/communications post atop a castle tower. (There's no telling just what a search of all unit records would uncover.)

Civilian populations of enemy countries felt the impact of strafing fire too. Policy of units I flew with prohibited "going after" or "gunning down" people that were observed in civilian pursuits. However, it was impossible for the enemy civilian population to be totally separated from all strafing.

In early 1945, Alfred E. Schey was a German high school student living in Illingen, a village near Muehlacker and its railroad junction and yards, north of the autobahn between Karlsruhe and Stuttgart. We flew missions over this area from February until the French First Army took Muehlacker on 7 April. I'm deeply grateful to Alfred (senior master sergeant, USAF [Ret] and later DAF Civilian, Cold War Intelligence, in a 40 year career with the U.S. Air Force) for providing an account of life in rural Germany with U.S. strafers overhead, and to his son Eric for consenting to its use. Excerpts follow:

> Train busting in our area occurred daily, several times daily depending on associated track damage. The typical damage we received [to his parental home, near main rail tracks] was roof tiles shot out from strafing aircraft pulling out of dives, i.e. on shallow strafing runs against ground targets, e.g. trains, M/Ts, HDVs [horse drawn vehicles].
>
> ...
>
> Home owners became very nervous, of course, when they found German military vehicles seeking visual shelter under the trees next to their homes. I'll never forget the morning we found Tigers [tanks] next to our house. That was in preparation to the build-up for what later came to be known as the "Battle of the Bulge."
>
> ...
>
> While the cities were relatively well protected by AAA, the rural areas were wide open as you remember. Beginning in late summer 1944, the rural population infrastructure suffered the most from fighter-bomber operations. The general feeling among civilians was that it was impossible to be out in the open during day-

Unusual targets. We strafed a wide variety. *Top:* This round structure in Germany was reckoned to be a rail water supply, but auto-weapon fire came up from there; thus it proved to be a "flak tower." *Bottom:* We reported this as a "bus park" (gun camera, 86th Ftr Gp, World War II).

light. Farmers tilling fields were blown away with the result being that crops could not be harvested. Schools stopped operating. The students were subject to strafing raids in trains, on bikes or on foot.

...

One of the last times my friends and I went to high school over a distance of some five miles "in the open" we were chased by a P-47. Luckily, we could find cover in fox holes emplaced at about 50 meter intervals alternately on either side of the roads. These fox holes were dug earlier by 14–15 year old school kids, yours truly included, along the entire road network in the region. This was done on one or two Sundays and to this day I remember how scared we were about getting strafed. What saved us was the miserable weather.

...

The impact of fighter-bomber operations on the regional infrastructure has never really been evaluated. The typical four-ship fighter-bomber formation literally could stop daily life every day just by being in the region and without firing a shot.

...

After awhile the individual in the rural area would begin to think that every time he just hears a fighter-bomber [the usual military power high r.p.m. engine whine] the individual begins to assume that aircraft is after him personally, a real paranoia which transferred into a mass psychosis.

Schey's account also makes the point that heavy bomber raids on cities, although massive and devastating, were sporadic for the population there, while fighter-bombers over his area were present every day.

A few years back my brother sent me a newspaper with a story of another young fellow in Germany during the war. Klaus Main lived in the village of Niedereschbach, near Frankfurt. In early March 1945, his mother took Klaus, age 11, to visit family members in a town 25 miles away. They were traveling by bicycle and heard the roar of U.S. fighter planes all morning. For a short rest, it seemed prudent to stop under cover of trees. Approaching a small forest with that in mind, they saw a platoon of German storm troopers already using those trees as a campsite.

Wisely, Klaus's mother exclaimed, "Not here!" and peddled on. They were barely past the soldiers' camp when increased scream and howl of aircraft engines were heard—planes making an attack. Dropping their bikes, the mother took cover in the ditch on one side of the road and Klaus behind a large tree trunk on the other side—about 20 feet apart. Amid the roar of engines and clattering of machine-gun fire on the storm trooper position nearby, young Klaus wanted to join his mother. He made a dash across the road. While in the open a quick glance up at the sky revealed the yellow-painted cowling of a U.S. P-47—just above the treetops—which seemed coming straight at him but with the aircraft guns silent at the moment. Mother and son were unhurt in the strafing, and once the P-47s left the area, the two proceeded on their trip—with Klaus never to forget the sight of the bright yellow snout of the P-47 aimed at him.

Some forty-eight years later Klaus wrote a story of the experience in *Life*

Targets in cities, towns and villages. Pinpoint shooting lessened civilian property damage and casualties. *Top:* A vehicle was destroyed literally on a front doorstep without spraying bullets into the house. *Bottom:* A loco is hit by firing across the roof of a house with no hits showing on the roof (gun camera, 86th Ftr Gp, World War II).

and Times, Florida Today (Melbourne, Florida), in which he extended thanks to the pilot of that Thunderbolt, whoever and wherever he may be, for keeping his finger off the trigger while Klaus dashed across the road. (This summary is from that article.) I am sure many other pilots kept their fingers off the trigger at other times and places and are thankful for it, as well as for receiving thanks from Klaus and others on the ground.

The population of Japan also came under strafing fire. Two P-47Ns (the long range version) on one of the earliest visits of U.S. fighters to the main islands of Japan arrived there at night to find the city of Kanoya, in southern Kyushu, brightly lit up with street and other lights. It was strafed.

Realistic simulation of strafing was not practical or sensible in training, but that did not keep all strafing overseas in the war. USAAF fighters on coastal patrol spotted a German U-boat off the east coast of the United States. The pilots used their guns to churn up water directly over the submerged sub, marking its position for the Navy, which sank it.

I have not tried to identify the "best" strafing plane of World War II. *The Army Air Forces in World War II* records that "The P-47 proved that the fighter-bomber provided the best answer to the long quest for an outstanding attack plane." Certainly the P-47 had features that made it a most formidable strafer: fighter performance, eight guns, radial engine (no vulnerable coolant system) and stable, rugged airframe. And P-47s did a tremendous amount of strafing in the war, thus the "Jug" (pilot nickname for the P-47) would be a top contender.

At the same time, the P-47 was not the best strafer in North Africa, Alaska, or the early days of the Pacific and CBI; it was deployed there until later in the war. The P-40s and others in the war at the time were best there. P-38s and P-51s strafed numerous targets beyond the range of the P-40 and P-47D (the most widely used "Jug" in World War II) in actions in the Pacific, at Foggia from North Africa, and on the Russian front from Italy. That made them the best in those operations. The same applied for B-24s and B-25s, plus late-war P-47Ns, on long-range Pacific missions. Navy/Marine Corsairs and others are noted too. But this book is devoted to the story of pilots and crews in strafing action in all types of planes—the history and heritage of the gunfighting, not who had the best plane. Duty, valor and sacrifice were not tied to type of plane. Any and all types could produce ultimate stories of war fighting.

I've dwelled on movie versions of strafing as a stream of bullet impacts racing along in a track across the ground or water. One film (which I have always remembered in content, if not in title) made during World War II showed a Japanese pilot raking a string of bullets across a surfaced U.S. submarine. Impacts started about half a mile short and continued the same distance beyond. Most pilots would never strafe a sub that way. They could easily "hold" all rounds on the "boat" itself. I have surely overworked my obsession that bullets should hit enemy equipment and hides, not open water or countryside. One additional example will shed other pilot and unit feeling on this.

Pilot Ken Thomas flew over 100 missions in the P-47, all in support of ground forces in Burma. He recently recalled that all ammo, fuel, bombs, etc., were flown in at a cost of seven gallons of fuel consumed for each eight pounds of payload, and his unit closely monitored how their precious loads of ordnance were used. They often placed a single bomb to do the job, and then went on to the next problem. Strafing runs were confined to three or four second bursts, which he noted was by calculation (range, airspeed, muzzle velocity) the maximum effective duration of fire. He further stated that he gets a great kick today out of watching on the Discovery Channel missions in other theaters where the trigger is held down while the tracers are falling 1,000 feet short and still held and visible after the break (this summarized from *P-47 Thunderbolt Pilots Association Newsletter*, January 1994).

Ken is not alone in seeing that on TV and video. The documentary *Thunderbolt* has one strafing run where the trigger is held down until the gun barrels burned out; bullets tumbled widely across fields, while the pilot weaved back and forth with no target visible. Such strafing scenes apparently have merit on the screen. Movie and video producers seem attracted to them. This shooting probably is more gripping and terrifying to viewers (and perhaps to people on the ground in war) than a pilot destroying a truck with a short burst of gunfire that hits nothing but the truck.

Out where the strafing was done, one fact was firm. The pilot had the capability and choice to put all bullets in a 15–20 foot spot if desired or he could send them far and wide or in a long stream. For example a P-47 at 350 mph, continuous 20-second bursts could be flown to send a path of bullet impacts about two miles long on the ground—even longer if a pull-up was made to toss bullets farther ahead; but the density of impacts from all eight guns in two miles would be only one bullet about every five feet along the way. The gun barrels would be trashed as a result, with most unit commanders making sure it did not happen again, or if it did the pilot might spend the war serving on the ground somewhere.

Thus, the crux of strafing history remains that pilots and unit leaders had great flexibility in how they shot. Their "generalship" in this regard is a huge part of their story. Evidence is clear that overwhelmingly the choice was "pinpoint" fire on enemy equipment and hides, rather than the movie and TV "cross country" shooting. Veteran strafers and leaders are united that this was the very basis—the secret—of the tremendous totals of enemy equipment and personnel taken out of the war by strafing. Almost every bullet fired was concentrated on a specific enemy target.

Some observers have noted that if the Japanese strafers at Pearl Harbor had been U.S. P-47s, in the same numbers—using "on-target" shooting instead of the wide spraying many Japanese pilots used—the P-47 strafers would have

A military post/barracks. *Bottom:* At this one in northern Italy a bus pulls up in front of a large building. *Top:* This P-47 pilot kills it and its occupants with good shooting and no rounds wasted. This was pilot "generalship," the secret to great utility and results (gun camera, 86th Ftr Gp, World War II).

had plenty of ammo to destroy all aircraft on Oahu, then go on to burn the fuel storage and play havoc with the base, dry dock, and yard at Pearl, as well as other military bases and Honolulu harbor, all with repeated strafing runs.

Most gun camera film released by the military for public viewing was selected from the best quality photography and the most spectacular or the most interesting action shots. Many of the films were certainly that—valuable releases to the public. At times, however, choice of good photography did not always show best gun shooting. Shown here is one case. It is a better photo than many others in this book, but a close look at target and bullet impacts show more miss than hit. Certainly not every "pinpoint" burst was dead-on each specific target. That was a risk in using the tactic. If the burst missed, that was it for that pass in most cases. But, with 4-ship flights standard in most units, chances were about nil that all four would miss. Most often they all hit as the majority of gun camera film in this book shows.

A misleading source of information to the public on strafing was in military news releases, but the public information officer was not at fault. It was instead caused by unit mission reports, and in turn summaries of those by higher headquarters, which lumped claims and results together under the heading "bombing and strafing." For example, one daily theater summary of activities included this notation: "Fighter-bombers bombed and strafed targets

Truck target. A fairly good photograph shows this pilot's close range pinpoint bullet impacts a bit off target high and left—and it's too late to correct aim without crashing into the ground (gun camera, 86th Ftr Gp, World War II).

Watercraft. This pilot's concentrated burst from longer range is a bit short of his barge waterway target, but he has time to adjust aim for direct hit and still pull out safely (gun camera, 86th Ftr Gp, World War II).

north of Rome, cutting rail lines and destroying 65 trucks, eight armored vehicles, and six locomotives." The odds are about a sure thing that what really happened was the rail lines were cut with bombs, and everything else listed was destroyed with guns—by strafing.

Trucks, armored vehicles, locos, etc., certainly were bombed at times, even singles and small groups. But when it came to identifying and confirming claims at each mission debriefing on mobile targets (or "movers") such as these, bombing and strafing were different stories. Most bombing results on "movers" (except for napalm) were not viewed close-up and not covered by gun cameras. Normally there was no means to determine details of destruction or damage to what and how many. But strafing results were seen close-up and covered by gun cameras (when equipped). It was relatively easy to determine details of destruction and damage to what and how many.

Two monthly claim/result summaries of the 86th Ftr Gp are shown with this text. They reflect several significant points in the story of strafing in World War II—first chart: December 1944, Italy, stalemate ground action that shows results of the 525th Sq's extra effort on "loco busting," including special bad-weather missions that month, while the other squadrons handled more of the rail cuts and direct support of ground forces; second chart: April 1945, fast

MONTHLY SUMMARY OF ACTIVITIES - DEC. 1944

	525		526		527		TOTAL FOR GP.	
	DEST.	DAM.	DEST.	DAM.	DEST.	DAM.	DEST.	DAM.
MOTOR TRUCKS	153	132	30	14	57	16	240	162
ARMORED VEHICLES			1	2			1	2
FREIGHT CARS	45	82	52	214	140	25	237	321
LOCOMOTIVES	72	39	6	4	2	3	80	46
RAIL CUTS		17		33		62		112
ROAD BLOCKS		3		6		4		13
ROAD BRIDGES	1	5	2	6	2	3	5	14
RAIL BRIDGES			3	10		3	3	13
GUN POSITIONS	20	24	8		14	8	42	32
SUPPLY DUMPS				1	1	3	1	4
BUILDINGS, C.P.S, ETC.		67	11	8	32	28	43	103
ENEMY A/C					4 (IN AIR)		4 (IN AIR)	

NOTE: These figures represent a careful estimation. Totals for the month may vary due to evaluation processes.

- 2 -

This is a fighter group claim summary for the month of December 1944, which is discussed in the text (86th Ftr Gp, World War II).

moving ground action that shows very similar operations and results by all three squadrons.

These actions were by one group of fighters. In April 1945, there were some 22 U.S. fighter groups in tactical air forces (9AF, ITAF), plus eight more joining them from the strategic air force (8AF), in doing fighter-bomber and strafing work in the ETO that month. Total claims of all come to massive figures for the theater. Certain claims in these illustrations obviously were from bombing—rail cuts, road blocks, most buildings—although many buildings were burned by strafing in Germany; but practically all that "moved or could move" was by strafing.

These particular summaries show almost no claims on tanks or armor, although just one month earlier the summary had numerous claims on armor in heavy ground fighting at the Siegfried Line. Many close support missions claimed no specific "kills" at all; there are only the FAC's comments, such as "All ordnance on target—good work." Summaries listed (by regulation) only certain categories of targets, not everything that may have been strafed.

Highly significant is that totally missing are claims of enemy personnel killed and wounded. Summaries seldom if ever listed figures on enemy casualties, although mission reports at times had estimates, such as "about 200

AMMUNITION

Rounds 50 Cal.	525 Sq.	526 Sq.	527 Sq.	Total for Group
Expended	551,745	509397	430,855	1,571,997

DAMAGE INFLICTED UPON THE ENEMY

Claims	Destroyed			Damaged			Total for Group	
	525	526	527	525	526	527	Dest.	Dam
M/T	237	249	62	373	329	138	548	860
Locos	37	18	15	56	84	25	70	165
RR Cars	95	99	81	250	521	159	275	930
HDV	0	74	742	0	3	11	140	14
Buildings	410	537	152	323	190	130	1099	643
Dumps	0	2	0	7	1	2	2	10
G/P's	48	3	2	43	23	14	53	80
Tanks	0	2	5	0	13	1	7	14
Rail Cuts	4	12	0				16	
Road Blocks	3	2	0				5	
A/C (Air)	2	6	3	1	5	4	11	10
A/C (Ground)	59	50	37	72	82	44	146	198

For the Commanding Officer:

PAUL E. VERESPUT,
Major, Air Corps,
Gp. Intelligence.

This is the same group's claim summary for the month of April 1945, which is discussed in the text (86th Ftr Gp, World War II).

troops killed in ditches along the road" and "over 400 enemy killed strafing a snowbound troop train." Even though casualty figures were not shown, it was recognized in each unit at the time that the largest claim figure for each summary period was that of enemy personnel.

On many missions that strafed troops in battle and in rear areas a great majority of all targets strafed had operators, crews, drivers, gunners, mechanics, passengers, guards, etc., in or near them. This was characteristic of almost all strafing targets, which were in-use, active equipment and positions. One small claim of two trucks burned in a German town killed 30 workers and maimed numerous others; a glance at these summaries with that in mind projects some huge figures of total enemy personnel killed and wounded by aircraft machine guns in the war.

As *The Army Air Forces in World War II*, vol. 3, notes, "The effect of strafing attacks directed against personnel was fearful, and the enemy estimated that only 20 percent of those wounded by air returned to duty as against 40 to 50 percent wounded in ground action." There is little doubt that cal-.50 API rounds were very destructive on humans as well as on a wide variety of equipment. Overall, strafers were highly prolific killers of enemy personnel, perhaps at the top of "gunfighters" in the war, with certain strafers having gunned down more of the enemy than most other warriors. This may not be a cherished memory by all strafers; nevertheless, evidence seems to make it fact. The great difference in fame for "dogfighters" and the lack of it for "strafers" surely rests in the award of air-to-air "kills" to individual pilots and crews but no award for ground "kills." Air "kills" were officially accumulated in records of individuals. Ground target "kills" were not.

Some numbers in air war history well known to the public are 5, 26, and 40. Five is the "score" of air kills to become an "ace," 26 is top American ace Rickenbacker's score in World War I, and 40 is top American ace Bong's score in World War II. (Some later bookkeeping gave Rickenbacker 24.33 or so, but it stays 26 in record and to the public.) By comparison, back in World War I a pilot killed "60 horses and a like number of men" on one mission. But no ready account is found of his total kill of "horses and men" in the war, or the totals of any other pilots. Strafers did not have total "scores" back then, nor in World War II, and they still don't.

In World War II there was no Army regulation or USAAF directives allowing award of accumulated credits to pilots and crews for enemy equipment and supplies destroyed or damaged and personnel killed or wounded by strafing. Theaters and air forces varied in policy: 8AF gave accumulated credit for aircraft destroyed on the ground; 12AF (and others) prohibited that. (Later all such credits of aircraft on the ground disappeared in published reports of official victories.)

Some literature has mentioned "locomotive aces," a designation assumed to be based on five or more "killed." Yet, most overseas air forces had no system of such "scores" or status. Some pilots kept unofficial accounts on their own. Some units may have too (but none I am aware of). My unit prohibited awarding individual accumulated "scores" of ground kills to pilots because it was nonregulation extra workload and likely a source of adverse effects on morale from the complexity of such scorekeeping.

Most strafing operations maintained integrity of four-plane flights or

Official credit for "victories" and accumulation of them in pilot records was given only for destruction of enemy aircraft in the air, not for anything on the ground or water, whether a plane, ship, big gun, or field kitchen. One exception was that 8AF gave credits for aircraft on the ground (79th Ftr Gp and U.S. Air Force).

elements of two. Often the lead pilot "killed" a loco, vehicle or gun position on his pass. Even so, following pilots normally fired on those kills too, which improved odds of killing operators, crews and passengers and insured targets were fully destroyed and could never be repaired. Also, against well-defended targets certain pilots of a flight often fired on the flak guns while others destroyed locos, aircraft, etc. Thus a "team" killed most targets, not individuals. It might follow that each team member could have been given a share of the team results. While that was not officially authorized or done, a look at some cases is quite revealing history about strafers.

On the first mission I led, eight pilots destroyed three freighters. Each pilot could have received credit for .38, or just over ⅓ of a ship destroyed. But no such entry went into our records. The only official record was the mission report: three ships destroyed. My squadron was known as top "locomotive busters." Just the 4-plane bad weather "Specials" destroyed 10 locos per mission. Leading all nine of them flown, my share would have been 22.5 locos destroyed on those missions alone (plus more than double that on regular missions), but no such entries went into my Form 5 (flying record) or 201 File (personnel records).

The 525th Sq destroyed or damaged 131 planes on the ground in Germany in April 1945. At that stage of the war we were low in pilot strength. Some 20 pilots achieved these results, about 6.5 kills per pilot. But no such breakdown of "victories" was awarded. The same pilots destroyed or damaged 630 vehicles that month, an average of 31.5 each, but no entries were recorded in individual records.

Missions with massive results can also be considered. Seven P-47s at Montelimar set up destruction of a German army resulting in 33 miles of solid wreckage and carnage in the Rhône Valley. Yet neither they nor pilots of following missions received any individual "scores" on the thousands of "kills" accomplished. Missions of the 27th and 86th groups set off huge explosions in rail yards, but the pilots got no official "scores" of either a fraction of a rail yard destroyed or of locos and rolling stock in it. If pilots and crews had received accumulated "scores" of ground targets destroyed, those figures would surely have brought more attention and fame to strafing and strafers. They would have had totals to compare with and to be "ranked"—among counterparts the same as air aces—stuff loved by the media and public. While that observation involves an "if," the clear fact remains there is no "if" about those individual "scores" themselves. They were achieved. The "if'" applies only to the matter of awarding and recording totals. Thus any practical means of showing at least a scope of what individual scores were seems significant. They are history, whether credited or not.

One case I can give a feel for is my own. With 208 missions flown, averaging over four strafing passes per mission, some 1,000 total (numerous cases of multiple targets and firing bursts per run) and part in several "mass" kills, my "score" of "kills" by "shares" could have been compiled in the ball park of 15 enemy planes on the ground, 45–50 locomotives, 150–200 vehicles, 20–25 flak guns and the same for watercraft, plus several tanks, other armor, artillery pieces, railroad wreckers, staff cars, motorcycles, plus considerably more as "damaged."

Of course each pilot and his combat experience was a case in itself—varying by theater, phase of the war, and more—which would require examination of results on each mission. But from the unit summaries with this chapter and missions covered throughout this book, it is apparent that all pilots flying full tours or more in intensive strafing operations had very substantial "scores" of "kills." One thing holds true for me and all other strafers in any system of computing "scores" by "shares." Regardless of what a pilot's "kills" came out to be , he actually had engaged in four or more times (up to 8–12) that amount of strafing results. To receive credit for one "kill," he had strafed in four or more "kills." Thus he has an actual record of vastly more bloody gunfighting than his "scores" would ever indicate. Of course, no system of "scores" would have given the full story of actual destruction he put on the enemy because of so many missions on which specific claims were not made—such as cargoes in trucks, trains and ships, FAC comments of "guns silenced," "enemy retreating," and similar notations—and especially claims on enemy personnel killed and wounded. Without total scores of ground target kills to be highlighted, news releases to hometowns on strafers often noted other accumulations: (ETO to *Waycross* [GA] *Journal Herald*, May 1945): "A Fighter Squadron Commander.... One of the European Theater's top fighter pilots or any other theater ... Major Colgan, despite his youth, has accumulated more combat missions, decorations, narrow escapes and friends [ground forces] than the vast majority of other American airmen in the present war. "

Missions and decorations were well understood by the public. So were narrow escapes in meaning, if not in how they occurred. Unit operational summaries showed the number of planes per squadron per month that returned from missions with battle damage. One set of those figures was a high of 54 damaged planes in 506 sorties flown, or 11 percent. Rates of damage and losses by sorties were important and useful to commanders and staffs in decisions on operations, repair and replacement needs, etc. But rates by sorties failed to tell the story of narrow escapes by pilots, neither all pilots on any one mission nor any one pilot on all the missions he flew.

A notable case of pilot experience with battle damage was Capt. Glenn Moore, 86th Gp, who had 18 planes shot up in 118 missions flown, or 15 percent. With great skill and will he flew all those planes back to friendly territory. My experience was some dozen cases of damaged planes, mainly by enemy auto-weapon fire, but also from targets exploding and a few collisions with obstacles—a cable, a gun barrel, and over four feet of wing cut off by a steel tower on a rail line in a mountain valley. I had very little damage from trees,

Many strafers flew battle-damaged planes back to friendly territory. Some landed normally, some the way pictured here, and many bailed out (86th Ftr Gp, World War II).

just from nips of treetops. I was wounded once, crash landed twice and forced to bail out once. Like Moore, I flew back to friendly lines each time before crash landing or bailing out. The extent of this being done by other pilots is reflected in the war album of the 525th Sq. Over twenty pilots became members of the Caterpillar Club (lives saved by an emergency parachute jump) when they flew planes home so severely damaged that flight control was insufficient for landing, either normal or crash, and the pilots were forced to parachute to safety. It should be noted that the pilot handbook on the P-47 recommended a belly landing, if practical, over a bailout because of the danger of the person bailing out hitting the aircraft tail in the latter. Further evidence on the extent of being shot down in low-altitude operations in World War II is found with German ground attacker Hans Rudel. He flew over 2,500 missions (according to his book) and was reported shot down 30 times. My experience jived quite closely to that, with 208 missions, shot down 3 times. Rudel's percent was .012, mine .014.

Flying terribly damaged aircraft home certainly was not limited to strafers.

Many close calls were never entered in records at all, such as this near crash into a German village (gun camera, 86th Ftr Gp, World War II).

Bombers were famed for "coming in on a wing and a prayer." Carrier pilots had special challenges. But all pilots faced the same ultimate danger. Some of the narrowest escapes were never known at the time, such as a bullet or shell that missed by only inches; and there were near disasters from weather, crowded skies, slick PSP strips, and more. Yet, strafers overall had a wider variety of things to escape from than pilots and aircrews in most other operations. One in particular created a unique demand in flying skill if escape was to be made and that was a massive target explosion.

Accompanying gun camera frames record such an explosion in the face of a pilot. From the instant of set-off in the lower frame, he is in a violent steep pull up to avoid the blast, but was being overtaken as the fireball and all in it shot up to over 10,000 feet high. He could not miss it. It was both too big and too fast, facts evidenced by an examination of the elapsed time covered by the three stills of movie footage shown. The overrun feature of the camera shows that the pilot quit firing immediately when the world under him exploded. Then that "overrun" recorded his attempt to avoid the still-rising blast (and also shows secondary explosions of munitions jetting out above the main blast), then the camera automatically shut off filming, which was just before he went into the mess. Camera "overrun" filmed only a second or two after trigger release, thus this entire sequence of frames was less than two seconds.

As this film exists, obviously the pilot and plane survived to return and land. But the film shows nothing about that part of the story. When engulfed by the explosion the plane was near vertical, slow speed; then it was blown violently to a yet more unusual attitude (almost surely with damage to the aircraft as well), hardly an ideal situation from which to undertake instrument flying at a low altitude. The unforgiving truth of strafing was always there: a slip in flying and the ground will get you, whether the enemy does or not.

Once engulfed by the explosion, the flying had to be on instruments, and odds were the attitude indicator had tumbled. Still the pilot had to keep flying, and above all prevent a steep dive, spiral, or spin if possible. Explosions did not have low ceilings or bottoms for a plane to break out of and possibly recover before hitting the ground. To survive, breakout had to be flight in some direction other than steeply down. A large explosion could stretch miles across as well as up. It took only a second or two to become trapped in one. It could take up to 20 or more seconds to get out of it. That is a long time to be grappling with instrument flying (likely only needle, ball, and hopefully airspeed available) amid violent turbulence, fireball, secondary explosions and debris.

The leader of the eight P-47s set off this explosion in southern Germany. The lead flight of four was engulfed. Even the second flight flying cover could not totally avoid it. Most planes suffered damage. For the lead flight that damage consisted of some holes and punctures, paint burned off, and windscreens and canopies seared or smoked over, cutting visibility from cockpits. Instrument flying was not over even after the planes broke clear. Fortunately their canopies could be opened. The second flight pilots joined on them, then led the first flight pilots (who could fly close formation looking out the side) back to base and down to formation landings, which were practical because our group was flying from a prior Luftwaffe jet test base with a wide concrete runway.

The public rightly viewed impressive scores of air kills in dogfights as feats of flying skill and cunning, including courage of course. Air-ground gunfighting, with no comparable scores of kills, simply did not create similar images for the public. But strafing certainly had its full share of flying skill, cunning and courage, much of it unsurpassed or unequaled anywhere. Overall, the story of strafing and strafers appears to be found in "what it was like" rather than in either individual credits or in command summaries. That seems to apply even for the ultimate numbers in the history—the lives lost.

Back in World War I the French pointed out the deadly nature of strafing in terms of life expectancy: 17 hours overall, 2½ of those spent strafing. Earlier chapters in this book have noted continuance of that bloody nature in World War II, such as two squadrons of the 79th Gp losing one-third of their pilots in two months. A further example of low-altitude losses is found in a USAF Project Warrior Study, *Air Interdiction*. Gen. John W. Vogt, USAF (Ret), relates that the fighter squadron (8AF) he commanded in World War II "lost

fifty percent of the squadron in fourteen days." That was in an all-out effort to provide direct support, and salvation if possible, to the beleaguered Allied forces in the Market Garden operation in Holland in September 1944.

Capt. Glenn Moore's book, *Dear Mom and Dad*, has a subchapter titled "Memorial Day," which describes services held by the 86th Fighter Group in Germany in May 1945 to honor personnel of the group who would never return home from World War II. His text includes these words:

> Following conclusion of the service, I moved into the operations shack to wait for the return of the fly-over pilots and I began to analyze the casualty list in the program. We had helped compile the information for the 525th Squadron and I wanted to examine the file. The 525th had forty-one names on their list of which thirty-nine were pilots.... Captain Blackwell [Intel officer] had helped Group Headquarters prepare the program for the service and I wrote on my program some of the information he had tabulated. A total of 154 pilots had flown one or more combat missions with the 525th Squadron before VE Day. The thirty-nine pilots we honored that Memorial Day represented a loss ratio of one out of four or twenty-five percent. I had thought the casualty rate was much higher.

In recent years I made similar computations from records of several other squadrons in fighter-bomber work in the ETO and MTO—heavy on strafing, high-threat targets, tough gunfighting. The KIA rates (those killed in combat and those carried MIA and never accounted for) were from 19 to 27 percent, averaging a fraction under 25 percent. Such a figure of "killed-in-action" is very grim history in itself. Yet, in the minds of pilots back at the time, figures were not the full story on losses. A key aspect of that is found in Capt. Moore's words: "I had thought the casualty rate was much higher [than 25 percent]."

Pilots while in combat did not know an exact KIA rate in their unit. Many losses were carried MIA until their actual fate was determined later. What pilots mainly went by was their own daily observation (and feelings) of losses among pilots with whom they had joined the unit, whether in original complement or as replacements later. I have asked a number of veteran fighter-bomber pilots of World War II what they thought the pilot loss rate was in their units while they were in combat. In every case, as with Capt. Moore, their answers were much greater than 25 percent. In many cases that was for such sound reasons as "Eight of us joined the squadron together; four were shot down the first month."

Other factors supported such beliefs. All units had pilots and crews shot down in enemy territory who survived, and then evaded or escaped capture or became POWs. But strafing was such low-altitude work that when a pilot was

Opposite: The pilot's strafing sets off this huge ammo/munitions explosion, blanking out his world ahead with fireball, smoke, flying debris and further exploding ammo. *Bottom:* The explosion erupts, instantly filling the camera's field of view. *Center:* The pilot is in a violent pullup trying to avoid it. *Top:* It is overtaking him; he can't stay out of it (gun camera, 86th Ftr Gp, World War II).

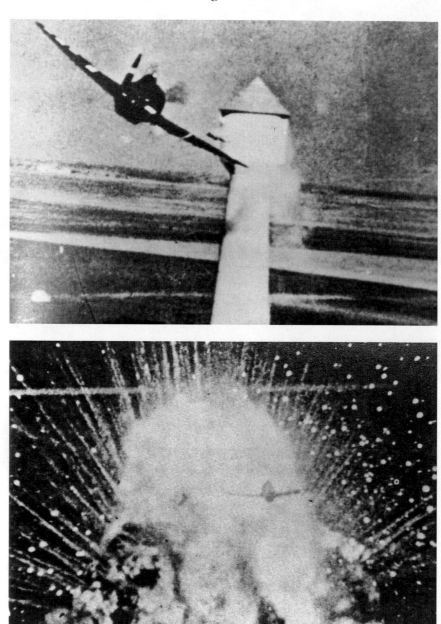

Two of strafing's most publicized still photographs from World War II. A P-47 pilot takes on German gunners in a gunfight with a flak tower, and a P-47 pilot sets off another massive target explosion (U.S. Air Force).

Another look at one of strafing's many millions of unpublicized frames. Shown here is the destruction of a locomotive in clouds of steam by concentrated "on target" shooting, a core staple in the story of strafers (gun camera, 86th Ftr Gp, World War II).

hit by enemy fire or collided with obstruction—and was still physically able to bail out—often he was unable to gain sufficient altitude for his parachute to open. His only option then was to stay in the plane even if it was out of control or rough terrain was the only place for a crash landing. Many strafers were killed because they never had the chance for successful bailout and possible survival via evasion or as a POW. Numerous strafers who did evade and escape or were POWs reached that status only because they lived through crashes into the ground or obstructions, some that were beyond belief that survival was possible.

Pilots were well aware prior to each mission that with strafing the odds were greater of being "hit" by flak, especially the deadly auto-weapon ground fire, or "flying into something" than on most other missions. They also knew that when that happened the odds of survival were less than on most other missions. That combination was a formula for such a high actual KIA rate and for pilot estimates of an even higher rate, and it has played strongly in strafing's historical record and reputation as air war's bloodiest gunfighting. Still, even while full well knowing that, pilots and crews worldwide pressed on in relentless, aggressive strafing of the enemy, a huge percentage of it undertaken on their own decision and initiative, their own doing, being "their own generals."

They took aircraft guns and cannon into point-blank range of the enemy and his defenses on land and sea in every theater, and generalshipped the time-of-fire of those guns and cannon to do so many different things in so many times and places. Those actions were often over and above use of other munitions, often when no other attack would do the job, often where no other ordnance was at hand, and often simply as the best "killer" anyway. It often was acknowledgment that strafing came out as the most used, most versatile, most paralyzing, and most telling form of direct "killing" hurt from the air on enemy combat and supporting forces in the war.

There has been no extensive published history, study or evaluation on strafing in World War II such as *The Strategic Bombing Survey*. Thus, the above words on the role of strafing and strafers in the war are not taken from such references or archives and files; they come instead from the low-altitude skies around the world and are an ultimate story of duty, devotion, valor, and sacrifice.

· 13 ·

Those Who Followed

The Korean War,
the Vietnam War, and Beyond

After World War II victory in Europe, when I arrived back in my hometown from Germany in October 1945, I was certainly grateful for and honored by the welcome I received. Two items from my combat were of top interest to friends, neighbors, and news people. Those were my "scores": first, me versus FW 190s and Me 109s in dogfights over Anzio (my 2 kills, 1 probable, 1 damage), which were well publicized at the time; and second, my number of missions (208), which were recognized as three normal tours. Strafing received less interest and questions, except when talking with German POWs working in the officers' club at the deactivating local Army air field. The POWs linked a P-47 pilot to JABO and "strafer."

My first assignment was to Peterson Field, Colorado, in P-47Ns, the long-range version used in the Pacific. Flying over the Rockies let me compare rail lines there with those of the Brenner Pass; but I had no urge to make strafing dry runs on trains, to again make 10–12 G pullouts skimming rocks or to fly into cables. This was a quick peacetime reminder that to duplicate the flying of strafing in training was not practical or sensible. However, "peacetime" was not the theme for very long. The world entered the early stages of the Cold War, which locked the two superpowers, the U.S.A. and the U.S.S.R., in a struggle over nuclear war for half a century, with accompanying clashes of Free World versus Communist goals in some "limited" but very real shooting and killing wars.

This brought forth a world of new nomenclature and terminology over World War II. Some came from the establishment of the Department of Defense atop our service departments. The Army Air Forces/Air Corps became the United States Air Force (USAF) on 18 September 1947. World War II "Groups" became "Wings," but Groups still existed under Wings (and some World War II vets were never clear thereafter on USAAF Groups versus USAF Wings). Aircraft designations changed, such as "P" for pursuit to "F" for fighter. Major "Air Commands" were created over the "numbered air forces" and included Strategic (SAC), Tactical (TAC), Air Defense (ADC), and U.S. Air Forces in Europe (USAFE) and Pacific Air Forces (PACAF).

At Turner Air Force Base in Georgia, we of the 31st Fighter Wing, flying F-51s in 1947 and 1948, (TAC then, later SAC) under a new USAF had no change in mission from World War II. A fighter unit mission still called for both air-to-air and air-to-ground combat. In the 309th Sq, with a mixture of air aces such as Bob Stevens and strafers such as me, our gunnery scores followed no pattern of aces best in aerial and strafers best in ground. Some strafers had top scores in aerial and some aces top score in ground. Firing six "50s" with a K-14 lead computing gun sight was loved by all for aerial; but ground was still fired with fixed "pipper."

My experience leading the wing firepower demonstration team opened up a special part of strafing history to me. These were "live fire" munitions events before many spectators, military and civilian, on both Air Force ranges and Army reservations, where air-to-ground gunfire could be the star. Its great accuracy and dependability allowed it to be shown safely, actually destroying targets, close enough to spectators and maneuver participants for striking effects

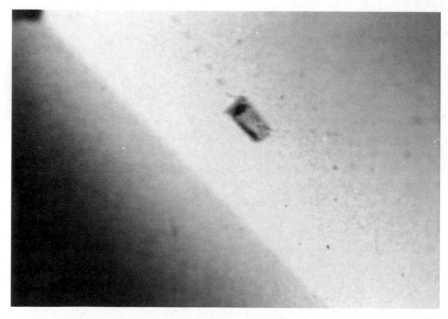

Fighter pilots continued to train in both aerial and ground gunnery. Here, a pilot is pulling off of a pass on an aerial gunnery towed banner target (gun camera, 31st Ftr Wg).

in view, sound and feel; it was not practical or safe to show comparatively close air-to-air "kills" or high explosive bombing. Nor did aircraft guns require the safe corridors of approach and departure (avoiding over-fly of populated areas and spectators and troops) demanded by externally carried bombs and napalm. Thus guns could be used in far more locations and maneuver situations than other live munitions.

Over the years, events of air-to-ground automatic-weapon fire, representing combat strafing, have been viewed by millions, both live on the scene and via film and video, forming its own chapter in history. That gunfire in demonstrations and maneuvers was made possible by the same great utility as in combat; and it has played a distinct part in military education, training, readiness, and public affairs. Yet, as is the case in combat gun camera film, while these events have been eagerly viewed, they have never translated into wide media and public recognition of strafing's role in war or the story of pilots and crews.

That also seems to be true for another noncombat part in the history of strafing. One of my assignments (1949–50) as a regular USAF officer with the Oklahoma Air National Guard highlights this. While I was there the 125th Fighter Squadron, Tulsa—commander, Lt. Col. Joe Turner; ops officer, Maj. Staryl Austin—won the Spaatz Trophy, an award of "top Air Guard squadron." Criteria for judging this high honor covered major areas of unit flying and ground operations, with gunnery scores being definite factors.

In squadron armament was Lt. Bob Greninger, who following recall to active duty in 1950 and completed a career as one of the USAF's top experts in fighter armament. He held assignments from fighter wings and air divisions to requirements for new armaments at TAC. A real clue to his expertise is that he invariably was given the job of preparing aircraft for gunnery qualifications, exercises, readiness inspections, etc., and especially for gunnery team meets, including the Air Force Gunnery Meet at Nellis AFB, Nevada. This was high impact, high stakes stuff, and a chapter of its own in the history.

An example of gunnery scores in the 125th at Tulsa while Bob Greninger was there is pilot Jim Ayers' 368 hits out of 400 rounds fired, or 92 percent, and that on an undersized ground target of 6 by 6 feet instead of the standard 10 by 10 feet. Ayers said the secret was "close in and short bursts." All "top guns" would concur with that as being part of "flying the plane right"; good guns and precise bore sighting also contribute to high scores.

Certainly no story of strafing is complete without due attention to guns and bore sight and those who handle them. I asked Bob's help here, and am most grateful to him for the following material of great value he provided and to his wife, Patty, for agreeing to its use. His comments follow:

> You probably remember that we bore sighted the F-51 aircraft of the 125th Fighter Squadron, Oklahoma ANG (Air National Guard), Tulsa, in the north door of the hangar. We bore sighted at 1,000 feet, for airspeed of 274 M.P.H.,

F-51 of Oklahoma ANG. Expert bore sighting and top scores were priority goals in units as gunnery competitions and "meets" became inherent in the history.

placed wing jacks under each wing and put digging bar through the tail, a hole just in front of the horizontal stabilizer. We made a harness and connected it to a hoist in the ceiling at the hangar door. We then placed sand bags on the horizontal stabilizer to prevent the aircraft from tilting over on its nose. Leveling lugs in the wheel well were used for wing leveling. With the leveling lugs in the cockpit just under the canopy, right side, using a straight edge and a protractor or caliper, you adjust the aircraft to the desired angle of attack. This scale is taken from the tech order as to speed and load factor. A gun sight line level indicator is used to get the target up on a level line with the sight image.

This is a device that hangs over the sight glass and levels the line of sight. The aircraft is aligned by the "plumb bobs"—two screws under the fuselage, one forward and one near the tail provide a fastener for the strings. I hang the weights in cans of heavy oil to prevent the "bobs" from swaying in the breeze or wind.

Now you sight down the strings, moving either the aircraft or the target left or right until they are aligned. Now you are wondering about the parallax between the gun line and sight line? Well, if you close the parallax at 1,000 feet this provides for bullet drop. Your impact at 900/1,000 feet is small and your gyro computing sight will compensate for it.

As you remember at Tulsa we used a yellow jeep wheel mounted on a crane boom as target. We raised it and moved it any direction necessary. Now, we have the aircraft aligned with the sight and are ready to adjust the guns. The gun bays are opened, 50-Caliber guns charged open. Each gun is bore sighted on the yellow jeep wheel. A bore sight mirror is placed in the breech, sight through the bore. By looking down the barrel you see three round images: the breech, muzzle and target. The rear gun mounts are adjustable. Carefully crank the guns up, down, left or right until all are aligned. This method is almost as good as firing-in on a bore sight range/butt.

On a firing range/butt you find that guns have a cycle pattern, but usually the dry method is very close. Some gun patterns can be closed down to a tighter pattern by closing the headspace a click. But tight headspace may cause the gun to stop, freeze when hot. Consequently, keep a loose gun and change gun mounts and/or guns to tighten pattern. This is done in gunnery teams, especially with your best gunner. On a bore sight range/butt you fire 10 round bursts to develop firing patterns of each gun.

Pilots were well aware of, and had full appreciation for, the role that bore sighting played in all shooting. This showed every time they pulled the trigger. Obviously the tasks of gun maintenance and ammo loading were essential too. If possibly the latter seems rather mundane, some pilot experiences might dispel that.

In occupation duties in Germany after the war, my group's mission required we have loaded guns at all times and certainly for special ones, such as escort of President Truman's plane to Potsdam. This was done during a mass turnover of wartime personnel. With shortages, plus training replacements including infantry transfers, pilots often loaded their own guns. This had been done at times in the war too.

One P-47N pilot, Ed Hodges, related one case from the Pacific in the *Jug Letter*. With his group on Saipan, awaiting movement to Ie Sima (off Okinawa), some proficiency missions were ordered against the Japanese on bypassed islands. The group's armorers had already moved out. Pilots had to load the guns, and the task of putting 250 rounds in eight guns per plane had not been previously realized. After removal from ammo boxes, each round was checked with a "go-no go" gage to insure no "short" or "long" rounds were loaded (which could jam a gun). Relinking 50 and 100 segments to make a 250 linked load was done before carefully folding it into the ammo bay of each gun, then the top round was clamped into the gun feed, and finally the gun was charged to put that round into firing position. Ed noted that it took him all afternoon to arm his plane and that such a workout was a real lesson in appreciation of your ground crew. It is hoped these bits on the ground crews' part to keep aircraft ready for gunnery—and for combat—will give wider appreciation and offer a salute to those "who kept them flying" in all wars.

By the late 1940s jet fighters had replaced propeller types in most all USAF units and many ANG units. A few comments on jet capabilities are noted here for better understanding of following combat flying and fighting. The first production fighters of the jet age were, in chronological order, the F-80, F-84 and F-86. Their major features included increased speeds of some 600 mph or more over the 400 plus of World War II piston-engine types. The jets were extremely stable, with ease of flight control trim and no engine torque. Pilot downward visibility was vastly improved, and jets had a knack for "slipping up" on people on the ground better than propeller planes did.

Checking and linking Cal-.50 API ammo prior to loading in aircraft. Note the pile of empty ammo cans in the truck (79th Ftr Gp, World War II).

Among new considerations in operating procedures was the jet's high fuel consumption at low altitude. Some early models were slow in engine acceleration, required pilot anticipation, and were critical in takeoff distance, especially at high field elevations or hot weather. Much new terminology was involved. The jets used kerosene for fuel, designated JP-1 (and later as -4, -5, and -8) instead of gasoline. The power of a jet engine was rated in "thrust," not horsepower. With jets came use of nautical miles for distances and knots for speeds. Ejection seats brought terms of "squeeze out" or "punch out" in place of "bailout."

These early jets had six .50-caliber machine guns. They were grouped in the nose of the F-80 and F-86. The F-84 had four in the nose and one in each wing root. Common ammo loads were 300 rounds per gun. At first glance this may seem no more, or even less, firepower than World War II fighters. But the main gun of this era was the M3 version of the Browning "50," with rate of fire increased to 1,200 rounds per minute per gun versus the 800 of earlier guns. Six M3 guns put out 7,200 rounds per minute, 120 rounds per second impact on target, while it would take nine World War II M2 guns to equal that impact power. Thus this was an increase in firepower. Remembering that "time of fire" is what a pilot employs in strafing, these jets had some 15 seconds of fire, continuing the trend from World War I through World War II of suc-

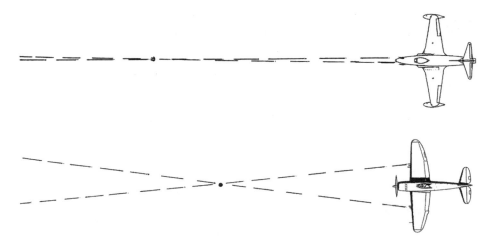

Comparison of bore sight patterns of wing gun P-47 and nose gun F-80 jet. Lower: P-47 at 750 feet. Upper: F-80 at 1,000 feet.

ceeding fighters with greater kill power at some reduction in time of fire. With that was recognition of the need for accuracy on targets and not to squander any of the shortened time of fire.

Gunnery, and subsequent combat, involved some differences in pilot and armorrer challenges, especially so in units changing from wing-gun planes to nose-gun jets. Gun bore sight remained essential, and was usually done for convergence range of 1,000–1,200 feet in the jets. However, the specific distance became a less severe and complicating factor for the pilot in varying combat conditions. The converging fire of close together nose guns (and even the wing root guns of the F-84) was an extremely small angle compared to that of wide apart wing guns. Besides an extended bore sight point, these jets had a greater distance beyond that point in which the bullet pattern remained compact. This, combined with the jet's good stability during changes in engine thrust and speeds, allowed the pilot to shoot further out, going faster, without comparable loss in accuracy and effectiveness, as occurred with wing gun prop fighters.

Gun sights were factors too. From World War II on, fighters had gyroscopic computing sights such as the K-14 and K-18, initially with manual ranging. Electronic sights such as the A-1C and A-4 were introduced in some models of the F-84 and F-86, some adding radar ranging. For ground gunnery and strafing, pilots had new options in use of sight functions. They could use sight "ranging" and aim with the "pipper" in compute mode or they still might cage the sight and shoot with "fixed pipper" of old, which had merit in certain situations of weather and terrain.

Gunnery scores of numerous pilots improved in jets (some said "soared"). Combat veterans could foresee some relief from the "point-blank" range needed

Author in F-84E, 136th Fighter Wing, Korea. Six Cal-.50 "M3" guns gave slightly more impact power than eight "M2" guns of World War II.

in much World War II strafing. Yet, as close in as practical gave the pilot better view and ability to precisely aim on specific hard spots on targets such as engine louvers of tanks; close-in hit hard too. Thus "close-in" was not past history. Greatly improved "farther out" was a distinct advantage over-and-above it, giving yet greater capability and flexibility.

At the same time, the public heard predictions from some sources that jets would be no good for strafing because their great speed spread bullets too far apart on the ground. This was obviously ridiculous to fighter pilots. We did not have to spread bullets at all unless desired, and if so we could control how much. Yet we realized the public, just as before the war, probably viewed strafing as spraying, and likely would believe that jets spread bullets too far apart. One pilot's wife asked if that was a fact. He told her it's the same as delivering newspapers. You toss them on driveways OK from a four cylinder car. But a faster eight cylinder car will spread them too far apart. She said, "With the paper boy we have, that could happen." He said, "You've got the picture." Regardless of such ill predictions before the public on jet fighters and strafing, most pilots never feared spreading bullets too far.

These early jet fighters underwent numerous and rapid improvements of various modifications, greater engine thrust, and updated systems. For example, early F-84Bs, Cs and Ds failed to meet all requirements and had safety concerns.

But by 1950 the F-84E, overcoming those problems, was in production followed shortly by the F-84G, which became one of the most successful and notable planes in USAF history. In 1950 jet fighter units were pressing on at being fully combat ready, with gunnery receiving much attention in that aspect, and these jets produced the best results ever.

On Sunday, June 25, 1950, North Korea invaded South Korea. The main attack was by ground forces north of Seoul. Yak fighters strafed both Kimpo and Seoul airfields, destroying several Republic of South Korea (ROC) aircraft and an American USAF C-54. Thus the first shots fired on U.S. forces in this war were strafing, just as in World War II. However, other than that, the strafing action of early days in Korea was not similar to that of Pearl Harbor and the Philippines in 1941. Enemy planes did attempt a few more strafing attacks in following days. One on Suwon destroyed several U.S. planes, but other attackers were largely turned back or shot down by our F-82s and F-80s. Instead of enemy strafing being a key element in ruling the skies, as in 1941, this time the enemy attack did result in another strafing victory. But it was a victory in reverse, one by American pilots and crews on North Korean forces and one of the greatest in history.

That history is found in various references, including *The United States Air Force in Korea, 1950–1953*, from the Office of Air Force History. A small force of U.S. aircraft, mainly the 8th Fighter Wing F-80s, a squadron of F-82s, plus one B-26 (Douglas), took on initial tasks of covering evacuation of Americans from Korea, closely followed by orders to attack enemy ground forces south of the 38th parallel and then into North Korea as a rapid build up of air capability started. This included F-80s of the 35th and 49th wings, B-26s of the 3rd Wing (with "hard nose" versions, 14 Cal-.50 forward firing machine guns) all F-82s and F-51s in theater, plus some 150 of the latter from the States, a major B-29 bombing effort, and Navy and Marine units, along with increased cargo, recce, FAC and support capabilities.

A few examples of early combat action include missions of F-80s that tore into concentrations of tanks, vehicles, artillery and troops north of Seoul, leaving fires visible for 50 miles; B-26s, F-82s and F-80s in close support action (initially with improvised FAC contact on the ground, later with TACP and airborne T-6 "Mosquito" controllers) that scored large kills of vehicles and troops; B-26s that destroyed 25 enemy aircraft on the ground in North Korea, and also hit trains moving south and; U.S. pilots and crews that made mass kills on tanks, vehicles and troops jammed up attempting to cross Han bridges.

As the North Korean Peoples' Army (NKPA) moved south with strong attacks on our forces who were courageously holding the shrinking Pusan Perimeter, a strong effort on close support produced results such as 117 enemy trucks and 34 tanks destroyed, with many NKPA troops killed in front of the 24th Division. Major Louis Seville, with a mission of F-51s, after bombing their target, led strafing attacks on the enemy. His plane hit by enemy fire, he

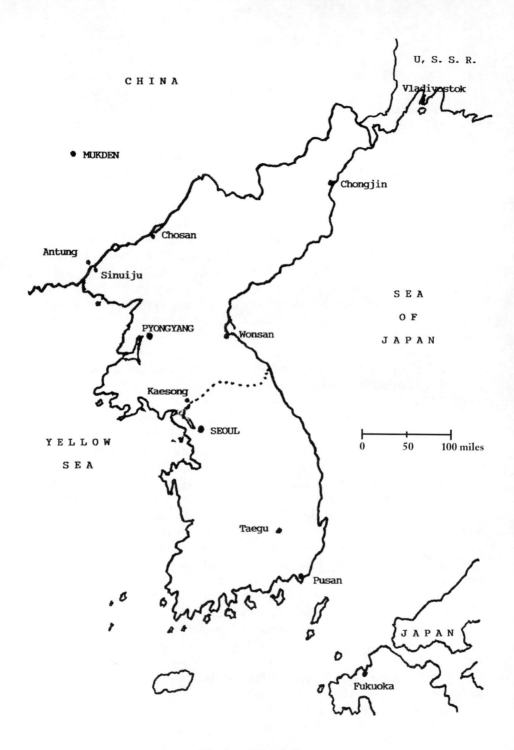

North and South Korea.

pressed on into yet another pass, was further hit and his plane crashed into the enemy concentration. He was awarded the Medal of Honor.

A captured NKPA soldier said the destruction and casualties from American air attacks had great effect on his division's morale and effectiveness, as they had to stop combat and rebuild. A report from the U.S. 2nd Division confirmed destruction of 1,500 hostile soldiers and their equipment by air support. Interdiction to prevent enemy reinforcement was pressed too, and strafers historically were the champion killers of enemy "movers."

These are only scant tokens of the total air actions involved. Statements by ground force commanders may better reflect the bigger picture. In early September 1950 Maj. Gen. William B. Kean, commander of the 25th Division told newsmen "The close air support strikes rendered by the Fifth Air Force again saved this Division as they have many times before." After the end of the Pusan crisis on 12 September, with the perimeter saved, Lt. Gen. Walton H. Walker, commander of the U.S. Eighth Army in Korea, made a statement that is found in numerous references: "I will gladly lay my cards right out on the table and state that had it not been for the air support we received from the Fifth Air Force we would not have been able to stay in Korea."

Strafing is specifically noted in some of the above reports along with the existing situation of units, planes and operating conditions. In the early stages the F-80s were the bulk of U.S. fighter capability and were credited with flying 70 percent of the sorties and as being responsible for 85 percent of enemy losses in the earliest days. What isn't spelled out is that overwhelmingly their aircraft guns were the main weapons available—another case where strafing was there when little else was, and in fact saved the day, as it had before in the world wars. Enemy attempts to base aircraft inside North Korea resulted in immediate U.S. air attack, mostly by strafing.

Increased outlook for victory in this war came with the Inchon landing and rapid advance north of our troops all the way to the Chinese border, but reversed to grave concern as Chinese forces entered the war with a massive attack on 26 November. The valiant fight of vastly outnumbered U.S. forces during withdrawal in the notoriously cold winter in "Frozen Chosen" (the troops' term for Korea) is among the greatest chapters of duty and courage in military history. The following are a few accounts of strafing among many during that ordeal (from *The United States Air Force in Korea*).

On 29 November at 0130 hours the U.S. 25th Division was so hard pressed by enemy assault that air support was requested even though it would be very close to friendly troops at night—not normal operating procedure at all. The following is an account of the response: "[L]ight bombers (B-26s) arrived within thirty minutes and poured round after round at machine-gun fire into targets within fifty yards of friendly positions identified to the bombers by white phosphorous smoke shells fired by infantry mortars.... The surprise and supreme accuracy of the fire had a marked effect on the Chinese for it came

Closely grouped guns in the nose of the F-80 (this one at the U.S. Air Force Armament Museum) played a major strafing role early on.

at the crisis of the fight when it seemed doubtful ... that any part of the company could survive."

    After performing the rear-guard mission for the U.S. Eighth Army withdrawal, the 2nd Division started to move back, only to find a strong enemy force behind them and set up to put murderous fire on the Americans as they withdrew through a narrow gap known "'The Pass." Their report of air support reveals that "U.S. fighter-bombers flew so low and close in the pass attacking the Chinese that napalm spilled down off the cliffs onto the road; rock fragments chipped off by .50-caliber bullets flew about everywhere; several friendly personnel sustained concussions from rocket blasts; but no friendly troops were known to have been killed by the air strikes." The division commander reported that they might not have ever weathered the enemy fire in the pass without air support.

    One mission of F-51s bombed and strafed enemy positions 80 yards in front of friendly lines. In addition to the destruction and casualties achieved, over 100 of the enemy surrendered, saying they had taken enough of U.S. air attacks and strafing.

    Chinese efforts to support combat units met with disastrous results. One report cites over 30,000 troops and huge amounts of equipment lost in less than two weeks. Our attacks, especially time of fire of guns, made enemy movement too costly and slowed the Chinese advance. History records that the Chinese did retake Seoul and a portion of the south again, followed by a UN drive back north with heavy fighting that set battle lines in late June 1951 roughly along the 38th parallel, where they would generally stay through the war, in active strong fighting, not just static holding.

By July 1951 the order of battle of U.S. aircraft had been changed and continued to be changed substantially. For fighters and fighter-bombers, some units that had previously switched from early F-80s to F-51s in initial actions were reequipped with F-80Cs. USAF F-84s and F-86s as well as latest U.S. Navy and Marine aircraft had entered the war, rapidly building in numbers. Almost all were based in South Korea, along with FAC, recce, rescue, and Marine units.

Operational plans and procedures saw developments too. For armed-recce, main rails and routes were covered by fighter-bombers by day and B-26s operating with and without C-47 flare ships at night, also Navy and Marine fighter and bombers with C-47s operated at night. Corsairs and F-51s were put over assigned zones behind enemy lines during daylight hours to "grub out" small movements and hiding vehicles. RF-51s worked in teams with F-80s and F-84s. Use of T-6 and ground FACs became standard operating procedure (SOP) for close air support.

Fifth Air Force claims on enemy vehicles rose from 599 destroyed and 683 damaged in January 1951 to 1,366 destroyed and 812 damaged in February 1951; and then the numbers went to 2,261 destroyed, 1,326 damaged in March 1951. At the heart of these results was armed-recce and at the heart of armed-recce had always been strafing—the shudder of the guns and the pilots and crews.

Amid high-level agreement that air power had saved South Korea, General Otto P. Weyland, commander of the Far East Air Forces, made a statement specifically about the early and critical days of the war: "I am afraid that too little attention was given at the time to what happened to the enemy as a result of air attacks. It was not until our army had broken out of the Pusan perimeter that its leaders became aware of the magnitude of the air destruction." As I recall, that was much the case for the news media at the time too. Had the war gone on as mainly a ground force struggle with air support, perhaps greater attention and publicity would have evolved on that destruction and the pilots and crews who did it; and perhaps there would have been more recognition of strafing and the strafers' part in it. But that was not to be.

The Chinese Air Force made a serious challenge for air superiority, mainly with MIG-15 jet fighters. While engagements with U.S. F-80s, F-84s and B-29s were also involved, the U.S. F-86 jet fighters took on the role of maintaining control of the air. The air battles of Saber versus MIG became legend, among the most gloried in the history of air combat. News of dogfights, victories, aces, and "MIG Alley" dominated news coverage of air operations in the Korean War from then on. Little publicity was given to air support of ground forces or to strafing and strafers.

"Firing-in" the guns of an F-84 at night, a portrait of the type of gunfire so key in the airpower that ground commanders say "saved the day" in Korea (U.S. Air Force).

As I departed for duty in Korea in October 1951, that lack of news attention to fighter-bombers was not really different than it had been in World War II. However, much about my trip back to war *was* different. Back during World War II I said good-bye to a young bride at a train station full of others in uniform on the way to war too. This time it was good-bye to her and two young children at an air terminal with no military uniforms or other evidence of a war showing anywhere. In Tokyo, personnel officers at Far East Air Force (FEAF) headquarters suggested my experience in World War II warranted a change from "F-84" shipment to "F-86"; but they added that the need for unit commanders in F-84 units was paramount, and they also made a point not heard in public back home that "this is a fighter-bomber war." They and others at the headquarters and the officers club freely used another expression not publicized back home: "those poor bastards flying F-84s." However, the reason behind that was known to me and other pilots—all blood and guts without any glory.

I joined the 136th Fighter-Bomber Wing, located at K-2, Taegu, Korea, flying F84Es. It was the first Air National Guard combat unit to see action in war. From Texas, its squadrons were the 111th, Houston; 182nd, San Antonio; and 154th, Little Rock, Arkansas. I had fired gunnery in the F-84, including a recent two weeks camp, which was all with two guns loaded. Korea was my first shooting of all six guns in a jet. It added one more feel of the "shudder of the guns" for me. With four guns in the forward fuselage quite close to the pilot, there was a more direct transfer of "shudder" than with wing guns. While the pressurized cockpit kept out much of the smoke and smell of earlier nose guns, the pilot's view through the gun sight just above and behind the firing guns saw more muzzle blast than from wing guns.

As the original Guard personnel completed tours, I took command of the 111th Squadron from Lt. Col. Ira Susskey. In the winter of 1951–52 combat operations of the 136th were primarily "rail cutting" with high explosive bombs, dive-bombing. That was on the main rail lines from the Chinese border south to Pyongyang, under MIG Alley. From Taegu, most of these were long range missions (made possibly by the excellent range of the F-84E) invariably in weather with severe jet stream winds, calling for precise letdowns in target area and on critical tight approach back at K-2 amid mountains. They were flown as group missions, two or three squadrons participating, usually 16 to 24 aircraft launched to attack while F-86s were airborne as cover.

General flying conditions in Korea played a major role in combat mission planning and in pilot airborne decisions, which some factual lore can explain. One F-86 pilot called the control tower that he had run out of fuel and needed to make a flame-out landing. The tower replied, "Roger, you are cleared to land—as number three in the flame out pattern." Cold hard facts made a clear point. A flight of Marine jets forced to land at K-2 in bad weather failed to stay high enough in the teardrop pattern feeding into a narrow final approach gap in mountains. The entire flight crashed into the mountainside; there were no survivors.

My flying was primarily as group lead of these large missions: get the group to the target and cut rails, without flying into mountains or across the Chinese border while coping with enemy ground fire and at times MIG attacks, and then get them back to and down on home base. Strafing was not planned or expected on these missions, but we did some anyway in a few cases.

Leading one such mission to MIG Alley, as I pulled off the rail line target I spotted two Chinese Army tanks headed south on a nearby road. The leader of the second flight, who was the designated alternate mission leader, was ordered to complete the attack and take the mission out to sea on the planned normal withdrawal. I took just the lead flight of four aircraft back around for a quick strafing pass on the tanks, then rejoined as the rear flight of the mission. This kept mission integrity at full strength in case we were jumped by MIGs, and since the lead flight uses less fuel en route to target, our fuel state on return was no lower than that of a normal tail-end flight. We reported two heavy tanks strafed, both hit with solid bursts, but no specific claims. Headquarters was surprised and concerned at this strafing while on a large mission just below the Chinese border. It remained a rare case, not standard procedure by any means.

Harsh weather of "Frozen Chosen" had an effect on tactics and in-flight decisions.

The photos from my gun camera film on that mission were of very poor quality, but did verify several things. It was not unusual for F-84Es and Korean weather to produce such useable but sad pictures. The shooting is farther out than most World War II pinpoint strafing. This started over 2,000 feet out and allowed us to put a good burst into one tank then hit the other one hard on a single pass. Each burst shows about as compact on target as the other. Our speed was around 400 knots, but faster or slower would not have had any great effect on the accuracy. All of this is characteristic of jet fighter strafing capability, especially in the extremely stable F-84. But very precise aim and aircraft control was demanded for accuracy at greater distances, thus there was no relief at all from "flying the aircraft right" in a jet.

While this type of add-on strafing was rare on these particular missions, there was a lot of it done in other ways. Flak suppression flights were a regular part of our rail cutting. They involved strafing and airburst HE (high explosive) and frag bombs. A case of downed airman triggered rescue operations and strafing support. Any time the enemy attempted to base aircraft within North Korea, we could expect orders to strafe there.

On a mission against rails in central North Korea, we had an F-84 pilot shot down just after the 8th Wing had an F-80 pilot downed in the same area. Lead flights of both missions flew cover in intense ground fire until a mission

Pilot's view through an F-84 gun sight. This was at high altitude en route to a target over North Korea. Note the solid cloud cover, which was usually worse than this almost all winter.

of F-51s arrived to assume that role. In radio contact with both pilots, the F-51s repeatedly strafed and slaughtered numerous advancing enemy troops as they were called out by the downed pilots. Rescue "choppers" encountered icing, plus hits from ground fire. Still the F-51s kept strafing while losing three aircraft. Next morning I led a mission back to that area to resume rescue attempts, but we had no contact with downed pilots and received no ground fire. Many other rescue efforts in Korea had more successful endings, but none anywhere else were with greater valor.

In the spring of 1952, we began flying more varied missions. Some were large efforts on military installations, storage facilities, and even factories. In addition to the primary bombing, we strafed heavily, both in dive-bomb runs and on follow up passes. We flew many smaller missions of four- or eight-ships, sometimes working with airborne target finders, but also armed recce on our own for targets of opportunity. In general this was flown similar to World War II but a bit faster and higher; in much of North Korea at 3,000 feet or more above a route, a fight missed mountain ridges by only a few feet. Live targets, "movers" and "hiders," were found and immediately pounced on, but much "grubbing" also was involved in looking for targets. On rail lines, when train targets were lacking I looked for rail work crews and equipment and people at adjacent support and warehouse facilities. We did well in slipping

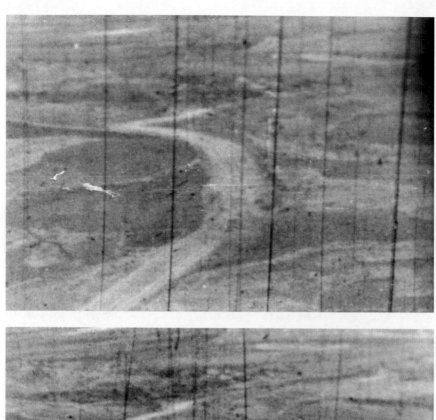

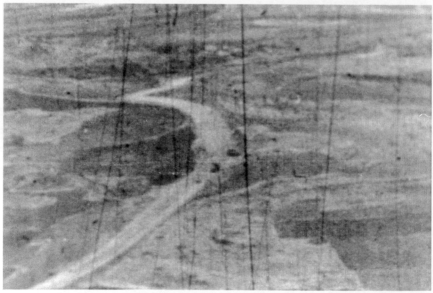

Vague photograph, but sharp shooting. *Bottom:* The two dark blobs on the road are two heavy "movers." *Top:* Our firing is farther out in this pass than most World War II pinpoint shooting, and puts bursts on both targets in one pass. Key is precise aim (gun camera, 136th Ftr-Bmb Wg, Korea).

up on people working on and around rail lines and we sent much "time of fire" into those workers.

As summer approached, we began flying close air support too, mostly in the center to eastern MLR (main line of resistance—the same as front line between enemy armies), including the Punchbowl, Bloody, and Heartbreak Ridge; but we also flew some to the west in areas of Old Baldy and Sniper Ridge. Spending a day with our ground forces at the front lines, I had two sets of incoming artillery and mortar fire impact much too close to suit a visiting flyer. The fact of an obviously active enemy was kept in mind on CAS (close air support) missions, and my squadron regularly offered extra strafing passes after bomb and napalm drops. These were gladly accepted. We often saw results of fires and explosions and the FACs could report more from their view. In one example, a Mosquito FAC called that our napalm caused troops not caught in the fire to break from that area and flee to a nearby hillside. We made repeated strafing passes gunning them down. Maximum strafing, using all ammo, on CAS was SOP for us.

Varied strafing in these jets put critical demands on pilots in judging how close in to press passes. Much strafing was in varied conditions of weather and terrain, and pullouts had to be started far enough out to safely clear obstructions. Most of us did not want to try pulling 12 "Gs" or more to miss something as was often done in World War II. An accompanying photo shows a pass on vehicles in a valley with steep cliffs behind, a "solid" hazard to be cleared.

Summer brought other operating changes. Takeoff distances were longer, which was critical on a rough PSP strip with Korean workers alongside to run out between aircraft takeoffs and knock down jagged rips in the PSP with sledge hammers. JATO (rocket bottles to assist takeoff) put out heavy smoke that often cut visibility to zero on the runway. Running short of F-84Es, replacement F-84Ds were sent in but experienced wing failures. Then F-84Gs began to arrive, a great airplane. The 136th designation was returned to the ANG. We became the 58th Fighter Bomber Wing, with a legacy of action in the Pacific in World War II, and we began flying limited night missions. Pilots quickly learned to keep one eye closed when firing rockets at night or else be blinded for a spell; they also had to remember that the muzzle blasts of the nose guns were in their view too.

Night operations were a major part of the air war in Korea. Various aircraft were involved, including Navy Corsairs, but USAF B-26s of the 3rd and 452nd and 17th wings, including a specialized night-trained 731st squadron, were the main story in that. Various munitions were used, with and without flare aircraft. Strafing was often primary on targets; also as add on after bombs and rockets. The book *Every Man a Tiger: The 731st USAF Night Intruders Over Korea* recounts strafing runs that started from 3,000 to 4,000 feet, dives of 20 to 30 degrees, firing beginning 2,000 to 1,500 feet out, speeds reaching 325 to 350 knots at pull-up around 200 feet, with weather and terrain often dic-

One vehicle has already been "flamed" on this valley road (right side of photograph) below steep hillsides. This pass is going in for more kills. Pilots had to judge "how close in" they could fly and still pull out without crashing (gun camera, 136th Ftr-Bmb Wg, Korea).

tating adjustments. The enemy was active in movement each night and a huge amount of destruction and killing was inflicted on them.

F-86s are famed for air kills of MIGs in Korea, but in some cases they also dropped down to strafe rail traffic and workers. Late in the war, F-86s replaced F-51s and F-80s in two fighter-bomber wings, and thus joined "those poor bastards in F-84s" as strafers too.

Much of the material here has involved my experiences and F-84s, which were the overall majority "fighter-bombers" of the Korean War. I asked a close friend, Col. Jack Porter, who flew F-80s with the 8th Wing, if he would provide some thoughts from his experiences. I am most pleased and grateful to include his valuable contribution to this effort and to the "inside story" in the overall history and legacy of strafing. I also thank his wife, Judy, for consenting to its use. A few of Jack's words follow:

> [On strafing]: Here the pilot was afforded the dubious opportunity of becoming a little more closely associated with his enemy and his defenses.... To the pilot the effect of strafing is immediately clear. The consequences of six fifty caliber guns can wreck [*sic*] havoc on almost any target unless it is dug in deep under earth.... He can work his rounds into the target or hold it in effectiveness. He knows what he is shooting at and he knows whether his attack was effective. He sees the results of his work. The concentrated machine-gun fire is psychologically frightening. Enemy troops will break and run from it. Truck drivers appear to be so

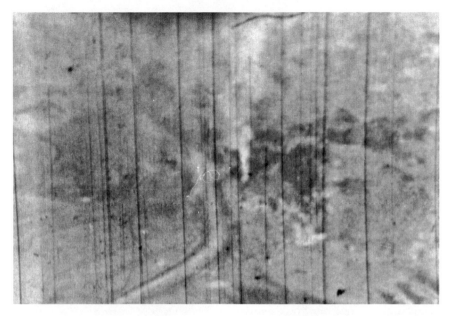

More poor-quality film, but it records the search for and kill of targets "off roads" as well as on them. Here such a vehicle is found and burned (gun camera, 136th Ftr-Bmb Wg, Korea).

frightened that they will do nearly anything to escape its effect. I observed one truck driver in the Wonsan area run headlong into a tree and I had not yet fired at him.

[On enemy defenses]: Enemy fire was pronounced and visible.... In addition to gun emplacements the enemy had the disconcerting habit of stringing cables across valleys and between peaks to discourage low angle strafing. Gun emplacements were placed high on the sides of hills to allow the gunners to fire down on unsuspecting pilots. It seemed that they would use any method at their disposal to discourage strafing.

[On Strafing's effects]: Ships can actually be sunk with fifty caliber machine-gun fire. A flight of four of us sank what appeared to be a motorized junk along the east coast of North Korea.... We carried (on a four-plane mission against massed enemy troops) four 5-inch rockets, two cans of napalm and 1,800 rounds of 50 caliber ammo each. The rockets and napalm were effective but did not compare to what the machine guns did in that little valley. They were devastating.

[A specific case]: On one early morning mission my flight was contacted by a forward ground controller who was seeking help for one of our "RESCUE" units on an island off the west coast. At that time period several small islands off the coast changed hands back and forth between us and the North Koreans. The island under assault was close enough to the coast of North Korea that when the Yellow Sea tide was out[,] the island was connected to the main coast by "mud flats." The enemy forces had planned to capture the island under darkness but probably because of the slowness of navigating the mud flats they were caught out in the open when daylight came. The enemy were slogging through the deep mud and had no protection at all. Our 50 calibers appeared to open up the mud down to the hard pan. The troops actually seemed to disappear under the 50 caliber attacks. It was not a pretty sight.

Col. Porter's comments on strafing in the Korean War are strongly allied to, and in step with, my experience and those of most other pilots I served with or know who flew fighter-bombers in that "fighter-bomber" war.

I returned home from Korea just before Christmas 1952, having spent seven months in combat, before being hand-picked by 5thAF and FEAF (without being asked if I wanted the job, which I didn't) to command a new large three-wing F-84 rear echelon maintenance organization. My assignment back home was to attend Air University's Air Command and Staff School. This gave me the opportunity to discuss the ongoing war with many other officers. I received frequent questions on comparisons with World War II, such as "Which war had the most and deadliest antiaircraft fire?" My answer was "both." I was shot at more intensely on more different types of missions by the Germans, but North Korean, Chinese, and Russian guns were definitely no less a threat at many times and places.

Certainly no one pilot's experience would reflect the whole. In Korea I had battle damage to only one plane on 72 missions. On the many of those that I led, only one pilot was shot down. My squadron lost no pilots while I was commander. Yet, overall losses in Korea became so high the 5th Air Force issued an order prohibiting fighter-bombers from flying under 3,000 feet. That drastic order, a real shocker to pilots and viewed by most of us as a godsend to the enemy, was short lived and we returned to full low altitude flying and killing of the enemy. Yet, it is evidence, if most unusual, that low altitude in Korea was deadly, just as in prior wars.

Several years after the end of fighting in July 1953 Gen. Weyland said, "[O]ne thing is certain; air power was triumphant in the Korean War. The legacy of strafing and strafers is ever so prominent in that—from saving the war in the early days on to major role throughout—despite being the most unknown action of the 'unknown war.'"

On graduation, I was hand-picked again for a task. And this time I was overjoyed and most grateful, as the Air Proving Ground Command, Eglin AFB, Florida, made me project officer for the operational suitability test and development of tactics for fighter aircraft to carry and deliver atomic bombs. This testing went well and was highly successful on the F-84G, and I continued to fly nuke delivery and other operational testing of "Century Series" fighters (F-100, F/RF-101, F-104 and F105) as I held positions of commander, Fighter Test Group, and chief, Test Operations, Air Force Operational Test Center. These fighters were a new breed of jet—supersonic, capable of speeds above Mach 1, some Mach 2—and they brought in a new era of aircraft gun armament.

None had the famed Browning "fifty" machine gun, which meant I had seen my last time to ever fire that gun. In two wars of strafing, I had made

Close air support. Smoke from the bomb burst rises above the hilltop. Much strafing was done in terrain such as this in close air support.

over 1,000 strafing passes. With multiple bursts on passes, plus gunnery and firepower demos, I had pulled the trigger to fire those guns some 2,000 times. Only once had they failed to fire, and for good reason: one time I didn't have the gun switch on.

The F-100 and F-101 had revolver type 20-mm cannon in the nose. Firing those in the F-100, two each side almost under the cockpit, led me to rate them tops in "shudder of the guns" to the pilot. Their firing was felt not only as "shudder" but also as the aircraft "wiggling" a bit. Much of our testing was in aerial gunnery, but when fired ground, the impact of 20-mm rounds was impressive even on panel targets, and certainly so in tests on actual vehicles and armor. The F-100 would in time do much strafing.

Most people at Eglin AFB in the 1950s had exclaimed at least once, "What the heck was that?" It was a sound. Some, especially the kids living on base, called it a "growl," but most doubted anything earthly could growl that powerfully. That sound was test firing of the aircraft cannon of the F-104 and F-105. It was a modern version of the old Gatlin gun, the multiple-barrel, hand-cranked machine gun used in the Civil War and the Spanish-American War.

The version under test, which became the M-61 20mm cannon, was six

Much strafing was also in the open, mostly in the flat western coastal areas and some valleys of central North Korea, and the enemy antiaircraft fire was most intense there too. Here F-84s of the 136th Ftr-Bmb Wg are shown strafing a train locomotive in a central valley (painting by Gary Trout).

barrels and power driven. The type of drive and feed system could vary rate of fire, ranging from 3,000 rounds per minute up to double that. The F-104 and F-105 each had a single gun mounted in the nose. Very slight bore-sight angle and improved sights and avionics in this gun greatly reduced "bore-sight distance" as a critical element in gunnery. Firing three thousand feet or more out could be accurate effective shooting. In tests, an F-105 with a high rate of fire M-61 and 1,029 rounds had some 10 seconds' time of fire. In firepower demos, this new gun wowed viewers in several ways. In the F-105 it put out a brilliant show of muzzle blast on the port side of the nose, sending up to 100 rounds per second into a target with shocking destructive force. Its rate of fire squeezed any repetitive sounds of past "machine-gun" shooting into a solid blast of noise or roar, which to a degree compressed "shudder of the guns" into a feel of pure force.

Operational suitability testing had strong qualitative input by highly experienced combat pilots such as Jim Jabara, Lonnie Moore, Bill Haning, Henry Brown and others. As computers came into greater use, the ops analysts and scientists at Eglin devised "models" to use in testing. Some of these worked out well for certain operational concepts and plans. But then they undertook strafing.

F-100, first of the "Century Series" supersonic fighters. This one was at the U.S. Air Force Operational Test Center, Eglin AFB, FL, in the 1950s (U.S. Air Force).

Our top combat strafers, this writer included, doubted that strafing could ever fit into a "model." It had never had a published operational concept or manuals of standard procedures, even though standardization had become a high priority in major air commands. But we gave full cooperation and input into the effort; and the more we did, the more the analysts saw this vast, varied, and multifaceted gunfighting as nonconforming. Attempts at a strafing "model" were abandoned. Expert pilot judgment and results in shooting gunnery panels and varied real targets on ranges remained the primary operational testing of strafing. Recommended strafing tactics for the Century Series fighters and their guns were not a totally new ball game in speeds, altitudes, and firing ranges; but new capabilities and options available were, to include speeds up into supersonic range and firing as far out as the pilot could effectively aim.

My experience in fighter nuke testing resulted in my next assignment, to headquarters of United States Air Forces in Europe (USAFE) from 1959 to 1962. But I did fly F-100s with the 49th Fighter Wing. In the early 1960s the Air Force had yet another new fighter entering the inventory. It flew Mach 2 plus, but otherwise was much out of common with the Century Series fighters. It was an in-service U.S Navy air superiority fighter that with a few changes would become an Air Force tactical fighter. Initially designated the F-110 but then changed to F-4, it had a two man crew, with radar and missile air-to-air

The author while chief of Test Operations, U.S. Air Force Operational Test Center, Eglin AFB, FL, in the late 1950s (U.S. Air Force).

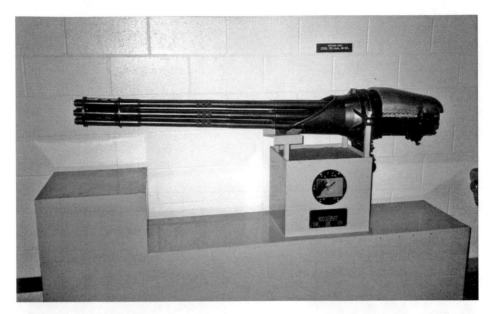

Top: M-61 20mm "Gatlin" aircraft cannon on display at the U.S. Air Force Armament Museum. *Above:* The F-104, the first fighter to be equipped with the M-61, is shown here with the author at the U.S. Air Force Operational Test Center, Eglin AFB, FL (U.S. Air Force).

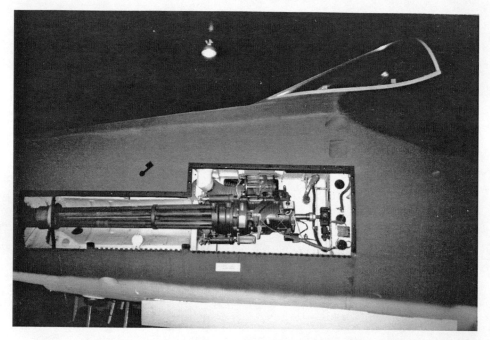

M61A1 installation in the F-105 fighter is shown at the U.S. Air Force Armament Museum.

armament; but it had no gun, only a provision that "If needed, an air cannon could be added."

In tests of the Century Series fighters at Eglin, air-to-air missiles were highly effective new capabilities on tactical fighters. The same was true for new air-to-ground weapons such as dispenser and cluster munitions. Pilots fully recognized they could take out targets that in the past were mainly hit by guns. Some pilots may have hooted "hooray" at times over any likelihood of less strafing, but there was never mention in pilot evaluations of new weapons ever replacing the gun. To us the gun was there "over and above" all other weapons.

I first learned of this "no gun case" during a VIP front seat flight in an F-4 in Europe. Asked afterward in a staff meeting for views on the F-4, I joined in with others who were impressed with its two-engine afterburner performance, but I added my flat horror at there being no gun in it. As I saw it, missiles could not handle all situations in air-to-air combat, nor could external munitions handle all needs in tactical air-to-ground combat. The enemy will benefit—both enemy pilots and enemy ground and surface forces. Inventories of tactical fighters without guns would remove the enormous amount of inherent versatile "over-and-above" ace-in-the-hole gun and cannon killing "time of fire" we now have. We must demand a gun in this other tactical fighter.

After a year of Industrial College of the Armed Forces, mention of my next stateside duty can help introduce a salute to strafers of the Vietnam War. In 1963 I was assigned to Tactical Air Command, Directorate of Operational Requirements (DORQ), which was responsible for the "Specific Operational Requirements" that stated performance and capability needs of future weapon systems—aircraft, armament, and munitions for tactical air forces worldwide including USAFE and PACAF—and for needed improvements in current systems. This included participating in and insuring fulfillment of those needs through birth, development, engineering and operational testing. In my six years there, first as head of TAC Systems, then as overall director, some of the major systems involved were the F-111, F-4E, F-5, A-7, the FX (F-15), and early stage work for a "Lightweight Fighter" (F-16)—all equipped with an aircraft gun/cannon (including the later model F-4E).

We also represented overseas commands in urgent and immediate needs, which included the Vietnam War, with a special category of Southeast Asia Operational Requirements. Some of the major new capabilities that came to be and were used in Vietnam included gun pods for the F-4C/D, the gunships (AC-47, AC-119, AC-130), the sensors and fire control systems for the AC-130 and numerous other aircraft, laser guided bombs, special operations systems, and hundreds of other items from personal equipment to a world of advanced capabilities in electronic warfare. Of course the TAC centers played an enormous role in all this, and other agencies were involved too. For example, no mention of electronic warfare should be made without citing the key player in the birth of ECM (electronic countermeasures) pods and "Wild Weasel" surface to air missile (SAM) hunters/killers. That player was Col. William B, Williamson, of Headquarters USAF, later of the 7th Vietnam, and then commander, Fighter Weapons Wing, Nellis AFB.

I had special responsibilities on certain programs. One was on the F-X/F-15 to represent and speak for the planned using commands and combat pilots in all phases of requirements, requests for proposals, and evaluations thereof. Another was with the Southeast Asia requirements, which resulted in temporary duty stints of 4–6 weeks there heading teams to set up the system and then to stay in step on details of each need with the warfighters (which were valuable back home in fighting off attempts by the Department of Defense [DOD] to rejudge needs); and I participated in some dozen combat missions toward that aim.

Thus the following coverage of the Vietnam War is not undertaken as being firsthand in combat, as was much regarding World War II and Korea, but as one in contact on it. What this information on my position can help introduce is the scope of strafing in Vietnam. Everything mentioned above in both Cold War and Southeast Asia requirements and systems (except F-15 and F-16) played very real roles in Vietnam. Yet they are a mere token preview of the vast and varied operations of that war. If strafing of past wars could not be fit into a "model," the strafing of Vietnam compounds that nonconformance manyfold. Vietnam's enormous scope of strafing will not fit into anything, in or out of history, other than itself.

Just an attempt to list all aircraft and models, plus special programs (one of a kind, etc.) involved would probably dwarf a major city phone directory, much less describe the varied types of shooting done. Thus, this salute will strive to reflect to some degree the gigantic extent, and accompanying duty, valor, and sacrifice, of stafers.

First there is the magnitude of the war. It is generally recognized that the United States actively fought the Vietnam War for some 12 years, from 1961 to 1973, the first years in an advisory and special ops role, then from 1964 with major military force, then that force declining in the 1970s. The ground war was primarily U.S. forces (and South Vietnamese) fighting the enemy (Viet Cong and North Vietnam) within South Vietnam (but with exceptions). The air war was another story, and was popularly recognized as three distinct "wars": (1) In-country, within South Vietnam; (2) Out-country, over North Vietnam; and (3) Over Laos. Yet other actions can be cited, including Cambodia and nonmilitary operations. There also were breakdowns of wars within those wars, identified with side names such as "Rolling Thunder," the air operations over North Korea, and "Linebacker," the late war massive strikes there. In Laos there was "Steel Tiger," the interdiction of the Ho Chi Minh Trail, and "Barrel Roll," the support of the ground war in northern Laos. Many more code-named operations occurred, including "Arc Light," the B-52 strikes.

Photographs with this text show two groups of aircraft employed in the Vietnam War. They include combat and training planes dating from World War II as well as latest inventory aircraft of the day. Every plane shown that had a gun was used for strafing by

Southeast Asia, the Vietnam War.

Static display, Hurlburt Field, FL, in the early days of the Vietnam War. Terms of "Jungle Jim" and "COIN" were involved, but "Air Commando" and "Special Operations" have become lasting designations and legends. These "old timer" aircraft had roles in Southeast Asia (U.S. Air Force).

the Air Force, in addition to others, such as F-4s and A-7s. Not shown are the many types of Navy and Marine aircraft in the war; nor are civilian aircraft strafers shown. The Army played a huge role in strafing with some fixed-wing planes and a huge force of rotary-wing aircraft, both mobility and attack types. Helicopters of all services were regular strafers.

The varied operations of the air wars and threats faced in different situations were so broad and diverse that they defy comparison with previous wars. In the "in-country" air war a pilot might bomb and strafe enemy Viet Cong under his own base flight pattern but also do the same on massed North Vietnamese Army forces such as those at Khe Sanh. Over the Ho Chi Minh Trail auto-weapon defenses were a definite threat, while in other areas of Laos there were friendly troops on the ground. One war was certain in threat. That was over North Vietnam, especially Route Packs 6A and 6B (Hanoi/Haiphong areas), heavily defended by guns (auto weapon to heavy AAA), surface-to-air missiles, and first-line fighters (MIG-17/19/21) in the most advanced defenses faced to that point in history. Before the war was over, SAMs, including low-level SA-7 heat seekers, joined enemy auto-weapon, machine gun and AK-47 fire found in all the wars.

In each air war, over 12 years of war fighting, strafing took on many forms.

Static display, Eglin AFB, FL, late 1950s. From the "Century Series" fighters and recce versions of the inner half circle (plus the F-4) to the bombers of the middle half circle and cargo/transports of the outer half circle, all of these aircraft and more (including helicopters) of the USAF served in Vietnam along with almost all Navy/Marine and Army fixed and rotary wing aircraft (U.S. Air Force).

Some went back to early World War I days as pilots and crews fired individual weapons out of cockpits, windows and doors of planes at the enemy on the ground. The most prevalent individual weapon in Vietnam was the M-16, an automatic. On the high end of the scale, the F-105 Wild Weasels were using the best available aircraft, electronics and gun developments to strafe SAM sites in bloody gunfighting over North Vietnam. In between was a range of strafing across every known type of air operation.

Close air support of U.S. ground forces in-county employed aircraft from World War II and Korean vintage attack planes to supersonic jets. These planes supported search and destroy operations, mobility, any case of troops in contact, and, of course, all ground campaigns; they also repulsed the heavy enemy attacks of later years. Protection of bases and installations of all services was a major operation day and night. In Laos and South Vietnam interdiction, targets of enemy troops and "movers"—vehicles, carts, animals, sampans and people—were strafed by aircraft ranging from civilian light planes to the most modern fighters. Strafing support was essential for airlift, rescue, special operations and more.

A-1, a stalwart of USAF Special Operations and Vietnamese Air Force operations (U.S. Air Force).

The Air Force gunships brought in a new chapter of strafing history. That chapter started with the AC-47, which was equipped with a Gatlin mini-gun, and was known as "Puff the Magic Dragon." It was followed by the AC-119 and AC-130, the latter with 20mm Gatlins and 40mm and larger cannon. The guns were mounted to fire sideways out doors and windows. Switching to as high an altitude as practical (instead of the diving low passes of most other strafers), the gunships fired in a level banked turn that aligned the side-firing guns on a target below. From earlier daytime and night flare operations mainly in-country, the more advanced AC-130s became top night truck hunters and killers of the Ho Chi Minh Trail. However, the gunship support over friendly bases, camps and positions that were under enemy attack was surely their most appreciated role by our troops below.

Another new chapter in the history of strafing was the expanded role of Army (and special operation) helicopters as strafers in this war. Whether from mounted forward-firing guns on specific attack or "gunship" choppers or from crew members or passengers firing an "automatic weapon" out of doors or perched on the skids of any type, air-to-ground fire from helicopters was inherent in the enormous use of those helicopters in ground combat operations as well as in convoy escort, rescue, medical evacuation, special mission, and other tasks.

AC-47 "Gunship," a new ball game in air support of friendly troops and bases (U.S. Air Force).

With new forms of strafing making new history, various new terms were applied, too. Some of those terms were often used interchangeably with "strafing" in official and media reports and included "suppressed ground fire," "made cannon passes," and simply "covered." In the news these tended to reduce public exposure to the term "strafing."

Yet, with just the above scant information on the war, if we recall the official DOD definition of strafing—"the delivery of automatic weapon fire by aircraft on ground targets"—we are reminded that the scope of strafing involved every round fired from every kind of automatic weapon carried aloft in every kind of aircraft employed in the 12 years of war. Published figures that show USAF air munitions expended in the Vietnam War was three times (in millions of tons) that of World War II can further spotlight scope.

It was not even necessary to be airborne to observe much evidence of strafing in Vietnam. From almost any base, or even cities, flares were seen almost nightly in nearby skies lighting targets for gunships or other planes. Planes and choppers were seen and heard almost constantly and if you were in position to watch any of them return to base, you would inevitably see guns being reloaded for the next mission.

A unique and most impressive picture on the extent and valor of strafing in the Vietnam War is found in the award of the Medal of Honor to U.S. Air Force personnel. In World War II only a small fraction of the 38 awards to airmen involved strafing. In Vietnam 13 Medals of Honor were awarded (two

Flares of air support operations in the night sky, a common sight from most all bases and many cities in Vietnam each night.

won in POW status), with a major percentage for acts of strafing or direct involvement in strafing actions. Those include the awards to Major Bernard F. Fisher, Captain Hilliard A. Wilbanks, Captain Merl Dethlefsen, Lt. Colonel Joe M. Jackson and Captain Steve Bennett.

The Tet Offensive is widely recognized as a milestone of the war. The Viet Cong and North Vietnamese attacked our installations and cities in force all across South Vietnam, and in turn they were defeated. But it also has been citied as having great impact on the future of the war in an opposite way with the public. For this salute it is a key event because it triggered beyond doubt the most intense strafing action in all history.

One early alert on the Tet Offensive came from Tan Son Nhut when a C-47 took off around 0330 on 31 January 1968 and received heavy ground fire from the end of the runway. Responding Army gunships were overhead and firing into the enemy forces almost as they began their ground attack. Of some eight gunships, seven were reported hit by ground fire, but hundreds of Viet Cong bodies were found along the perimeter of the airport. In the end, the enemy attack was contained, then totally repelled.

With numerous other air bases and installations under attack or infiltrated, a number of gallant actions were involved in saving them. One was by USAF base security forces. Another was quick action by U.S. ground forces, such as elements of a division that made a headlong dash into and through enemy forces to reach Saigon. And there was our airpower, of which strafing was the most available and the most suited.

Strafing was also the quickest reaction. Planes and choppers were always ready to strafe, whether loaded with other munitions or not. Then too, you do not want to bomb your own runways, ramps or flight line facilities if it's possible to keep from it. Strafing was the choice to kill and defeat enemy foot soldiers on our bases without blowing craters and crippling our bases and operations. Our troops were also mixed up with, or in close proximity to, the enemy. In cities and towns the enemy was among the civilian population. U.S. personnel were holed up in off-base billets and risked travel through enemy held streets to reach bases. There were American civilians, along with some dependent wives and children, living in cities and towns.

Bombs and napalm could not be used within bases and cities without high risk of hitting our own people. The huge bomb loads of the B-52s could not even be considered. Strafing accuracy, and the ability of pilots to control impact patterns—to fire pinpoint on target or limit spread of rounds as needed—was the only option for close support. If Viet Cong were in the field behind the BX (Base Exchange), strafers could pump gunfire into that field and have all of it go there and none into nearby defenders or buildings. Stafers had the time of fire of the guns to move over and do the same near the chapel. Strafing was the air power in our victories of saving bases and installations and billets in cities during the Tet Offensive. General William W. Momyer, commander of the 7th Air Force, said (in meetings with staff where the author was present and in *USAF Warrior Studies*) strafing was all he had in fighting Tet.

Of course, not all Tet battles were short operations against mainly Viet Cong; they were also extended large-scale struggles against forces and weapons of the North Vietnamese. One was the epic retaking of the city of Hue. Another was the lengthy battle to hold Khe Sanh, which actually was attacked before Tet, and which involved some 22,000 fighter-bomber and 2,400 B-52 sorties with a full array of bombs and munitions, plus guns.

My participation in combat included an A-1 mission from NKP Air Base, Thailand. It had a primary target task in North Vietnam, then a brand of Vietnam armed-recce—not of rails and roads, but of rivers and waterways in the jungles. From above little could be seen of enemy activity on the waters, but flying very low looking under the tree canopy revealed enemy watercraft, supplies and people along shorelines. (It made me think of doing much the same on German autobahns to find enemy aircraft in forests in World War II.) We found several enemy bullet holes in the plane after landing at NKP.

Another mission was on 6 March 1968 with a FAC (call-sign of Nail) out of NKP over Laos. It was diverted to Khe Sanh, then involved several hours' FAC work at the height of fighter air support there with a hand in much of what was done that afternoon. The loads of modem munitions from F-4s and F-105s hitting enemy positions far surpassed anything of past wars, and M-

The AC-130's 20mm cannon barrels in action (U.S. Air Force firepower video).

61 cannon fire impacting on the enemy seemed to have an impressive nature of its own.

A mission onboard a late model AC-130 gunship out of Ubon, Thailand, in 1969 gave the most graphic evidence of new air-ground gunfighting capabilities. On a dark night over Ho Chi Minh routes at altitudes far above past armed-recce altitudes, truck after truck was sighted, "locked on to," and killed. Not once was there a miss, and this went on most of the night. While a system of sensors to signal passing vehicles on the ground had been in use for some time, it was the onboard airborne sensors and displays, fire control, and highly professional teamwork of the crew that showed that showed most in capability. There were a few "breaks" as auto-weapon flak was encountered, but then they went right back to killing trucks.

As TAC director of requirements I had the good fortune to fly several missions in the A-7 test and evaluation on a range in Texas. As I had once used "needle, ball and airspeed" instruments and a fixed "ring and bead" gun sight in combat, the cockpit instrumentation, fire control and heads-up display of this small agile attack plane was a totally new world in weapon delivery and strafing for me. That was the case for all the first line weapon systems of the Vietnam War. It was a new era in strafing capability and history. (It was a new era in nomenclature too. Many past two-word names had been combined in military usage, such as: gunsight, gunfighting, gunsmoke, boresight, warfighting, and others.)

Among literally millions of pilot and crew mission experiences, mention of a few specific instances may help show a bit more of their varied nature. Lt. Col. Cal Ellis and another pilot, on duty with a South Vietnamese air unit, were airborne in A-1s when a FAC called in need of air support for a ground unit under attack and in danger of being overrun. With no external weapons onboard, they had loaded guns, and were the first aircraft to reach the scene. When they departed, after repeated strafing runs and now empty guns, the FAC reported the day saved, the enemy withdrawing and leaving over 100 dead.

An article titled "Shine's Boatyard" in *Ghost Wings* magazine by Don Harten is about some "river" strafing by fellow pilot Anthony Shine while flying Mach 2 F-105s from Takhli. Harten describes gun camera film from Shine's plane that was shown at a wing commander's briefing in 1968. There was graphic display of jungle and muddy water of a river in North Vietnam flashing by some 25 feet below; then large barges under the jungle overhang came into view, with cannon fire tearing into a barge, flame, explosions and people leaping into the water. This film was taken on Shine's 97th mission, when he had only three more to go to finish his tour.

With those three missions completed, gun camera film was shown at Shine's hundred-mission party—again the river, barges, cannon fire and explosions. Attendees cheered and praised what great strafing that had been on the 97th mission. In his going-home speech, Shine put in a by-the-way that the film just shown was not from the 97th mission, it was from that morning on the 100th mission. The squadron pilots named the place "Shine's Boatyard" and kept tradition going by strafing there on future missions. The article advised in conclusion that Shine had been lost in combat flying an A-7 over Vietnam in 1972 and that, in his honor, the USAF Fighter Pilot of the Year Award is known as the Lieutenant Colonel Anthony C. Shine Award.

The Easter Invasion by the North Vietnamese with some 40,000 troops and 400 armored vehicles in March 1972 brought on an open major enemy military force versus U.S. air power. The enemy attack was turned back. An article, "Chico the Gunfighter," in *Flight Journal* magazine, by Warren E. Thompson, is about one strafing operation in that action. This was by the 366th Tactical Fighter Wing. Two squadrons had F-4Es, with an internal M-61 cannon and 630 rounds of 20mm ammo. The wing identified itself as "The Gunfighters" and their patch showed a blazing M-61. External gun pods (SUU-16) with an M-61 and 1,200 rounds of ammo were also available for F-4s. (With strong calls of need for guns in F-4s from commanders and key pilots when F-4C/Ds first entered combat, crash programs had resulted in the gun pods and a cannon in the F-4E.)

Col. J. Dudley Pewitt, the director of operations, figured a well armed F-4 airborne just before dark could catch some early movers of the main enemy night traffic. He configured an F-4E with two pairs of Mark-20 Rockeye II cluster bomb units (CBUs) and two SUU-16 gun pods under the wings, plus

An ammo load for a F-105 (U.S. Air Force).

the internal gun. This gave armament of cluster bombs plus three M-61 cannon with 3,030 rounds of ammo. Approval to fly it was obtained, limited to Pewitt and certain other pilots, with the call sign "Chico." A few missions are summarized here.

An urgent FAC call was received for air attack of a superior enemy force crossing a river to attack a friendly unit. Chico arrived, was greeted with enemy ground fire, and began strafing passes at speeds around 425 knots, firing 3–4 second bursts. Cannon fire accurately covered the area of enemy troops. In a sixth pass Chico ran out of ammo as the FAC reported the enemy retreating and many bodies left on the riverbank and in the water. The Rockeyes had not been used in this situation. They were too dangerous that close to friendly troops.

On a search and destroy mission an enemy tank was spotted. Setting up a pass to fire into the tank broadside using all guns, Pewitt reported the results to be amazing, as the rounds converged into the tank with such force that they knocked it over against a hill, nearly flipping it.

Another mission brought a gunfight with a 21.7mm gun that was trying to shoot Chico down. Pewitt put his sight pipper dead on the enemy gun and fired all three of his M-61s. They all impacted exactly where aimed. All that was seen at the target was puffs of gray smoke; nothing at all was left there.

The tremendous scope and utility of strafing in uses and forms in varied situations in this war certainly warrants a special place in history, along with the story of pilots and crews and their shudder of the guns and their generalship of their time of fire to provide that great and telling contribution. Certainly their devotion, valor and sacrifice deserves a proud place there. Most air operations in the war depended on them.

The author while commander of the 326th Air Division, Pacific Air Forces, 1970–1972 (U.S. Air Force).

My final duty was as commander of the 326th Air Division, Pacific Air Forces. I flew F-102s with the Hawaii Air National Guard. This was my only flying that did not include firing aircraft guns or cannon, but it was a privilege and honor to be with this outstanding organization. We hacked two ORIs (Operational Readiness Inspections) with high flying colors. The direct link with the Marine Air Wing in Hawaii was also a pleasure and honor.

Retirement in late 1972

sent my wife, Anita, and me to settle in the Eglin AFB area of northwest Florida, which is home to several military bases and is dense with military retirees. Talking of experiences among the latter was certainly expected, and one case was a real gem of a story on strafing. It was about "what it felt like for German tank crews when hit by P-47 strafing." It was told by a fellow retiree, an Army officer, about an infantry platoon leader in Europe as American troops pushed into Germany. On patrol into enemy territory, his platoon came across a new German Panther tank on a road. The crew was outside sitting on a fence eating lunch. The U.S. troops slipped up on the enemy crew, who gave up and were captured. The U.S. platoon leader recalled being taught to start and operate a tank back in officer training. He and a sergeant boarded the Panther and cranked it up. They were moving in a German tank, in German territory, when two American P-47s came overhead. The pilots must have had enough ammo remaining for one good pass each—because that is what they made on this tank.

The platoon leader in describing the experience when the first burst of cal-.50 API rounds (probably 100–200) hit the tank said it was beyond ordinary words—whether he was trying to tell of the ungodly sound or the equally ungodly impact shock and shudder transmitted from steel tank hull into his body, which in combination left both occupants dazed. Then, while they were in that state, the second pilot's strafing hit the tank. This was another dose of the same, but it somehow seemed worse yet and left both occupants lacking in full sense and function. The tank stopped, apparently by a "dead man's" switch. The occupants had to be helped out and they rested for a while before the platoon returned to their unit positions with the POWs.

I told the storyteller that we normally strafed in flights of four; thus a German tank crew would normally get four doses from us. He said he doubted that human bodies could take four or more strafing runs like that and be capable of normal operation of a tank for some time. I would be surprised if this experience is logged in official records; but if one wanted to research that, some of the story leans toward the 9th Division around the time of the "Remagen" bridge.

With wars after Vietnam, I was of course mainly dependent on the media for current information on the flying and fighting, just as the rest of the public was. The Gulf War opened with heavy news on stealth, cruise missiles, smart bombs and other precise weapons, along with a new array of aircraft in combat that included the F-117, F-15, F-16, A-10, F/A-18, AV-8, advanced USAF and Army "gunships."

About the first news I recall that headlined "strafing" was two A-10 pilots who destroyed enemy vehicles approaching a downed Navy pilot as a helicopter came in and picked him up. Ever more use of terms such as "suppress" might well include strafing but not publicize it. A few mentions of cannon passes were made in A-10 armed-recce in search of Scud missiles. A very clear ref-

Top: Fighter and attack aircraft stalwarts of the Gulf War in a single formation: clockwise from top left: F-4E, A-10, F-16, F-15 and F-111 (Test Operations, USAF Air Armament Center). *Above:* Advanced versions of the AC-130 were key Special Operations strafers of the war. This is a photograph of a display at the U.S. Air Force Armament Museum.

erence to air-to-ground gunfire action came in news of the loss of AC-130 Spectre gunship *Spirit 03* and its entire crew while supporting Marines at Khafji, an especially hard-felt loss to the Hurlburt Field family and this community.

I don't actually remember any other publicity specifically on strafing during the war. However, when photos were shown of a mass of destroyed, damaged and abandoned military and civilian vehicles of many types on the highways north of Kuwait City toward Basra—some photos captioned "The Road to Basra"—it didn't matter whether strafing was mentioned or not. Pilots and aircrews of mass kills in other wars knew full well what had gone on there. Such a target had always triggered a strafing frenzy. A close look at "Basra" photos can further add to a belief of strafing frenzy. With wreckage strewn widely on and along the highway and on out into the desert, nowhere does even a single bomb crater show, nor evidence of extensive use of cluster or incendiary weapons. This fits with a mass strafing kill.

Of course in postwar years, from both published works and war stories, considerably more strafing actions have been brought forth, including opening shots of the war to A-10 tank killing, as well as some pilot gripes that units were controlled on the "Road to Basra" and did not all get to barrel in and strafe "at will" as in past wars. Obviously this war was not the "mother of all strafing wars." In fact it was much the opposite of strafing's tremendous role in Vietnam. There seems to be good reason for that. New and advanced weapon systems destroyed targets with precision from greater standoff ranges. Besides that factor, the overwhelming airpower in an aggressive air campaign for weeks before a quick and total ground war victory reduced situations of both scheduled strafing and the dire need for its help. What does stand out about strafing in this war is that the air-ground gunfighting done (which was surely publicized) followed the heritage of past wars. When needed it was there in its great utility and capability, with greater firepower than ever before. Certainly, it carried on in the ultimate story of warrior duty, devotion, and valor.

Shortly after the Gulf War I read an article praising the A-10 for its strafing ability, in both aircraft design and multi-barrel 30mm cannon with special ammo. The article then went on to add the undying belief by some that the great speed of supersonic jet fighters sprayed bullets too far apart when strafing. At about the same time, I watched a video of a firepower demonstration on Eglin ranges in which an F-16 put a burst of 20mm precisely into what appeared to be an armored personnel type vehicle target from probably a 2,000 feet range. Not one round was seen to hit anything but the target in the split second before the vehicle erupted into a great flash of fire and smoke. The only "spraying" seen was vehicle parts and pieces flying out across the range, with not much vehicle left intact. Instead of considering it as no good for strafing, I can think of times and places back in World War II and Korea that I would not have minded having an F-16 to strafe in—and perhaps especially in which to climb up out of the Brenner Pass valleys in the Alps.

Much strafing history is often hidden in overall histories. The DOD document *Conduct of the Persian War: An interim Report to Congress*, July 1991, weighs about four pounds. Yet, in scanning it, I never saw the word "strafing" or any comment on air-to-ground gun and cannon fire as being separate or

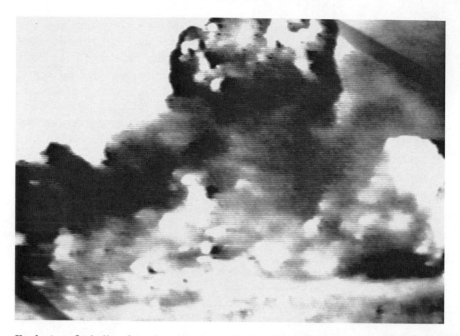

Explosion, fireball and smoke were the result of an F-16 "cannon pass" in a firepower demonstration. Concentrated cannon fire, all impacts on target, set this off— definitely not a case of "bullets spread too far apart" (U.S. Air Force firepower video).

different from "ground attack" or "suppress." On the other hand, the long held USAF worldwide weapon delivery competition titled *Gunsmoke* put strafing in a separate category from all other forms of weapon delivery. Much the same as back at Eglin when strafing's great utility would not fit into a "model" for testing, it would not fit into any standardized attack or strike rules of competition either.

If the trend is for less strafing by fighters and fighter-bombers today than in past wars, so much the better to get the air war job done without more time spent at history's bloodiest air gunfighting. But evidence is that gunfighting is not over by any means. An article in *Air Force* magazine (April 2005) notes that in the battle of Takur Gar, Afghanistan (March 2002), a helicopter insertion operation encountered resistance and a team of Special Operations Forces/Rangers came under heavy enemy fire. Two rescue helicopters were shot down. Repeated close air support missions were pumped in. That need for maximum firepower on the enemy included F-15Es (sophisticated strike version of the Mach 2+ fighter) adding strafing passes in their CAS missions. Successfully rescued were 38 of the 40-man team. When needed, fighter and fighter-bomber guns and cannon are there.

Strafing has been there ever since Maj. Harold Hartley, commanding officer of the 1st Pursuit Group back in World War I, reported his expectations of a real future for strafing aerodromes. On ground war he had this to say: "Before and during an offensive enemy concentrations will be strafed and machine gunned from low altitude. Indeed the possibilities are unlimited" (from the *U.S. Air Service in WW I*). The major would likely be astounded at the extent and forms those possibilities have become in all subsequent wars and in the capabilities of today's aircraft and helicopters. He probably never dreamed of some evolvements, such as the following two.

An item in *Elks* magazine (April 2005) cited a letter from a Marine serving in Iraq. The letter expressed thanks for a care package sent by an Elks lodge and added a few words on her duty there to this effect: "My job is to fly Huey helicopters, crew chief and door gunner. Not many women get to shoot .50-caliber machine guns."

In the early 2000s the Air Armament Center at Eglin AFB announced successful development of a new type of barrel for the Browning .50-cal machine gun. Already the record holder for weapon of longest active use in U.S. military service, there is every indication this gun will continue beyond a century of U.S. strafing and other war gunfighting.

Moving on to the time of the "surge" in Iraq, we see Hartley's predictions still holding. The article *Not Fade Away*, by Marc V. Schanz in *AIR FORCE* magazine, June 2008, tells how the Maryland Air National Guard showed the A-10C as an oldie but goody. In that article, the excellent capabilities and performance of the updated Thunderbolt II with a variety of munitions are

An A-10 in a firing "cannon pass" (U.S. Air Force video).

covered. It also cites pilot statements that a frequent choice of weapon was the seven-barrel 30-mm gun for its rate of fire and precise explosive rounds and that on a target with friendly forces nearby, the gun was a lifesaver.

That pilot view has held solid and firm throughout the history of strafing. It applies to the total role and use of strafing in air warfare. For me, and many other veterans of strafing action, aircraft guns and their time of fire have been by far the most valuable weapon we had in multi-mission air operations. For this writer, that applies to all wars of my active experience. With guns I killed far more, destroyed far more, and paralyzed far more enemy military personnel and equipment, and did the same to enemy direct supporting people and systems, than with all other weapons and munitions combined. That could well serve as concluding words toward my goal in this effort. Still, one more "pass" is judged necessary toward mission accomplishment, and that is about multiple or repeat strafing passes on a target or targets. Of course that subject has been

involved in and regularly discussed in almost every mission covered in this book. What has not been noted before on that subject is the views of people not directly involved—the public, media, historians, and buffs, who have been a part of the history from way back. An example for me was the regular comments I received from numerous friends regarding a pilot from our hometown who was killed in action in Korea: "You know, he was on a fifth strafing pass." I have had many other questions about repeat passes over the years. A recent one was in a letter on the subject from a historian, which cited a pilot killed in Europe in World War II while making a sixth strafing pass on an enemy airfield, along with a quote from a ditty by a World War II fighter pilot on strafing: "One

The author in retirement in northwest Florida.   pass and on your way, live to fly another day." No doubt the deadly record of strafing compared to some other air combat could fuel such wisdom as the ditty. Some strafers have said much the same in bar talk and even in interviews. Even so, strafers and all other warriors fight in the real world of troops in war and with the demands of duty and performance in the face of the enemy.

In cases of one pass, which totally destroys the target(s) and fully accomplishes the mission, then "on your way" is valid, your duty done. That was often so for 4-plane kill of a loco, MT, etc. But for untold thousands of other cases over the long history of strafing it was not so at all. I would ask these questions: Would one pass and on your way have been better than the repeat passes actually made on several specific missions? Should pilot MacArthur, at the Marne in World War I, have made "one and run" instead of "pass after pass" expending all ammo on missions all day as German troops continued to pour across the river all day? Should the pilots of the 79th Ftr Gp at Valance Airfield in World War II have quit on one pass as enemy bombers attempted takeoff on a mission against us, rather than stay as they did and make as many passes as possible to destroy as many bombers as possible? Should the pilots of the 58th Ftr Gp have quit after one pass on a Japanese naval task force bearing down to attack our beachhead on Mindoro, instead of making pass after pass using all ammo? The same question could apply on many more missions of all wars, all with a firm "no" for answer. What these pilots did was their duty. "One pass and quit" in the above examples would have brought forth some of the ugliest words in the Code of Military Justice, such as cowardice or failure to perform in the face of the enemy.

The citation for the award of the Medal of Honor to Lt. Raymond Knight for strafing an airfield in Italy in World War II cites numerous repeat passes in the destruction of enemy aircraft. Every level in the chain of command from the squadron to the top approved that award. Obviously, there was no belief by any of those commanders that "one pass and on your way" was a compelling criteria in pilot decisions on strafing.

Perhaps this book will reverse some apparently continuing public beliefs that "one pass only" was the "right" or "best" pilot decision on strafing missions. Most of all, this matter of multiple passes again, and further, reinforces the fact that so often it was the decisions of pilots—in fact, being "their own generals"—in use of the great utility and "time of fire" of the guns for each situation that made aircraft guns such valuable tools of war in multi-mission air warfare. Thus, may this book give enough of the ultimate story and heritage of strafing—duty, devotion, valor and sacrifice—that readers better know and understand what strafing and strafers did, and be thankful for it.

Bibliography

Books

The Army Air Forces in World War II. Vols. 2, 3, 5. Washington: Office of Air Force History, 1983.

Barnes, G.M. (Maj. Gen., USA [Ret]). *Weapons of World War II.* Princeton, NJ: Van Nostrand, 1947.

Blank, Chester L. (Lt. Col., USAF [Ret]). *"Every Man a Tiger": The 732nd USAF Night Intruders Over Korea.* Manhattan, KS: Sunflower University Press, 1987.

Bowen, Ezra, and editors of Time Life Books. *Knights of the Air.* New York: Time Life, 1980.

Burke, Lawrence G., and Robert C. Curtis, comp. *The American Beagle Squadron, 2nd Fighter Squadron, 52nd Fighter Group.* Lexington, MA: American Beagle Squadron Association, 1987.

Chinn, George M. (Lt. Col., USMC). *The Machine Gun.* Vol. 1. Washington: Department of the Navy, 1951.

Department of Defense Dictionary of Military and Associated Terms. Washington: Joint Chiefs of Staff, 1989.

The Falcon, 79th Fighter Group, 1942–45, Austria, and the 79th Fighter Group, 1946.

Gurney, Gene (Col., USAF [Ret]). *Vietnam: The War in the Air.* New York: Crown, 1985.

Hallion, Richard P. *Rise of the Fighter Aircraft, 1914–1918.* Baltimore: Nautical and Aviation Publishing Co. of America, 1984.

Hartley, Harold E. *Up and At 'Em.* New York: Doubleday, 1971.

Hudson, James J. *Hostile Skies: A Combat History of the American Air Service in World War I.* Syracuse: Syracuse University Press, 1968.

Knaak, Marcelle. *Post-World War II Fighters, 1945–1973.* Washington: Office of Air Force History, 1986.

Longstreet, Stephen. *The Canvas Falcons: The Story of the Men and Planes of World War I.* New York: World, 1970.

Military History, Editors of. *Desert Storm.* Leesburg, VA: Empire Press, 1995.

Mitchell, William (Brig. Gen.). *Memoirs of World War I.* New York: Random House, 1960.

Moore, Glenn C. *Dear Mom and Dad—I'm OK.* Nowata, OK: Moore, 1990.

Nowarra, H.J., and Kimbrough S. Brown. *Von Richthofen and the "Flying Circus."* Litchworth, Hefts: Harleyford, 1958.

O'Leary, Michael. *USAAF Fighters of World War Two in Action.* Poole, NY: Blandford, 1986.

Palmer, Bruce, Jr. (Gen). *The 25-Year War.* Lexington: University Press of Kentucky, 1984.

Piser, Robert. *The End of the Line: The Siege of Khe Sanh.* New York: W.W. Norton, 1982.

Prange, Gordon W. *At Dawn We Slept.* New York: Penguin, 1981.

Rudel, Hans Ulrich. *Stuka Pilot.* New York, London: Bantam, 1979.

Stewart, James T. (Col.), ed. *Airpower: The Decisive Force in Korea*. Princeton, NJ: Van Nostrand, 1957.
The United States Air Force in Korea 1950–1953. Washington: Office of Air Force History, 1983.
U.S. Air Service in World War I. Vols. 1, 2, 3, 4. Washington: Office of Air Force History, 1978.
Williamson, Murray. *Air War in the Persian Gulf*. Baltimore: Nautical and Aviation Publishing Co. of America, 1995.

Other Publications

Air Interdiction in World War II, Korea and Vietnam. USAF Warrior Studies. Washington: Office of Air Force History, 1986.
Air Superiority in World War II and Korea. USAF Warrior Studies. Washington: Office of Air Force History, 1983.
Conduct of the Persian Gulf Conflict: An Interim Report to Congress. Washington: Department of Defense, 1991.
Daedalus Flyer. Randolph AFB, TX: Order of Daedalians, 1988 forward.
Greenhous, Brereton. *Evolution of a Close Ground-Support Role for Aircraft in World War I*. Manhattan: Military Affairs, Department of History, Kansas State University, 1974.
Gropman, Alan L. (Lt. Col., USAF). *Airpower and the Airlift Evacuation of Khan Doc*. Maxwell AFB, AL: Air War College, 1979.
Jug Letter. New York: P-47 Thunderbolt Pilots Association, 1988 forward.
Une Mission de Guerre, 28 Aout 1944, no. 2375 (Colgan, Bagian, Jennings). France: Association Rhodanienne Pour Le Souvenir Aerien ARSA, 2003.
Schneider, Donald K. (Maj., USAF). *Air Force Heroes in Vietnam*. Maxwell AFB, AL: Air War College, 1979.
Waycross (GA) *Journal Herald*, daily editions, 1941 forward.

Index